P9-CLD-142

Sect Ideologies and Social Status

Gary
Schwartz

Sect Ideologies and Social Status

The University
of Chicago Press
Chicago and London

International Standard Book Number: 0–226–74216–4
Library of Congress Catalog Card Number: 72–120598
The University of Chicago Press, Chicago 60637
The University of Chicago Press, Ltd., London

Printed in the United States of America

To My Mother and Father

Contents

Acknowledgments ix

1. Introduction 1
   - Ideology and Religious Belief 1
   - Religious Ideologies and Secular Societies 9
   - Evangelical Christianity and Separatist Religious Movements in the Non-Western World 18
   - Participant Observation and the Study of Religious Belief 27
2. The Problem of Sect Affiliation 32
   - Social Stratification and Religious Affiliation in America 32
   - The Problem of Sect Affiliation—The Relationship between Religious Belief and Social Structure 35
   - Status Deprivation and Sect Affiliation—The Structural Sources of Pentecostal and Adventist Ideologies 39
   - Religious Ideologies—The Link between Social Structure, Religious Doctrine, and Social Action 50
3. The Sect as a Sociological Construct 56
   - The Church-Sect Typology 56
   - Contemporary Sociological Approaches to the Problem of Sect Affiliation 69

Ideological Consensus, Group Cohesion, and the Problem of Sect Affiliation 71
4. Seventh-day Adventist Belief 79
Religious Belief and Ritual Action 79
Pentecostal and Seventh-day Adventist Belief and the Christian Tradition 85
The Scope of This Treatment of Pentecostal and Seventh-day Adventist Theologies 89
Seventh-day Adventist Belief 90
5. Pentecostal Belief 137
Pentecostal and Holiness Belief 137
6. Socioeconomic Status and Sect Affiliation 182
The Organization of the Seventh-day Adventist and Pentecostal Congregations 182
Pentecostal and Seventh-day Adventist Status Trajectories 194
7. Conclusions 211
Sectarian Belief and the Social Order 211
Seventh-day Adventism and Pentecostalism as Transformative and Redemptive Social Movements 216
Some Theoretical Considerations
Appendix 1 Methodological Considerations 231
Appendix 2 Interview Schedule 245
Index 251

Acknowledgments

Like others who have sought to understand the relationships between religious belief and social life, I have accumulated many intellectual debts along the way. Although it would be fruitless to recapitulate my complete intellectual history, I think it is necessary to mention the role that Bryan Wilson's work, particularly *Sects and Society*, has played in my own research. Although I take issue with some of his theoretical formulations, I have found that his analysis provided a firm empirical foundation for my efforts to illuminate the significance of sectarian ideologies.

The summer fieldwork program of Brandeis University gave me my first opportunity as a graduate student to study sectarian religious movements. I am grateful to Robert Manners for his counsel during this initial field experience on a small West Indian island and to David F. Aberle for his advice and criticism during the formative stages of the present study. David Kaplan and Benson Saler were most helpful and encouraging when I was preparing my doctoral dissertation, from which this book is derived.

Perhaps the most significant influence on my intellectual development was the opportunity to work as a research assistant on David M. Schneider's American Kinship Project at the University of Chicago. During this time, I saw at first hand how an anthropologist could perform a distinctively cultural analysis on extremely complex data collected in an urban setting. I am especially appreciative of the effect this experience had on whatever analytic skills and theoretical sensitivities I am able to bring to bear on my own materials. In addition, I would like to thank him for many kindnesses which go beyond the bounds of scholarly courtesy.

I must express my gratitude for the patience and goodwill of my friends and colleagues Don Merten and Cal Cottrell, who were always willing to listen. I would like to thank my wife Angela and our children for keeping this project in proper perspective. Carolyn Rosenthal and Fran Behan typed an often messy manuscript without the slightest complaint. I would also like to thank the Wenner Gren Foundation for financial support provided by a predoctoral fellowship in anthropology. I would like to thank the Institute for Juvenile Research and its research director, Dr. Nöel Jenkin, for the time taken from my regular research duties to prepare this manuscript for publication. Finally, I am most indebted to my informants, who taught me that those who hold unconventional beliefs are capable of leading lives marked by great personal integrity and by a renewing sense of the meaning of human existence.

I Introduction

Ideology and Religious Belief

This study examines the religious ideologies of two sectarian groups in American society—the Pentecostals and the Seventh-day Adventists. By religious ideology, I mean those ethical doctrines and theological dogmas which not only reflect secular exigencies but also influence ordinary social conduct. Thus, this study looks at both the social roots of sect affiliation and the impact this commitment has upon the believer's everyday existence.

Ideologies are ideas which move men to action. Religious ideologies tell men how to achieve salvation. But, more than that, religious ideologies diagnose the bearing of various natural, social, and supernatural realities on their adherents' spiritual fortunes, and they propose to remove the obstacles which stand in the way of salvation. For the believer, then, religious ideologies accurately portray the forces which affect his spiritual welfare and, at the same time, point to a safe way through the diverse contingencies which might prevent him from reaching this goal.

Ideologies are not the product of dispassionate inquiry. To those who accept its teachings, an ideology's credibility is not easily dissipated by evidence which challenges its validity. Moreover, men with similar material interests and needs habitually espouse certain political, social, and economic doctrines and reject others. Competing ideas have a differential appeal to persons variously situated in the social structure.

These observations have led some scholars to conclude that ideologies confuse values with facts.[1] In their opinion, this failure to separate normative and existential judgments is due not merely to a lack of logical sophistication. Rather, it results from the ideologist's desire to convince others that his view of a situation is morally right and intellectually valid in a manner which conceals his unstated interests in it.[2]

Following this line of reasoning, ideology is seen as a source of perceptual error.[3] Ideologies prevent those who subscribe to them from assessing a situation veridically.[4] According to this

1. See Gustav Bergmann, "Imperfect Knowledge," in *Readings in the Philosophy of the Social Sciences*, ed. May Brodbeck (New York: Macmillan Co., 1968).

2. This follows Karl Mannheim's discussion of the nature of a "particular" ideology (*Ideology and Utopia* [London: Routledge and Kegan Paul, 1949], esp. pp. 50–54), but it does not correspond, as is popularly thought, to the Marxian conception of ideology. On the latter, see Norman Birnbaum, "The Sociological Study of Ideology (1940–60): A Trend Report and Bibliography," *Current Sociology* 9 (1960).

3. For instance, Werner Stark says that "the doctrine of ideology thus deals with a cause of intellectual error, rather than with the social element in the pursuit and perception of the truth." *The Sociology of Knowledge* (London: Routledge and Kegan Paul, 1958), p. 53. Gunter W. Remmling observes that this view has its sources in the French Enlightenment: "The French philosophers of the Enlightenment viewed 'ideological' distortion of thought—or prejudice as they actually called it—as a psychological problem: man deceives himself when he permits prejudices and superstitions to penetrate his reason. They distinguished three causes of prejudice: idols, interests, and priestly fraud. These they considered the causal determinants creating a psychological sphere of error that clouds man's perception and his grasp on reality." *Road to Suspicion: A Study of Modern Mentality and the Sociology of Knowledge* (New York: Appleton-Century-Crofts, 1967), p. 111.

4. However, George Lichtheim (*The Concept of Ideology and Other Essays* [New York: Vintage Books, 1967], p. 20) points out that ideologies do not necessarily distort historical actualities but rather are bound to the particularities of a given time and place.

view, ideology and science are basically incompatible: what is accepted as scientific truth today may be exposed as ideological distortion tomorrow. Hence, ideologies are potentially falsifiable propositions, and it is the social analyst's task to subject them to empirical scrutiny.

This fusion of cognitive and moral standards of validity undoubtedly accounts, in large measure, for an ideology's capacity to induce men to adopt a given program of action. Ideological rhetoric attempts to convince those to whom it is addressed that moral desiderata follow logically and inevitably from its analysis of the forces which determine the present and the future course of human affairs. Yet I find the conceptions of ideology discussed above unsatisfactory as they stand. They suggest that a social analyst can take discrete ideological propositions from the larger body of thought in which they are embedded and test each one against scientific knowledge *without a critical loss of meaning*.

This sort of intellectual dissection is, of course, a common tactic in political debate. It may inhibit an opponent's political effectiveness but it does not explain why he continues to rely upon his ideological presuppositions when their empirical foundations are seriously undermined. In other words, an ideology's ability to motivate men to pursue certain goals and to avoid others resides in those properties it retains as an integrated *system* of beliefs.

Certainly, men do not commit themselves to an ideologically sanctioned code of conduct on the basis of the credibility of its isolated propositions. If this is so, then on what grounds are the adherents of an ideology persuaded that it is indeed true? To answer this question adequately, we must keep in mind three analytically distinct dimensions of an ideology.

First, ideologies are recognizable as such only to an observer. To the believer, they are veracious representations of reality. Mannheim puts this quite well:

> If I take, for instance, a theoretical statement simply as an idea, that is, "from within," I am making the same assumptions that are prescribed in it; if I take it as ideology, that is, look at it "from without," I am suspending, for a time, the whole complex of its assumptions, thus doing something

> other than what is prescribed in it at first glance. . . . For we do not stop at the suspension of intrinsic interpretation but, at the same time, relate the intellectual content to something outside it, as the *function* of which it then appears.[5]

Second, ideologies not only arise in a particular social milieu but also often have a decisive impact upon it. If one thinks of the connections between thought and action in terms of simple cause and effect, this assertion appears tautological. Such an excessively mechanical view of this relationship ignores what Parsons calls the complex interpenetration between the ideal and real elements in a concrete social situation.[6] Insofar as they shape as well as reflect the social circumstances in which men must act, ideologies dramatize the universal dilemma between the pressures of environmental constraints and the possibilities of cultural innovation in social life. As a collective attempt to resolve common problems, ideologies are free, within certain limits, to impose their own interpretations on the sources of man's ills. In any case, they are not direct symbolic representations of material realities. Ideologies, then, locate the causes of common suffering and prescribe a remedy for them.

Geertz observes that ideologies reduce the uncertainty which surrounds action undertaken in perplexing situations: "And, it is, in turn, the attempt of ideologies to render otherwise incomprehensible social situations meaningful, to so construe them as to make it possible to act purposefully within them, which accounts both for their highly figurative nature and for the intensity with which, once accepted, they are held."[7] Social conflict, economic deprivation, and a host of other distressing conditions frequently generate indecision and inaction when men can least afford to remain passive—they are temporarily paralyzed by forces and events which escape their ordinary modes of understanding and control.

5. Karl Mannheim, "The Ideological and Sociological Interpretation of Intellectual Phenomena," *Studies on the Left* 3 (1963): 56.
6. See Talcott Parsons, "An Approach to the Sociology of Knowledge," *Transactions of the 4th World Congress of Sociology* 4 (1959).
7. Clifford Geertz, "Ideology as a Cultural System," in *Ideology and Discontent*, ed. David Apter (New York: Free Press, 1964), p. 64.

Ideologies serve as a symbolic bridge between the debilitating effects of these difficulties and positive efforts to overcome them. An ideology mobilizes man's hope that he can resolve his most recalcitrant problems by offering to provide a lasting solution to them. Thus, ideologies are not ameliorative; they promise much more than the partial alleviation of the pain of personal afflictions. They promise to remove man's most onerous burdens forever. Salvation is never a halfway measure.

The agency responsible for this total transformation of an individual's life situation is never *solely* suprahuman. This process is set in operation by the individual's initial free choice between morally tinged alternative responses to his situation. According to ideological programs for spiritual redemption, an individual can transcend the morass in which he is presently mired only by opting for the alternative which is both right and true. Thus, by recognizing historical necessity, the individual secures his freedom from spurious and potentially destructive future contingencies. In exchange for a truly secure and certain future, ideologies exact a commitment to a pattern of conduct which specifies the terms under which its adherents can legitimately expect to reap its benefits.

The third dimension of an ideology concerns the conditions under which it becomes believable. What convinces its adherents that the promise of a more perfect mode of existence in the future is, in fact, realistic, and, furthermore, that their own rather limited efforts on its behalf will alter the course of history? Ideologies per se have no intrinsic qualities which somehow automatically set man in motion. Only those already converted to a particular ideology are willing to give their lives a wholly new direction and significance. The simple promise of future rewards in return for present sacrifices in the service of an idea scarcely explains the passion with which its proponents defend these changes in their way of life.

To those who believe in them, ideologies work in the present. For the believer, the truth of ideological postulates about the nature of reality is evidenced by a normatively engendered transformation of his daily life. As an answer to those who doubt the truth of his creed, the ideologist points to his personal experience. He avers that such a fundamental reconstruction of his being would have been impossible if it were predicated upon false doctrines. Thus, the meaning of an ideology does not reside solely in its utopian imagery. Instead, an ideology's credibility is grounded in its ability to demonstrate workable solutions to what at first appear as insuperable problems. Ideologies, therefore, afford their adherents increased instrumental control over a hazardous natural or social environment. Predictions about a state of affairs yet to be realized are prefigured and, hence, to the believer, verified by changes he can see in the present.

Concrete results alone are not a satisfactory measure of an ideology's appeal. The pragmatic effects of an ideology are created, in part, by its philosophical bias. What people will do depends upon how they conceive of the world in which they must act. Of course, men sometimes discover an approach to a previously confusing and difficult situation which yields handsome dividends without experiencing the slightest desire for ideological justification. Therefore, belief in a model of reality which has practical implications does not necessarily qualify as ideological commitment.

Moreover, in my opinion, ideas that serve as convenient rationalizations for an advantageous position in the struggle for scarce social resources are the least enduring forms of ideological commitment. These notions are usually hastily contrived in response to immediate political and economic opportunities and then are freely discarded when they lose their effectiveness. In any case, a person can abandon or replace these sorts of ideological commitments without jeopardizing his sense of reality—his cognitive equilibrium remains undisturbed.

People believe that an ideology is true because it satisfies their questions about the meaning of human striving as well as furnishing material proof of its value. Ideologies explain the failure or success of human endeavor in terms of its ultimate moral validity. All-embracing categories of good and evil are the center of a vision of the way in which natural and supernatural agencies impede or facilitate the attainment of primary values such as health or life-after-death. Ideological directives are binding not only because they are consistent with the highest standards of human morality but also because these ethical principles determine the allocation of these values. Conduct which violated these prescriptions would contradict the agencies responsible for human welfare. Such behavior would not only be immoral, it would be unrealistic. Only a fool would tamper with the mechanism of cosmic justice. Geertz makes this point most eloquently: "It is this air of the factual, of describing, after all, the genuinely reasonable way to live which, given the facts of life, is the primary source of an ethic's authoritativeness. What all sacred symbols assert is that the good for man is to live realistically; where they differ is in the vision of reality they construct." [8] In the final analysis, then, an ideology is believable because it embues its adherents' chaotic social experience with meaning. It links their place in a coherent moral order to those supreme realities in the universe which determine their destiny and the fate of mankind.

This does not deny, however, that people subscribe to ideologies because they "need" to believe them. There is an undeniably imperious quality to ideological commitment. Persons whose means of coping with a wide variety of existential problems are limited or inadequate often experience intense and recurrent psychological discomfort in certain social situations.[9] Once they are aware that their distress is shared by others, they become receptive to ideas which purport to explain their common predicament. At this point, the situation itself demands an ideology which exposes the causes of their suffering and suggests a way of eliminating it. Consequently, without the pressure exerted by these circumstances, ideological commitment is unlikely. On the other hand, situational stress does not dictate the cognitive terms in which it is grasped and appraised. Without the sense of factual authenticity imparted by a world view which delineates the relevance of cosmic occurrences to mundane human affairs,

8. Clifford Geertz, "Ethos, World-View and the Analysis of Sacred Symbols," in *Every Man His Way: Readings in Cultural Anthropology*, ed. Allen Dundes (Englewood Cliffs, N.J.: Prentice-Hall, 1968), p. 306.
9. See Neil Smelser, *The Theory of Collective Behavior* (New York: Free Press, 1963) for an impressive attempt to account for the various forms of collective behavior in terms of a model based upon situational stress.

ideological controls over secular behavior would lack their obligatory character.

In sum, this study of two religious movements at variance with the dominant culture not only examines the social forces which engender this opposition, but also focuses on the symbolic apparatus which attempts to mediate and resolve these differences. Social marginality and status deprivation sustain these sectarian forms of cultural protest; these ideologies are precipitated by the strains associated with an untenable social status. Nevertheless, one cannot discover the complete significance of a religious ideology solely by examining its material origins. Although resentment over the skewed distribution of social privileges and honors undoubtedly plays a major role in their genesis, religious ideologies are not simply statements of dissatisfaction with the social order in sacred guise.

Religious ideologies transmute their adherents' secular problems; they give them a new meaning. Mundane issues and concerns are transformed when they are endowed with cosmic import. They become the nodal points around which a universal ethical code is developed. This moral system, in turn, is grounded in a comprehensive religious world view which is the result of metaphysical speculation and of the elaboration of preexisting cultural postulates. It is not a direct reflection of environmental imperatives.

In a somewhat schematic form, this is the framework I will use to examine Pentecostal and Seventh-day Adventist religious belief. I will try to show that the specific intellectual content of these two quite different belief systems generates fundamentally diverse ideological responses to similar social circumstances. And I will also attempt to demonstrate that these ideologies shape the way their adherents construe ordinary social situations and, by implication, that they have crucial consequences for their secular conduct. Finally, I shall suggest, though not prove, a hypothesis about the social-psychological conditions which make it likely for a person disposed to seek a religious solution to a status dilemma to affiliate with either a Pentecostal or a Seventh-day Adventist group.

Religious Ideologies and Secular Societies

To those unfamiliar with its esoteric language, the relevance of much of current social research to vital human concerns is hardly self-evident. The opaqueness of technical discourse seems to suggest that social scientists, for the most part, have forsaken their humanistic origins and sought refuge from partisan disputes in the realm of pure science. Even though social scientists maximize their objectivity by assuming the role of disinterested spectators in the context of ongoing social activity, they are not free from the ordinary passions which motivate inquiry into human affairs. Short of schizophrenia, a social scientist cannot dissolve those values which define his personal community and cultural commitments—values which unite him to some men and separate him from others. Thus a completely "value-free" social science is not possible, and, even if it were, it is not desirable.[10] Therefore, aside from its possible contribution to the more or less parochial concerns of the sociology of religion, it seems reasonable to ask what relevance the study of the religious ideologies of two sectarian movements has to the social life of modern societies.

The Pentecostals and the Seventh-day Adventists are comparatively small and socially uninfluential groups whose theological stance is decidedly fundamentalist.[11] Their religious outlook is peripheral to the dominant religious ethos of Western societies.[12] And it appears quite unlikely that they will have a signifi-

10. On this point, see David J. Gray, "Value-free Sociology: A Doctrine of Hypocrisy and Irresponsibility," *Sociological Quarterly* 9 (1968), and Alvin Gouldner, "The Sociologist as Partisan: Sociology and the Welfare State," *American Sociologist* 3 (1968).
11. According to the *Seventh-Day Adventist Information File* (Washington, D.C.: Bureau of Public Relations, General Conference of Seventh-day Adventists, n.d.), there are about 300,000 members of the movement in this country. Nils Bloch-Hoell (*The Pentecostal Movement* [London: Allen and Unwin, 1964]) estimates that there are about 1,400,000 Pentecostals in this country. He notes that statistics about the Pentecostal movement must be taken with a grain of salt because so many congregations are not affiliated with any larger religious body.
12. See William McLoughlin, "Is There a Third Force in Christendom?" *Daedalus* 96 (1967).

cant impact, in their present form, on Western culture in the foreseeable future.[13]

In an era of increasing secularization, Christianity has lost some, though by no means all, of its power to shape its followers' prosaic social attitudes and moral commitments.[14] Yet in times of endemic social change such as ours people are often responsive to diverse and seemingly unpredictable ideological directives when their usual social routines and expectations are devastated by forces beyond their comprehension and control. The modern world is a fertile source of problems whose scale and complexity is so vast that most men trust, but rarely understand, the operations of the institutions designed to solve them. When these institutions fail to deliver the goods and provide the rationale which gives life its substance and meaning, modern man is confronted with many of the same existential dilemmas which in the past produced "bizarre" religious movements. Social crises are the handmaidens of the most unlikely cultural allegiances.

If we conceive of religion in its widest meaning as the search for transcendental legitimation for secular involvements, the cultural ambience of modern societies is not inimical to the emergence of "radical" religious ideologies. There are convincing parallels between the development of chiliastic and apocalyptic religious visions in earlier phases of Western history and contemporary revolutionary doctrines of both the right and the left.[15] Moreover, in modernizing states as well as in some modern states, "political religions" supply one of the principal ideological supports of revolutionary movements and regimes.[16] These movements do not always explicitly refer to the com-

13. See Werner Stark, *The Sociology of Religion*, vol. 2, *Sectarian Religion* (New York: Fordham University Press, 1967), chap. 3.
14. For a detailed analysis of this problem, see Gerhard Lenski, *The Religious Factor* (New York: Anchor Books, 1963).
15. See Norman Cohn, *The Pursuit of the Millennium* (New York: Harper Torchbooks, 1961), and E. J. Hobsbawm, *Primitive Rebels* (Manchester: University of Manchester Press, 1959), chaps. 4–6.
16. See David Apter, "Political Religions in the New Nations," in *Old Societies and New Nations: The Quest for Modernity in Asia and Africa*, ed. Clifford Geertz (New York: Free Press, 1963).

mands of supernatural figures to sanction changes in the traditional social order. Nonetheless, they mobilize their followers through appeals to transcendent moral values and thereby infuse their political programs with a sacred aura. This places overriding political goals beyond the pale of pragmatic judgments which would measure their potential worth against present costs and liabilities. In this fashion, the movement's political aims become inextricably tied to a historically necessary as well as an ethically desirable future.[17]

Modern societies, then, are not immune to ideological agitation. Even the so-called stable Western democracies experience periods of intense ideological excitement when many people see cosmological implications in mundane political events. Like their religious counterparts, these ideologies interpret ordinary human affairs in terms of categories of absolute good and evil. These visions of the moral dispositions of the contending forces in history expose the malaise from which the faithful are presently suffering, reveal the inherent strengths and weaknesses of the agents of oppression, and point to the road to victory in the struggle with the forces of evil. This sort of ideological challenge to the civic order of modern societies is not uncommon.[18]

17. According to J. L. Talmon, revolutionary faith in the inevitable transformation of the existing social order is "partly due to Judaic teachings on History as the story of election, sin, atonement and redemption at the end of days, partly to the millennial status of the Jewish dispersion as a minority. A nonconforming minority, persecuted or at least questioning itself and being questioned by the world on the meaning and purpose of its separateness must either assert a superior peculiarity and missionary destiny or regard its position as essentially provisional and its life as a kind of preparation for some apocalyptic denouement, after a violent spasm." *Political Messianism: The Romantic Phase* (London: Secker and Warburg, 1960), p. 80.

18. Perhaps the most fanciful, extravagant, and yet potent ideology of this sort is the vision of a powerful Communist conspiracy in this country which is presently held by many right-wing groups and which shaped the entire climate of political debate during the period associated with the late Senator Joseph McCarthy. This ideology asserts that the American Communist party, which has an infinitesimal constituency in this country, is capable of completely destroying American political institutions. It claims that our political structure is in such grave danger from those men allied with the global designs of "international communism" that any means should be used to eliminate them from the polity. See *Anatomy of Anti-Communism: A Report Prepared for the Peace Education Division of*

Whether they are politically right or left, these ideologies seek to generate a moral crisis. Once the integrity of those persons charged with implementing the society's central values becomes questionable, their authority is subject to erosion.

Analysis of the political intentions of these ideologies does not exhaust their significance. Regardless of their effect on the distribution of power in modern societies, these ideologies frequently crystallize new social identities and cultural styles. A glance at the current American political scene suggests that some people are dedicated to continual ideological ferment as part of their strategy for removing the gross inequities of this social system.[19] To this end, they create a counterculture which opposes the corrupting aspects of the dominant culture on every level of social life. Commitment to a revolutionary ideology becomes a matter of life style.

Persons motivated by political ideologies often use a vocabulary which has ritual overtones. They talk about "cleansing" the social fabric of "impure," "subversive," or "reactionary" elements. And they propose to "save" the misguided or misinformed from "alien" influences and, in the process, to regenerate dormant virtues in the service of a noble cause.[20] For these ideologists, the exhortation to attack or protect the prevailing social order is validated by eternal and self-explanatory values —that is, by spiritual values. In this manner, a religious rationale is embedded in ostensibly secular ideologies.[21]

---

the American Friends Service Committee (New York: Hill and Wang, 1969) for an excellent analysis of this ideology.

19. See Kenneth Keniston, *Young Radicals* (New York: Harcourt, Brace and World, 1968), and Jack Newfield, *A Prophetic Minority* (New York: Signet Books, 1966).

20. In their attacks on the complacency of their urban middle-class parents, participants in the early phases of the German youth movement emphasized the sacred quality of folk traditions which was symbolized by images of sacrosanct blood and soil. See Howard Becker, *German Youth: Bond or Free* (New York: Oxford University Press, 1946), and Walter Laquer, *Young Germany* (New York: Basic Books, 1962).

21. Edward Shils says that "ideology, whether nominally religious or anti-religious, is concerned with the sacred. Ideology seeks to sanctify existence by bringing every part of it under the dominion of the ultimately right principles." "Ideology," in *International Encyclopedia of the Social Sciences* (New York: Macmillan Co., 1968), 7:68.

One might grant that ideologies are a potent force in modern societies but still object that, whatever their specific form, Western ideologies have lost the salvationist impulse which identifies a distinctively Christian outlook. The argument admittedly becomes tendentious at this point. The evidence that the idea of salvation has undergone a change in character but has not lost its potency in contemporary Western culture is fragmentary and inconclusive. For the very empirically minded, there is no solid body of data which conclusively reveals the recrudescence of this motive in highly rationalized, if not rational, societies.[22]

Nevertheless, at the risk of a slight digression, I am willing to argue that the notion of salvation is not as foreign to modern sensibilities as the label of a secular era implies. Here the idea of personal salvation is understood as a persistent effort to preserve the self against the vagaries of time and nature and, at the same time, to intensify its qualities which partake of the eternal and the divine. Traditionally, this was accomplished through symbolic acts which united the believer's soul to a God willing to act in his behalf. In a more modern form, salvation involves attachment to collectivities (often pseudocommunities) which translate the individual's fear of existential meaninglessness and annihilation into a search for enduring sources of value and for modes of self-transcendence into these spheres of being.

Perhaps the strongest case for the persistence of the desire for salvation, despite its gradual demise in the established churches,[23] is its appearance in the one intellectual movement of

22. There are social scientists who think that American society has never relinquished religious modes of legitimating its central values. Following the work of W. Lloyd Warner, Robert Bellah discusses this in "Civil Religion in America," *Daedalus* 96 (1967). Similarly, Talcott Parsons argues that the value of "instrumental activism" is derived from our Protestant heritage. Parsons thinks that an individual's commitment to the betterment of the larger society is thus built into the achievement motive. See "The Link between Character and Society," in *Social Structure and Personality* (New York: Free Press, 1964).

23. See Bryan Wilson's incisive essay "Religion and the Churches in Contemporary America," in *Religion in America*, ed. Robert Bellah and William McLoughlin (Boston: Houghton Mifflin, 1968). From a global perspective, Peter Berger discusses secularization as part of the process of demythologizing the world. *The Sacred Canopy* (Garden City, N.Y.: Anchor Books, 1969).

our time where we would least expect to find it. In a study of some of the schismatic followers of Freud, Philip Rieff observes that their work marks the end of a cultural order in which salvation becomes possible through the renunciation of instinctual gratifications in the service of communal purposes.[24] This faith in the moral rightness of libidinal sacrifice, coupled with institutionalized modes of temporary remission from the guilt it engenders, was discarded for a doctrine of self-realization which recognized no prior cultural imperatives not consonant with personal needs. Here man is truly free to act as he feels.

Contrary to first appearances, this does not mean the end of religion but rather the emergence of a new faith. Rieff points out that, unlike the epochs of scarcity where the predominant cultural ethos demanded obedience to an ascetic ethic, the ascendant cultural therapeutic of our time allows the individual freedom to explore *all* the possibilities of his experience, save those which would damage the self or impair the autonomy of the ego:

> Cultic therapies of commitment never mounted a search for some new opening into experience; on the contrary, new experience was not wanted. Cultic therapy domesticated wildness of experience. By treating some novel stimulus or ambiguity of experience in this manner, the apparently new was integrated into a restrictive and collective identity. Cultic therapies consisted, therefore, chiefly in participation mystiques severely limiting deviant initiatives. Individuals were trained, through ritual action, to express fixed wants, although they could not count thereby upon commensurate gratifications. The limitation of possibilities was the very design of salvation. . . . What is revolutionary in modern culture refers to releases from inherited doctrines of therapeutic deprivation; from a predicate of renunciatory control, enjoining releases from impulse release, projecting controls unsteadily based upon an infinite variety of wants raised to the status of needs. Difficult as the modern cultural condition may be, I doubt that Western men can be persuaded again to the Greek opinion that the secret of happiness is to have as few needs as possible. . . . Men already feel freer to live their lives with a minimum of pretense to anything more grand than the sweetening the [*sic*] time.[25]

24. Philip Rieff, *The Triumph of the Therapeutic* (New York: Harper Torchbooks, 1966).
25. Ibid., pp. 15, 17–22.

Rieff suggests that the waning of traditional restraints on hedonistic pursuits inaugurates a "post-religious" culture where personal salvation is no longer linked to communal ideals. However, in my opinion, Rieff's austere reaction to the doctrine of self-realization through self-indulgence overlooks its similarity to what William James calls "the religion of healthy-mindedness." [26] This notion includes more than the conventional Christian theology of Norman Vincent Peale and the somewhat more mystical doctrine of "mind-cure" held by the followers of Mrs. Eddy, both of whom believe in a vague yet benign Deity dedicated to making a secure middle-class existence even more comfortable.[27] Those who subscribe to a creed of cosmic optimism believe not only that man is basically good but also that "the spiritual in man appears . . . as partly conscious, but chiefly subconscious; and through the subconscious part of it we are already one with the Divine without any miracle of grace, or abrupt creation of a new inner man." [28]

This outlook, stated as a libertarian social manifesto by some of Freud's heterodox followers, also underlies the less rigorous and recondite ideologies of those cultural elites Rieff sees as the vanguard of psychologically modern man. Among the affluent and well educated there is widespread interest in "encounter" or "sensitivity training" groups. In part, this phenomenon reflects the usual American infatuation with techniques of impression management which allows a person to treat his desire to control others as the spontaneous product of unrestrained sociability. But it also reflects a quest for the sacred remnants of a self subject to the anomie and alienation imposed upon those who have broken their ties to communities based upon residence and kinship and who are unable to commit themselves to the political surrogates for primordial solidarities. In ersatz primary groups, individuals struggle to find and regain the "authenticity of the self" in a context which, although not overtly religious,

26. William James, *The Varieties of Religious Experience* (New York: Mentor Books, 1958).
27. For a good description of Christian Science doctrine see Bryan Wilson, *Sects and Society* (London: Heinemann, 1961).
28. James, *Varieties of Religious Experience*, p. 92.

endows the person with sacred qualities, if only for the duration of this brief encounter.[29]

The urge to wring meaning from social experience devoid of preordained normative significance animates other current cultural ideologies which similarly affect secular banners. The life style of the "hippies" and their numerous and diverse sympathizers lacks conventional religious qualities, although its adepts affect a rather hedonistic sort of piety. Many of the members of this subculture are preoccupied with discovering the cosmic coordinates and the mystical implications of their particular place in the universe.[30] For some of them, a simple moral dichotomy divides the social universe into those who belong to the hypocritical (i.e., "plastic") establishment and those who are dedicated to a spontaneous and free exploration of the self and others. An often implied but rarely stated corollary to the injunction "to do one's own thing" is that people willing to "open" themselves to others in this manner are assumed to lack evil motives until proved otherwise. By abandoning all preconceptions about the significance of intra- and interpersonal experience, it becomes truly possible to know oneself. Salvation involves a process in which the seeker acts as a sentient siphon for the multitide of cosmic forces and prosaic events which affect his life. Salvation, then, arises out of a continuous openness to experience and is renewed by freely sharing the fruits of this enriched experience with like-minded others.

In sum, it is possible to discern currents of religiosity in the

29. Although he would probably disagree with my assessment of the significance of this phenomenon, I am indebted to Dr. David Orlinsky for this phrase. See William Schutz, *Joy: Expanding Human Awareness* (New York: Grove Press, 1967) for a general statement of encounter group ideology. *New Living*, a publication of the Elysium Institute of Los Angeles, describes the results of encounter group techniques which involve physical contact in the following terms: "All troubles, all anxieties, all depressions dissolved. A euphoric state of unity and oneness between all the participants transcended such considerations as status, wealth or sex. Everyone felt good about everyone else" (p. 31).

30. The data for this assertion are taken from tape-recorded interviews with persons affiliated with a West-Coast "hippie" subculture. The study is being conducted jointly with Dr. William Allen of the University of California, Santa Barbara, and Don Merten and myself of the Institute for Juvenile Research, Chicago.

ideological movements of advanced industrial societies. Here concern with personal salvation is phrased in an idiom of self-realization which, as Rieff so acutely points out, is the dominant motif in the faith of our time. If there is a useful historical parallel to this situation, perhaps the religious milieu in the later Roman Empire is the most appropriate. In this setting, esoteric mystery religions were not designed to effect a moral reorganization of the believer's life but rather provided access through various rites of purification to special knowledge about the universe and man's place in it.[31]

As the institutional structure of modern societies yields increasingly to rational principles of social organization, we might expect ideological reactions to the power of impersonal standards of efficiency and the like to determine a man's fate to exert a strong countervailing pressure on the larger society. Perhaps the "hippie" movement and allied phenomena are analogous to the Roman mystery cults insofar as they reflect personal needs and aspirations not fully satisfied by the institutional order. Collective attempts to redress the affective imbalance in modern societies may act on the not uncommon feeling that there is no effective and authoritative societal agency to protect one's spiritual welfare. Under conditions of social strain, men may become intensely conscious of their precarious status in the universe and may seek to revitalize the notion of salvation. Of course, this assumes that men cannot act purposively for indeterminant periods of time without ideologies which give their efforts more than temporal justification. And it is equally speculative to suggest that Christian conceptions of salvation which envisage messianic solutions to suffering and misfortune will again activate these movements. But it would be equally shortsighted to rule out the possibility altogether.

31. A. D. Nock says of those interested in the mystery religions that "such a man turned to the normal civic and private mysteries of the time and was initiated in some or all of them. What he found we do not often know: but it was probably for the most part ideas which he already had of the nature of the soul and its hope of bliss and of the symbolic expression of natural processes, and he gained a sense of intimate and special personal relationship to the universe and spiritual forces underlying its operations." *Conversion* (London: Oxford University Press, 1965), p. 115.

Evangelical Christianity and Separatist Religious Movements in the Non-Western World

As we have seen, the religious component of many Western ideologies leads a furtive existence. As long as religious faith is disguised as philosophical justification for ideological commitment, it remains respectable. Once it is exposed as a surreptitious desire for a transcendental solution to secular problems, however, the religious impulse offends the ruling technical ethos of our age and loses its potency as a goad to collective action. Most Western men cannot completely eradicate their submerged longing for personal salvation. On the other hand, they are equally incapable of wholeheartedly accepting a world view in which divine intervention into human affairs makes ordinary conduct the vehicle for its realization. Divorced from the normative structure of the larger society, the religious motive is fully operative only in those groups which refuse to accede to the secular temper of the times.

The situation is quite different in many parts of the non-Western world. Here many still believe that supernatural powers affect the outcome of vital human concerns and enterprises. Ethnographers report that belief in witchcraft and sorcery is extremely resistant to change in preliterate and peasant societies. In response to Western political and economic domination, religious movements emerge in the colonial and underdeveloped areas of the world which attempt to account for and to cope with the changes these forces impose upon the lives of these peoples. In varying degrees and ways, these religious movements assimilate certain elements of Christian doctrine and incorporate them into their own ideologies.

Along with many other evangelical groups, Seventh-day Adventists and Pentecostals try to convert the non-Christian peoples of the world.[32] It would be a Promethean task to disentangle the contributions of diverse denominations and sects to this effort. In the case of foreign missions, however, subtle doctrinal

32. For a detailed account of the efforts of different Protestant missions in a single country, see William Read, *New Patterns of Church Growth in Brazil* (Grand Rapids, Mich.: Eerdmans, 1965).

differences are usually much more important to the proselytizer than to the proselytized. It seems legitimate, therefore, to view Christian missionary activity as part of the growth of a new religious *oikumenê*.[33] Christian eschatology and moral ideals have influenced the religious outlook of nominally non-Christian societies in ways often unanticipated by and unacceptable to resident missionaries.[34] Although the dissemination of the Christian Gospel has not dissolved all religious boundaries between disparate societies, it has made the term "pagan peoples" progressively more anachronistic. Certainly from a Christian point of view it is no longer possible to draw unequivocal lines between the "civilized" and the "pagan" areas of the globe. Judging from the current theological debates on the "death of God" in advanced Western countries, these rather than the recently missionized societies may be in danger of becoming "pagan," at least as far as orthodox Christianity is concerned.

If nothing else, the Christian message of the fundamental equality of all men enables those groups subject to foreign control to meet their oppressors on common symbolic ground. For the subordinate group, Christianity supplies a flexible moral idiom capable of circumventing, if not directly breaching, otherwise impenetrable social barriers to communication with the superordinate society. In situations where interpersonal relationships between members of the ruling and ruled strata are systematically deprived of the richness and spontaneity that allows each to recognize the other's humanity, religion is the one language able to subvert, in intent if not always in effect, the

33. A. L. Kroeber says that "the old name Oikoumenê with a partial shift of meaning from the 'range of mankind' to the 'range of man's most developed cultures' thus remains a convenient designation for an interwoven set of happenings and products which are significant equally for the culture historian and for the theoretical anthropologists. . . . the Oikoumenê may perhaps be redefined as a great web of culture growth, areally extensive and rich in content. Within this web or historic nexus, first of all, inventions or new cultural materials have tended to be transmitted, sooner or later, from end to end." "The Ancient Oikoumenê as a Historic Culture Aggregate," in *The Nature of Culture* (Chicago: University of Chicago Press, 1952), pp. 379, 392.
34. For a well-documented case, see F. B. Welbourn, *East African Rebels* (London: SCM Press, 1961).

political motive which sustains this arrangement. Thus it is difficult for those in power to remain completely oblivious to grievances addressed to them in terms of an ethical vocabulary taken from their own religious heritage. Of course this tactic hardly guarantees compliance with these demands. Yet it explains, in part, why religious movements which adopt an overtly anti-European posture often do not divest their ideologies of biblical imagery.[35]

Most important, Christianity offers a means of widening traditional intellectual frameworks to accommodate change. Or it reinforces indigenous ideas which seem to account for significant aspects of the new social scene.[36] In either case, the vital cognitive process is a movement toward a synthetic grasp of a changed situation. Bastide remarks that Christianity becomes part of "an acculturation that affects the very structures of the mind and the emotions." [37]

Although not inconsequential, the effect of Christianity on the development of these religious movements is oblique. Specific ideological responses to Western intrusion cannot be precisely correlated with the presence of a particular church or sect in a given area. The influence of Christian doctrine on these ideologies is mediated through major shifts in the climate of religious opinion. New modes of metaphysical speculation and of historical interpretation are now available to the members of these societies.

35. For instance, the intensely antiwhite Jamaican Ras Tafari movement retains Old Testament prophets in its belief system. See George Simpson, "Jamaican Revivalist Cults," *Social and Economic Studies*, 5 (1956).
36. Lucy Mair says that "there are, of course, Christian sects which believe in the imminence of the millennium, and the best known of these, the Watchtower Movement, is at work in two of the three regions [Africa and Melanesia] that I have discussed and very likely among American Indians as well. In comparison with local cults it, like *Mission des Noirs*, has the prestige derived from the possession of its own doctrinal writings, which re-interpret the dominant religion in a manner favorable to the aspirations of the subject group." "Independent Religious Movements in Three Continents," *Comparative Studies in Society and History* 1 (1959):133.
37. R. Bastide, "Messianism and Social and Economic Development," in *Social Change: The Colonial Situation*, ed. Immanuel Wallerstein (New York: Wiley, 1966), p. 475.

Separatist religious movements sometimes retain much of the formal theological framework of Christianity after parting company with the missions. The crucial issue, however, concerns not how much is retained but how it is used: Which aspects of Christian doctrine are most consistent with the cognitive needs and practical aims of these religious movements? And how are they used to pursue ends not sanctioned by the superordinate society?[38]

Christian ethics maintain that the weak deserve and, indeed, are entitled to fair treatment from the powerful. To the peoples of the underdeveloped and colonial areas of the world, this suggests that cooperation and mutual understanding is possible between culturally distinct groups. At the same time, Christianity heightens their sensitivity to any social arrangement that denies the moral equality of all of its members. Evangelical Christianity proclaims that all Christians are brothers and are therefore equal in the sight of God. Missionaries tell their parishioners that conversion entails a basic transformation in their lives; to be converted means to be "born again, a new man in Christ." For peoples who do not rigidly compartmentalize the spiritual and material benefits of religious activity, this manifesto implies that a new status is available to them in the wider social and economic order.[39]

Christianity strengthens these peoples' already ambivalent feelings toward Western merchants, missionaries, and administrators. While their political ambitions are stifled by Western power, their appetite for material goods is stimulated by Western affluence. Separatist and revitalization movements arise when

38. Jean Guiart comments that with respect to cargo cults "up to now, few anthropologists have troubled to analyze Christianity in the area, as it has evolved over nearly two centuries. We talk of Missionization, as an external factor which plays havoc with traditional society. We look for the remnants of heathenism inside the existing Christian society. We rarely think of Christianity as a living factor inside the social structure, as being in many ways an entirely new phenomenon: the reinterpretation of occidental traditional religious ideas and structures by people who have chosen to make use of them as their own." "The Millenarian Aspect of Conversion to Christianity in the South Pacific," in *Millennial Dreams in Action*, ed. Sylvia Thrupp (The Hague: Mouton, 1962), p. 122.

39. Ibid.

the promise of political freedom and economic abundance is not realized. Ironically, Christian doctrine justifies this attempt to divorce themselves from the Western-dominated social order. The ideologies of these religious movements are replete with references to biblical prophets who answered God's commands to break the bonds of oppression and lead their people to freedom.

Pentecostal and Seventh-day Adventist doctrines are especially germane to the analysis of these religious movements. Pentecostals emphasize the accessibility of divine power to the believer through the medium of spiritual possession. Under the proper conditions, the Holy Ghost is said to enter into the body and mind of the believer and to bestow miraculous powers upon him. Seventh-day Adventists believe in a divinely instituted millennium in this world. They stress the rewards God will give the faithful and the punishment he will inflict upon those who refuse to heed his warnings.

Although these notions are not alien to Christian theology, they are subtly and unobtrusively woven into the fabric of orthodox thought. Conventional theologians view these sectarian doctrines as archaic vestiges of a faith that has outgrown its enthusiastic origins.[40] Pentecostals and Seventh-day Adventists amplify and intensify the meaning of these ideas. In this form, they coincide with the religious experience of many non-Western peoples.[41] They strike a responsive chord in the minds of those who are searching for ideas that will close the hiatus between the knowledge available to render change intelligible and the irreducible ambiguity that remains after attempts to do so have been made. When traditional verities are tested against contemporary actualities, the result is an interpretation of the present which draws upon the past and looks to the future.[42] In this process, Christian conceptions of immediate recourse to su-

40. For example, see Ronald Knox, *Enthusiasm* (New York: Oxford University Press, 1961).

41. See Mircea Eliade, "Cargo-Cults and Cosmic Regeneration," in *Millennial Dreams in Action*, and Walter Mischel and Frances Mischel, "Psychological Aspects of Spirit Possession," *American Anthropologist* 60 (1958).

42. See K. O. L. Burridge, *Mambu: A Melanesian Millennium* (London: Methuen, 1960).

pernatural sources of power and of a messianic solution to persecution and suffering do not go unnoticed:

> The continuing spiritual presence of these leaders (who referred to themselves as the Messiah and were called the Negro Christ) motivated the organization of a strong new church, unswervingly autonomous, polemical in regard to both the missionaries and the government, and founded upon old traditions but receptive to Christian ideas. What Georges Balandier points out in *Sociologie de l'Afrique Noire* applies to Matswa even more aptly than Kimbangu: Christianity, offering the example of a Messiah sacrificed to the blind intransigence of public powers no less than to the infamy of his enemies, yet rising triumphant for the redemption of the faithful, awakened in the natives a revolutionary spirit, from which Christianity itself had stemmed, and thereby set the seal of religious approval on the demand for religious and cultural independence and self-determination. The Christian promise of a "Kingdom" and a "Millennium" for the salvation of all mankind, inherited from the messianic tradition of the Jews, was heeded by the natives as a call against the repressive rule of the colonial powers. Worshipping its own martyrs, Matswa and Kimbangu, and guided by its current prophets, the natives' messianic cult was powerfully united by the Christian promise and by the more tangible reality of a struggle to be won against the European master and his white churches.[43]

Often the ideologies of these religious movements locate the ultimate cause of their distress in a mythical realm. Here the conduct of culture heroes symbolically reveals both the responsibility for and the solution to their plight. The supernatural actors in this mythical drama explicate the contradiction between their descendants' meager resources and their unlimited aspirations. Through this symbolic medium these people can envision cultural autonomy without relinquishing the dream of partnership in the new social and economic order. By positing moral parity with a superior power, these ideologies effect a "numinous translation from one order of being into another."[44]

The tension generated by unfulfilled needs frequently is relieved by predictions about the imminence of a this-worldly utopia. The members of these movements believe that they can induce or coerce spiritual beings to initiate a new dispensation of

43. Vittorio Lanternari, *The Religions of the Oppressed: A Study of Modern Messianic Cults* (New York: Knopf, 1963), p. 15.
44. Burridge, *Mambu*, p. xvii.

material goods and social status as long as they follow the appropriate ritual procedures and moral prescriptions. Messianic visions have retributive connotations. When the new age begins, the relationship between the subordinate and superordinate segments of the society will be radically reversed. The lowly are now clearly dominant, and the previous rulers are severely chastised for their immoral behavior. For politically powerless people, messanic fantasies express deep-seated antagonism toward those groups that deprive them of what they feel are their birthrights.

These ideas provide more than a relatively safe outlet for anger over racial discrimination and political repression. They serve many ends. For example, some scholars think that Melanesian cargo cults focus diffuse dissatisfaction with their current mode of living on the real source of their problems: the colonial social order. At the same time, this ideology gives indigenous leaders the opportunity to appeal for support on grounds which overcome local rivalries and particularistic social ties.[45] Other scholars claim that cult dogma adapts traditional beliefs about the creation of wealth to a social context in which the principle of moral equivalence is no longer established by ordinary productive and ritual techniques. Thus the cult searches for the answer to a persistent economic deficit in their relations with the whites. The members of cargo cults are certain that the magical key to the solution of this moral as well as economic equation is purposely concealed by the religious specialists of the dominant society. Consequently, changes in cult doctrine and ritual reflect the traditional experimental and instrumental attitude toward religious activity which holds that religious practices are true because they work. With each failure to bring the ancestors and the cargo, the cult tries another variant of its magical formula for compelling the spirits to deliver the goods for which the whites alone have the secret at the moment.[46]

45. See Peter Worsley, *The Trumpet Shall Sound* (London: Macgibbon and Kee, 1957).
46. See Peter Lawrence, *Road Belong Cargo* (Manchester: University of Manchester Press, 1964).

The meaning of symbolic action is multidimensional and overdetermined in the Freudian sense of the word. Those who participate in these religious movements can do so without always sharing exactly the same motives. They may pursue diverse ends without contradicting the substance of cult ideology. Furthermore, the extent to which consensus about concrete "definitions of the situation" is enforced by formal doctrines varies considerably in religious movements. And I suspect that these movements fall close to the undogmatic end of the continuum. In this respect, they differ markedly from Pentecostal and Seventh-day Adventist ideologies.

Thus it is possible to explain the significance of religious action at different levels of meaning. The cargo cult may represent a nascent nationalistic impulse. And it may also adhere to traditional conceptions of how wealth is acquired in its quest for Western goods. Whatever truth these explanations contain, Burridge, in my opinion, goes to the crux of the matter. He treats these movements as a creative attempt to endow a potentially anomic situation with a significance which transcends its unbearable restrictions and contradictions. Under the aegis of a collective mythical dream, these people imagine and try to build a viable culture out of their fragmented past. To do this, they must construct a moral order which resolves the incongruities in their relationships to the local missionaries and administrators:

> Let us say that the participants of a Cargo movement are attempting to find particular and relevant symbols which will express certain conflicts and the ideal solutions of them; and let us also say that they are trying to externalize and relate these symbols together into some durable form which will have validity for succeeding generations. . . . Unwilling to accept all that Europeans have brought, and unwilling to divide himself morally in two, a Kanaka can only find himself whole and entire within terms of a synthesis that contains both worlds and, is, therefore, larger than either. He must make a new man. And to do so he must resort to his learning and truths as he finds them.[47]

Predicated upon equitable principles and free from crippling moral deficiencies, this vision of the future constitutes the es-

47. Burridge, *Mambu*, pp. 32, 33.

sence of cult belief. Rather than depicting cargo cults as passive pawns caught in the grip of the inexorable movement of supra-personal historical forces, Burridge sees "that society is presented to each man as *a perspective of the future* and that this future penetrates to the heart of each one as a real motivation for his behavior."[48]

Christian belief not only corroborates the messianic expectations of these religious movements; it reinforces the idea that religious knowledge, authority, and power are gained through direct contact with supernatural beings. The notion that those possessed by the Holy Spirit are blessed with the "gifts" of prophecy and healing confirms traditional assumptions about the role of magical processes in social life. When the leaders of a separatist or revitalization movement openly disregard the authority of the dominant group, they face the possibility of punitive action. In a confrontation with a group that commands overwhelming power, the ability to foretell the future is of obvious value. Knowing the final resolution of their struggle, they can face any "temporary" setback with equanimity. Most important, prophecy is a critical source of charismatic validation for the leadership of religious movements which cannot depend upon outside support.[49] Along with healing, it demonstrates that the leader has a privileged relationship to supernatural beings and therefore can enlist their aid on his constituents' behalf.

In light of the foregoing discussion, it would be premature indeed to dismiss the study of esoteric religious ideologies as an antiquarian enterprise. At the very least, analysis of systems of belief which appear strange to the more conventional members of our society may illuminate the attraction which similar dogmas exercise on the ideologically less temperate masses at other times and places.

48. Jean Paul Sartre, *Search for a Method* (New York: Vintage Books, 1968), p. 96.

49. In his classic study of separatist churches in South Africa, Bengt Sunkler notes that "whether the Prophetic call has been conveyed by lightning or through dreams or visions, it is always thought of as being a call extended by the Holy Spirit. This is the foundation of the prophet's authority in the Church: the selective principle by which a budding prophet is brought out of obscurity into the limelight and to leadership is the claim to be a man of the Holy Spirit. *Bantu Prophets in South Africa* (London: Oxford University Press), p. 115.

Participant Observation and the Study of Religious Belief

This book is an anthropological study of religious belief, inasmuch as it relies on the traditional field method of participant observation. Later (see Appendix 1) I will discuss some of the problems I encountered as a participant observer in urban religious sects. But for the moment I would like to comment briefly on the special affinity between this method and the study of cultural systems. The association between participant observation and anthropology is not an adventitious result of academic history. Regardless of the structural complexity of the society in which fieldwork is undertaken, participant observation is the method par excellence for the empirical investigation of systems of meaning.

Participant observation not only is a technique for gathering data in natural social settings but has epistemological connotations as well. This method has an inherent phenomenological bias. Participant observers hesitate to explain conduct in terms of analytic categories which violate or ignore the substance of the actor's social experience. Merleau-Ponty states this more positively: "This process of joining the objective analysis to lived experience is perhaps the most proper task of anthropology. . . . The variables of anthropology . . . must be met sooner or later on the level at which phenomena have an immediately human significance." [50]

Unlike many other methods in the social sciences, participant observation eludes operational definition. In its most general form, participant observation involves a prolonged, multifaceted, face-to-face encounter between the observer and the members of a community that is designed to elicit their orientation to their social milieu.[51] The actor's social experience, in the terms in which he conceives it, plays a dual role in participant observation. On the one hand, it is the fundamental datum the observer

50. Maurice Merleau-Ponty, "From Mauss to Lévi-Strauss," in *Signs*, trans. Richard G. McCleary (Evanston, Ill.: Northwestern University Press, 1964), p. 119.
51. See my unpublished paper with Don Merten, "Participant Observation and the Discovery of Meaning" (Department of Sociology and Anthropology, Institute for Juvenile Research, Chicago, Ill.).

seeks to obtain in the field. On the other hand, along with the observer's conceptual schemes, the actor's "definition of the situation" serves to explain his behavior. With respect to the study of religious commitment, Carrier remarks that, from a phenomenological perspective, it is "the contents of consciousness which, from the subject's viewpoint, motivate his behavior; in this case the motive consists in a belief in divine action."[52] I would add that those ideas and feelings which have normative implications for the actor's relationship to both supernatural and human beings constitute what we might call the cultural component of the motivational grounds for his conduct.

An individual's relationships with others are always mediated by the meanings he imposes upon interpersonal events. Although the specific meaning he imputes to an act may be disputed by others, the cultural categories which render behavior intelligible to the members of a community are not commonly open to similar challenges. These relatively invariant notions about the nature and disposition of human and supernatural agents and agencies provide the cultural frame of reference from which an actor formulates his own projects and assesses those of others. In this sense, culture becomes an evaluative act through which the actor organizes his relationship to others. Culture, however, is not only a constellation of ideas and sentiments that exerts normative constraints on his behavior. As a symbolic process, it gains much of its behavioral validity through one of the principal means by which it is formulated: conversation.

The participant observer has a distinctive purchase on the study of culture because he has access to the symbolic processes by which it is manifested in everyday social interaction. He engages in a sustained dialogue about the meaning of the events and activities that directly impinge upon the lives of his informants. By talking about the significance of ordinary and unusual occurrences, the observer enters the fluid stream of social life. He participates in the very process by which the members of the

52. Hervé Carrier, *The Sociology of Religious Belonging* (New York: Herder and Herder, 1965), p. 74.

community reduce the ineluctable ambiguity of immediate social experience and thereby construct a durable model of social reality.

How does the participant observer immerse himself in the intricacies of ongoing social interaction, adopt a casual conversational style, and yet retain his analytic grasp of the social situation? In my opinion, he does so by consciously searching for the contradictions between his own assumptions about the meaning of an act and the motivational postulates that enable his informants to make sense out of the same behavior. In other words, he "gets into the situation" by contrasting his own vocabulary of motives with those held by his informants. It is the discrepancy between the observer's and his informant's explanatory schemes that ultimately allows the former to penetrate the experiential nexus between thought and action in a particular community.

If this is so, the observer's "subjective" reaction to unfamiliar beliefs and practices is an indispensable part of his analysis of their meaning. Moreover, those cultural phenomena that the observer designates as significant and worthy of systematic explication depend upon the way he perceives them as well as on his theoretical interests and empirical sensibilities. In fact, I believe that what the observer sees as problematic about a cultural system becomes so because its premises, to some extent, contradict the logic of his intellectual and moral experience. This methodological stance is consistent with what Michael Polanyi calls the "fiduciary" element in all knowledge.[53] Along these lines, Adorno remarks:

> The social scientist's experience does not give him undifferentiated, chaotic material to be organized; rather the material of his experience is the social order, more emphatically a "system" than any ever conceived by philosophy. What decides whether his concepts are right or wrong is neither their generality nor, on the other hand, their approximation to "pure" fact but rather the adequacy with which they grasp the real laws of movement of society and thereby render stubborn facts transparent.[54]

53. Michael Polanyi, *Personal Knowledge* (New York: Harper Torchbooks, 1962).
54. Theodor Adorno, "The Sociology of Knowledge and Its Consciousness," in *Prisms* (London: Spearman, 1967), p. 43.

In light of this rather abstruse discussion of participant observation, it seems appropriate to examine the problem this study seeks to resolve in terms of my fieldwork strategy. I sought to develop my sensitivity to the multiple meanings contained in the formal belief systems of these groups; I wanted to avoid treating these dogmas in a cursory or simplistic fashion—that is, assuming that "bizarre" religious doctrines reflect social and psychological pressures without looking at their capacity to generate rational modes of action, given the cosmological assumptions of a particular world view. I wanted to see how these notions were incorporated into the believer's action system; that is, how his theologically based interpretations of the world led him to construe social situations in one way and not another—what induced him to emphasize certain aspects of his environment.

Second, I was interested in the influence of religious ideas in nonritual contexts. Much of the anthropological study of the relationship between belief and the social order focuses on ritual settings. In the dramatic enactment of social relationships, the observer discerns the symbolic play and import of secular interests, tensions, and allegiances rooted in the larger social structure. Since I was concerned with the less visible or, at least, the less dramatic connections between belief and social action, I listened to theological discussions for references (however oblique, guarded, or disguised) to the ways in which believers ought to organize their lives, to the grounds upon which they should make moral judgments, and to the kind of social decisions and dilemmas they confront.

With these general objectives in mind, I spent much of my time talking to the members of these groups about the significance of their belief. In these informal conversations, I sought to discover the premises which gave their world view internal cogency and their lives a specific direction. The fieldwork, then, was a process of finding the intellectual and motivational basis of an integrated system of thought and action which I initially perceived merely as a disconnected set of not very credible propositions about the nature of the supernatural world.

Thus, the question which prompted this study and which it

seeks to resolve can be stated as a paradox. In the Seventh-day Adventist case, Why should people who firmly believe that God is soon to destroy all earthly systems of social rank and economic opportunity work so diligently against formidable odds to improve their own and their children's position in them? In other words, Why does a doctrine which should, on its face, create apathy or fatalism about one's present socioeconomic destiny lead to continuous striving to change that status? In the Pentecostal case, Why should people who believe that God is available for direct aid in every human contingency not utilize this power in their secular lives? In other words, Why is their attitude toward advancement in the socioeconomic system so passive and resigned if they believe that God is willing to intervene on their behalf in any situation which affects them adversely?

2 The Problem of Sect Affiliation

Social Stratification and Religious Affiliation in America

I will briefly discuss one aspect of the involuted relationship between social stratification and American Protestantism before turning to the principal concern of this chapter, the problem of sect affiliation. The links between social class and church membership are especially salient in contemporary American Protestantism. Although not stratified strictly along economic lines, Protestant denominations cater to congregations who are very sensitive to the religious concomitants of their social standing in the larger community. Consequently, a spirit of social exclusiveness pervades the organizational framework of the Protestant churches.

In his study of suburban churches, Winter observes that "much of this exclusiveness comes about 'naturally.' The style of life, manner of dress, form of worship, appointments, windows, clerical garb, and even the coffee hour serve to include some and exclude others."[1] And

1. Gibson Winter, *The Suburban Captivity of the Churches* (New York: Macmillan Co., 1962), p. 62.

Goldschmidt discovered in the study of a single community that:

> People like to "be with their own kind" when being with others means remaining always on the peripheries of participation. Yet people do not want to associate with people who are "beneath them." . . . The church members deny any policy of exclusion, and can document their denial with examples. Yet the exclusion is of such an insidious nature that it is felt at both ends, and there is a tacit recognition that certain churches are for certain people, and this is sometimes given overt expression.[2]

As national organizations, many Protestant denominations appear socially heterogeneous, but local congregations are usually homogeneous.[3] Church membership is closely tied to the major sources of social differentiation in American life—class, race, and ethnicity.[4]

Ritual often provides the symbolic medium through which Protestant churches imbue social etiquette with sacred value. In a very subtle fashion, the life style of a class or community gains religious attributes. Berger remarks that:

> The costume, speech taboos, and interior decorating regarded as suitable for churches offer a rich field for meditation on this subject. The flowered hats, the white gloves, and exclamations of "heck" or "darn" become integral parts of a liturgy of gentility. The sociability preferences of the middle class take on a religious color. Petty-bourgeois gregariousness is regarded as Christian *koinonia* and the back-yard barbecue takes on the aroma of the *agape* meal in countless church picnics or ladies'-aid gatherings. Needless to say, the details of this religious celebration of class aesthetics will vary with the precise social location in question.[5]

By pointing to these sorts of differences, churches which draw their members almost exclusively from overlapping social circles rationalize the covert but nonetheless undeniable barriers to

2. Walter Goldschmidt, *As You Sow* (New York: Harcourt, Brace, 1947), p. 134.
3. Nicholas J. Demerath III discerns high and low status modes of participation within Protestant denominations which he associates with church- and sectlike orientations to religious activity. *Social Class in American Protestantism* (Chicago: Rand McNally, 1955).
4. See H. Richard Niebuhr, *The Social Sources of Denominationalism* (New York: Meridian Books, 1959).
5. Peter L. Berger, *The Noise of Solemn Assemblies* (Garden City, N.Y.: Doubleday, 1961), p. 85.

fellowship with doctrinally like-minded Christians who happen not to share their social background. Thus, easy sociability rather than doctrinal agreement acts as the fulcrum of religious association; the church becomes a voluntary association composed of persons who feel comfortable in each other's presence rather than a community gathered together by their faith in Jesus Christ. Winter says that "the service of worship proclaims the sacredness of association by similarity in economic performance, symbolizing the insulation of one social rank against another rather than mutual dependence of rich and poor, insider and outsider, strong and weak, leader and led." [6]

In sum, the ritual symbols of social differentiation serve to validate a group's position in a status hierarchy and, more generally, to infuse its secular biases and interests with an aura of sanctity. Winter puts this graphically:

> The Church is now a reflection of the economic ladder. Ascent on this ladder is validated by escalation to congregations of higher social and economic rank. For every rung on the ladder there is an appropriate congregation, with ushers of slightly more refined dress, and somewhat more cultivated ladies affairs. Such small stylistic differences are the bread of life in a society dedicated to the service of productivity.[7]

Protestant congregations, sects and denominations alike, tend to assume that their ritual "superiority" extends to their entire way of life. They are therefore prone to interpret ritual differences as signs of moral dispositions and intellectual propensities.[8] This transforms religious conceptions about the tangible means of contact with the Deity into status symbols.

6. Winter, *Suburban Captivity*, p. 76.
7. Ibid., p. 77.
8. Seymour Lipset says that American religion is "explicitly concerned with values, with stating the proper modes of thinking and acting. And whether the religion of the privileged or deprived, it translates experiences into value terms, into concepts of right and wrong. Since religious groups must define the right as divinely inspired, their structure serves to institutionalize reactions to historical experiences as norms which are passed on to subsequent generations." "Religion and Politics in the American Past and Present," in *Religion and Social Conflict*, ed. Robert Lee and Martin E. Marty (New York: Oxford University Press, 1964), p. 119.

The Problem of Sect Affiliation—The Relationship between Religious Belief and Social Structure

If sacred symbols are supposed to heal antagonisms between groups and thereby overcome or, at least, periodically repair breaches in the social fabric, why should Protestantism split into separate and sometimes competing religious bodies, each with its own doctrinal and ritual peculiarities? In short, why are Protestant churches so responsive to the divisive concerns of social class?

The Catholic church has exclusive parishes, national (ethnic) churches, and religious orders, each with its own special organizational interests and point of view; yet the church retains a sense of its doctrinal and ritual unity which is alien to the Protestant world. The reasons for the greater susceptibility of Protestantism to organizational fission and ideological fragmentation are very complex. Without recapitulating the history of the not always successful Protestant impulse to divest religious commitment of all considerations other than those of the believer's conscience, perhaps a few comments on this question will enable us to understand why church affiliation is a critical issue in the Protestant tradition.

Catholics have a more "individualistic" view of the meaning of religious worship than Protestants, although theologians stress that certain of the priest's and the communicant's ritual acts involve the entire body of the church. As long as he fulfills his elementary religious duties, a Catholic's access to those sacraments essential to his salvation is unimpaired. His spiritual energies and interests, then, are focused upon the institutional instruments of grace, the sacraments as they are administered by the priesthood.[9] Underhill notes that "in the sacraments is ex-

9. Evelyn Underhill says that "at last, in fully developed liturgy, the whole drama of creation and redemption—God's loving movement toward man, and man's response in Christ is fully recapitulated. . . . Here, then, in a way which is concrete and homely and yet transcendental, the two major interpretations of the Christian Mystery—the redemptive sacrifice and the incarnation of the Word—are given

pressed the fundamental nature of the Church, the fact that Christ lives on in her. . . . Roman Catholic devotion since the Reformation has tended more and more to a personal and individualistic piety centered on the Reserved Sacrament."[10]

In contrast to Catholicism, Protestantism emphasizes the Word and its implications for ordinary life:

> The common worship of the Roman and Orthodox Churches is predominantly Eucharistic, and gives priority to the Ministry of the Sacraments. . . . On the other hand, the common worship of Continental and English Protestantism is predominantly Biblical, and emphasizes the Ministry of the Word and the ethical demands of Christianity. Here the celebration of the Eucharist is a special occasion, and not the heart of the Church's life.[11]

The Catholic interested in religious sustenance and not simply in Sunday sociabilitiy comes to the service principally as an individual communicant and only secondarily as a member of a particular local congregation. If circumstances demand it, he can worship alongside persons from different social backgrounds.[12] As far as he is concerned, the presence of others at the service, whatever their social origins, cannot materially affect the character or the validity of his religious experience.

On the other hand, devout Protestants are concerned not only about their own spiritual worthiness but also about that of the congregation as a whole.[13] Of course, like all Christians, Protes-

---

sacramental expression and made operative in each soul." *Worship* (New York: Harper, 1937), p. 122.

10. Ibid., pp. 249, 261.

11. Ibid., p. 336.

12. To verify this, one needs only to observe the socially varied clientel of Catholic chapels in urban centers.

13. Of course, this statement oversimplifies a complex historical development. Lutheranism, admittedly, focuses on the state of the believer's soul rather than on his behavior as the absolutely critical sign of salvation. Nonetheless, Ernst Troeltsch (*The Social Teaching of the Christian Churches*, trans. Olive Wyon, vol. 2 [London: Allen and Unwin, 1956]) suggests that the conception of the church as a group whose probity in secular dealings sets it apart from the rest of the world represents a central tendency in Protestantism. Acceptance of the Word as the sole authority for worship and conduct makes personal piety the standard for admission to these congregations. In the early part of this century, Max Weber ("The Protestant Sects and the Spirit

tants believe that each person is ultimately responsible for his own salvation. Nevertheless, they also feel that their fellow church members' state of grace reflects either positively or adversely upon their own. For Protestants, grace is closely related to the spiritual excellence which flows from a consistent pattern of moral behavior. Thus, the moral "tone" of a church indicates, to some extent, its members' collective state of grace.

Protestantism rejects an eternal, institutionalized source of religious and moral authority. Consequently the Protestant service is directed to the entire congregation, since in the final analysis it is the arbiter of theological and moral issues. In Protestant denominations, except for churches which maintain the principle of apostolic episcopal succession, each congregation or its representatives must decide upon the appropriateness of ritual or doctrinal innovations. Unlike the Catholic, if he takes his religious precepts seriously, the lay Protestant must sit in judgment upon questions that involve the relationship between divine commands and temporal interests. Only his conscience can tell him whether certain attitudes or actions are in keeping with divine imperatives. In situations of religious doubt and uncertainty he cannot rely, like the Catholic, upon the unequivocal authority of established dogma. When a Protestant who is committed to his faith suspects the spiritual capacities and moral qualifications of his minister or of his fellow church members, he is likely to question the righteousness of his church. And rather than knowingly depart from divine norms, he may leave the group.[14]

---

of Capitalism," in *From Max Weber: Essays in Sociology*, ed. Hans Gerth and C. Wright Mills [New York: Oxford University Press, 1958]) found that membership in diverse Protestant denominations in this country was generally taken as a sign of proved ethical virtue, and I would suspect that even today the members of most Protestant denominations believe that membership in their church is associated with a certain type of moral character.

14. This is particularly applicable to conservative denominations and, of course, to evangelical sects. Val Clear ("The Church of God: A Study in Social Adaptation" [Ph.D. diss., University of Chicago, 1953]) points out that Holiness groups reject the worldliness and seeming moral relativity of even fairly orthodox denominations. Originally members of the denominations, Holiness people began to question the denominations' position on proper Christian behavior and this led to

Protestant religious norms are consequently relative to the standards of a class or community in ways in which Catholic norms are not, and hence Protestant norms are more dependent upon local consensus. Thus, Protestant ritual and doctrinal conflicts are more open to the influence of nonsacred considerations.[15] In general, ritual and doctrinal differences often express a host of secular antagonisms, and prolonged conflict sometimes leads a person or faction to join or form a new church or sect.

Studies of the meaning of membership in Protestant churches have concentrated on one aspect of this problem: Why do the religiously inclined members of the various social strata usually gravitate to such *different types* of religious organizations? [16] More specifically, sociologists have tried to find out why the rich and powerful belong to the established denominations whereas the poor and oppressed join the evangelical sects.

In my opinion, sociologists have overlooked an important problem in the study of religious affiliation. It is related to but analytically distinct from the question of the social determinants of institutional affiliation (i.e., church type—sect, denomination, cult). This study asks why a person joins one rather than another kind of religious group when both have the *same type* of religious organization. The focus here is on two different belief systems associated with a single type of church organization, the evangelical sect.

---

serious doubts about the validity of the denominations' theology. Here we can see the familiar pattern of schism and the emergence of a new church dedicated to a new orthodoxy which either revitalizes or fragments Protestantism, depending upon one's point of view.

15. See Richard Sommerfeld, "Conceptions of the Ultimate and the Social Organization of Religious Bodies," *Journal for the Scientific Study of Religion* 3 (1968). He distinguishes between "democratic" and "dominical" forms of organization among Protestant groups and observes that the democratic type is most responsive to doctrinal disputes.

16. Charles Glock remarks that this concern has tended to obscure many of the significant differences between sects. He says that "classifying as sects the Father Divine movement, the Hutterites, the I AM Society, the Apostolic and Pentecostal Church and early Christian Science does not take into account the differences in the conditions out of which they developed, in the content of their theologies, in the constituencies to which they appeal, and in the form of their internal organization." "The Sociology of Religion," in *Sociology Today*, ed. Leonard Broom et al. [New York: Basic Books, 1959], p. 159.

This study, then, examines those circumstances which motivate an individual to commit himself to one rather than another religious ideology. This problem encompasses two distinct issues. First, What are the functional implications of membership in a Seventh-day Adventist or a Pentecostal group? That is, What needs and desires prompt a person to adopt either of these two very different religious doctrines? And, assuming for the moment that these motives are conditioned by the social structure, What role does sect doctrine play in their resolution or satisfaction? Although structural location may not determine sect affiliation in a simple cause and effect manner, at least it makes similar demands upon the members of a sect and generates a common set of problems to which they must respond. How, then, can we characterize the relationship between a person's position in the social order and the kind of religious belief he accepts as true and morally binding? Second, the question of why a person develops an affinity to a certain kind of belief system raises a vital issue in the sociology of religion. What impact do religious doctrines have upon a believer's orientation to his everyday, practical affairs? And how does a set of formal religious beliefs about man's place in the universe come to govern his attitudes toward ordinary conduct?

Status Deprivation and Sect Affiliation: The Structural Sources of Pentecostal and Adventist Ideologies

Weber's discussion of the genesis of the Protestant ethic (that ascetic, entrepreneurial attitude toward work, saving, and investment which was closely associated if not synonymous with the rise of rational bourgeois capitalism in the West) emphasized the austere implications of the Calvinist notion of predestination for the believer.[17] Weber pointed out that this distinctive pattern of secular behavior, which glorified active mastery over the material world and, at the same time, pressed a regime of personal asceticism on its adherents, was sustained by intense

17. See Reinhard Bendix, *Max Weber: An Intellectual Portrait* (Garden City, N.Y.: Doubleday, 1962), chap. 3.

religious anxiety. This anxiety was derived from a metaphysical assumption about the fate of men's souls and acted as the unconscious stimulus which reinforced the rigorous discipline of the Protestant ethic. Without this sort of emotional incentive men could not have been persuaded for long to renounce all immediate sensual gratifications in the economic sphere solely in the service of a religious ideal. Weber holds that the efficient cause of the Protestant ethic, the material agency which brings this moral code into being, is psychological. Or to put this somewhat differently, Weber argued that if ordinary Calvinists and Puritans did not worry constantly about their own religious status, whether their lives revealed the inner qualities of men chosen by God for salvation, they most likely would have reached some kind of accommodation to their moral ideals. Instead they sought religious reassurance through moral heroism.

Like the *Protestant Ethic and the Spirit of Capitalism*, this study is concerned with the problem of how formal religious doctrines and creeds become an intrinsic component of an actor's orientation to secular situations. Thus, I am interested in religious codes whose norms actually govern ordinary social and economic conduct: ethical prescriptions and proscriptions which the actor internalizes and uses to judge his own mundane social performances. If an actor merely estimates his behavior as generally satisfactory, exemplary, or lacking, then he most likely views these norms as a set of external religious ideals which may be approximated but never fully implemented in his daily routine. On the other hand, if an actor feels that a certain religiously sanctioned pattern of secular behavior is or should become an essential aspect of his character, then it has become, in my opinion, part of his orientation to ordinary social situations.

My analysis concentrates on the structural and cultural aspects of the complex problem of sect affiliation. As far as the actor's motive for joining a religious group is concerned, this study relies upon an elementary social-psychological postulate derived from relative deprivation theory:[18] People join sects

18. This is probably what Ely Devons and Max Gluckman would call a justifiably naive assumption. "Conclusion: Modes and Consequences of Limiting a Field of Study," in *Closed Systems and Open Minds:*

because they seek to redress the lack of deference and esteem they feel is rightfully theirs. Obviously sect members join these groups for a wide variety of reasons besides the public desire to achieve salvation. Devereux points out that people join highly "ideologized" social movements for reasons often unrelated to their official purposes and programs, especially when the overt goals of the movement provide symbolically satisfying psychodynamic cover for consciously unacceptable motives.[19] Despite the role that sect belief and worship plays in the believer's psychic economy, this analysis is restricted to those motives which are related to the problems of adaptation to a particular niche in the socioeconomic order.

If sect affiliation is shaped by social factors, which aspects of a person's location in the social order dispose him to adopt a particular religious ideology? More specifically, can we predict his religious outlook on the basis of prior knowledge about his position in societal prestige, occupational, and income hierarchies? Can we say that his religious ideology is determined by his life chances (his liabilities and assets in the competition for economic advantages in the marketplace) and by his social status (the amount of deference and esteem he can legitimately demand from others)?

I will argue that if a person decides to resolve his status problems (those which involve his self-respect with regard to his standing relative to others in societal economic and prestige

---

The Limits of Naivety in Social Anthropology, ed. Max Gluckman (Chicago: Aldine Publishing Co., 1964).

19. George Devereux, "Two Types of Modal Personality Models," in *Studying Personality Cross-Culturally*, ed. Bert Kaplan (Evanston, Ill.: Row, Peterson and Co., 1961). David Rapport points out that it is impossible to impute a single motivational significance to any overt pattern of behavior: "The remarkable thing about human behavior is that man often meets diverse stimuli by the same behavior, and identical stimuli often elict diverse responses. Likewise with motivations: the same motive may be expressed by a wide range of behaviors or satisfied by a variety of objects, and a great variety of motives may be expressed by the same object." "The Structure of Psychoanalytic Theory," in *Psychology: A Study of a Science*, ed. Sigmund Koch (New York: McGraw-Hill, 1959), 5:123. With respect to the problem of sect affiliation, this suggests that no single motive or complex of motives is likely to exhaust the meaning of sect membership.

systems) in religious terms (there are, of course, functional alternatives in our society), then his sect affiliation can be predicted both by his objective position in societal occupational and income systems *and* by his subjective assessments or expectations of the probability of future upward movement in the socioeconomic system.

At this point, I should caution the reader that this proposition attempts to account for only one aspect of the quite complex phenomenon of sect affiliation. It leaves two crucial empirical questions unresolved because we lack an adequate theoretical framework for dealing with them. In the first place, it is not possible to specify the conditions under which a person will seek a religious rather than a secular solution to a status dilemma. That is to say, we do not have a theory which explains why some people choose cosmic and others pragmatic means of resolving personal suffering. Why, for example, do some people who experience a diffuse sense of personal unworthiness or social insignificance search for help from God and others from a psychiatrist? Moreover, we do not know why some people actively try to remedy the situation and others remain passive in the face of considerable distress. Why should some people who discover that they do not command the respect of significant others endure a depreciated sense of self-esteem while others look for a concrete way of altering these disparaging judgments of their worth? Therefore, I invoke the concept of functional alternatives to sect affiliation in the proposition above because it avoids the issue of why a person adopts a specifically religious mode of dealing with his status problems.

Until now I have talked about sect affiliation as though a person joined such a group as he would any other voluntary organization. Conversion to a sect, however, demands a radical realignment of one's values and social identity and often heals what William James called a "divided self." This is particularly true if the convert believes that his previous mode of life violated the group's norms (this formulation, incidentally, applies to members raised in the group as well as to outsiders insofar as the former feel that they had "fallen away" from God at some point in their religious career). Formally, conversion refers to an uncoerced encounter between the believer and God, but nevertheless it has obligatory connotations. The idea of conversion implies that the believer's conscience demands that he confess his sins, and, in practice, groups which value this experience put a good deal of normative pressure on their members to achieve it.[20]

This in turn means that the convert is willing to explain his failures in a new light; he acquires a new personal history. In so doing he not only publicly admits to a sinful past but also accepts the burden of guilt for mankind's persistent rejection of the Savior. Thus, we encounter specific cognitive and emotional factors which predispose a person to join a sect. The potential convert must accept this interpretative scheme before he can embrace more practical solutions to his discomfort. That is, within the Christian universe, why should evangelical ideology appeal to some persons and not others, holding class, education, and other obvious sociological variables constant? Carrier has suggested some of the elements of an adequate theory of conversion to sects, but in its absence we must deal with this question at a fairly high level of social-psychological abstraction.[21] In light of the foregoing I prefer to regard the above proposition as a heuristic device for examining the connections between social status and sect affiliation rather than as a hypothesis about the causal relationships between them.

20. Charles Glock and Rodney Stark ("Social Contexts and Religious Experience" in *Religion and Society in Tension* [Chicago: Rand McNally, 1965]) suggest that we can account for much of what seems like deviant or exotic religious behavior in terms of the norms of the groups to which persons who undergo these conversion experiences belong. The argument that such behavior is "normal" within these subcultures is valid up to a point. Except for relatively self-sufficient religious communities, there are no communities in this country where ecstatic conversions are normative in the sense that the experience is a usual aspect of adult role behavior and where the experience is treated as part of the ordinary course of an individual's social development. Outside the precincts of the church, ecstatic religious conversions not only are optional but also generate normative commitments which sometimes conflict with prescriptions that govern role behavior in nonreligious contexts.

21. Hervé Carrier, *The Sociology of Religious Belonging* (New York: Herder and Herder, 1965).

I do not maintain that an individual's subjective status expectations are necessarily produced by his objective socioeconomic situation. In fact, to anticipate my argument, it seems that they are at least partly a function of sect ideology. At first this sounds paradoxical and perhaps even teleological, but, whatever the ultimate sources of his status expectations, once he is a committed member of the group its religious ideology legitimates his status aspirations or lack of them and validates his perception of his position on a moving status continuum—whether he is going somewhere, standing still, or falling in the prestige system.[22] I further hold that although Pentecostals and Seventh-day Adventists occupy the same sort of occupational and income positions in the social structure—they are generally stable working-class and lower white-collar workers[23]—their subjective attitudes toward the possibility of upward mobility differ radically. Seventh-day Adventists are convinced that they will move "up in the world" whereas Pentecostals are equally convinced that they will not undergo significant improvement in their socioeconomic situation.

However, they share an important corollary attitude: they are sensitive to imputations of a lack of "respectability." [24] Their

22. The idea of a "status trajectory" was suggested to me by Professor David F. Aberle (personal communication).

23. This characterization of the economic situation of the Pentecostals and the Seventh-day Adventists contrasts with some statements that the members of fundamentalist evangelical sects are drawn from the most disadvantaged segments of the society. If one correlated the location of these churches with the socioeconomic attributes of the urban areas where they are usually situated, I suspect that the greatest concentration of these groups (particularly Pentecostal churches) would be found in the poorer inner-city areas and among ethnic groups who suffer from racial discrimination. But the crucial question concerns those segments of the population under consideration who are recruited to the sects. Here I do not think we can afford to assume that sect members in these areas are sociologically equivalent to their neighbors.

24. Joseph Kahl points out that the prestige value of a high-school education, a white-collar job, and native birth—the traditional signs of a lower middle class status—have been progressively depressed by automation and by the high wages of union-protected blue-collar workers. This stratum holds clerical and semiprofessional jobs and includes "petty" farmers and businessmen as well as certain segments of the salaried working class. Kahl says, "furthermore, if asked most of these

state of mind, to take a term from C. Wright Mills, might be described as that of a "lumpen-bourgeoisie."[25] Although these people are marginally connected to middle-class occupations and life styles, they are very concerned about the negative connotations they associate with a lower-class status. Berger notes that "respectability has a generally middle-class character. But not only middle-class people are respectable. In fact, respectability may be more important in the lower or working classes, because the latter are much closer to the blatantly nonrespectable."[26] Basing his observations on studies of sect affiliation, Berger claims that the very act of church membership for these people symbolically allows them to differentiate themselves from the "lumpen-proletariat" and thus to identify themselves with the middle class. Although sect or church affiliation is not per se an unmistakable sign of a desire for upward mobility, it does reflect a vital interest in the degree to which others will classify one as belonging to that part of society which deserves general esteem and respect.

Both Seventh-day Adventist and Pentecostal sect members suffer from relative status deprivation. Here I follow Aberle's definition of relative deprivation as "a negative discrepancy between legitimate expectation and actuality. Where an individual or group has a particular expectation and furthermore this expectation is considered to be a proper state of affairs, and where something less than that expectation is fulfilled, we may

---

people would call themselves middle class (though with some hesitation and ambivalence). They feel superior to routine wage workers who drift from job to job without developing a specialty. Yet, when the interviewing is pushed, they recognize that they are not 'in the know' about important decisions; and they recognize that they do not make as much money as they need in order to live in an elegant style. They know they are not big people. Lower-middle class people are thus on the fence; they are more conscious of being in between than are any other group. They cannot cling too strongly to career as the focus of their lives, for their jobs do not lead continuously upward. Instead, they tend to emphasize the respectability of their jobs and their styles of life, for it is respectability that makes them superior to shiftless workers." *The American Class Structure* (New York: Rinehart, 1957), p. 203.

25. C. Wright Mills, *White Collar* (New York: Oxford University Press, 1953).

26. Berger, *Noise of Solemn Assemblies*, p. 39.

speak of relative deprivation."[27] Deprivation is not a simple quantitative measure of the extent to which an individual or group lacks access to highly valued goods. Rather, it refers to the way they feel about lacking certain attributes, resources, opportunities, or goods possessed by others. Seventh-day Adventists and Pentecostals do not come from the most disadvantaged stratum of our society, but they suffer from exclusion from the respectable centers of middle-class life. From their point of view, they justifiably belong to this more esteemed class even though they do not have the tangible, economic prerequisites for membership in it. They feel that they are not appreciated for their special virtues and often go to great lengths to convince themselves and others that their way of life is morally correct and thus different from the sensual, impulse-dominated life of the "lower classes." Although seriously disadvantaged people often feel antagonistic to dominant social strata and feel unjustly exploited by them, the emotional tone of the marginal strata is possibly better characterized as resentment. They feel slighted rather than exploited; they are "hurt" rather than angry about their exclusion from respectable, middle-class social circles.

Although Seventh-day Adventists and Pentecostals feel that the amount of deference and esteem they receive from others is less than they rightfully deserve, they differ in the extent to which they believe that their sacred status (as part of the elect or Christ's faithful, saving remnant church) should compel others to increase their opinion of their worthiness. In other words, they differ in the degree to which they willingly accept status assessments based upon socioeconomic criteria as legitimate.

Seventh-day Adventist and Pentecostal ideologies also differ radically in the degree to which they enjoin actions under the threat of negative supernatural sanctions which will, in the course of time, eliminate or ameliorate some of the external

27. David F. Aberle, "A Note on Relative Deprivation Theory, as Applied to Millenarian and Other Cult Movements," in *Millennial Dreams in Action*, ed. Sylvia L. Thrupp, Comparative Studies in Society and History, supplement 2 (The Hague: Mouton, 1962), p. 209.

obstacles to their increased self-respect; that is, actions which will increase their earning power and improve their social demeanor. Here I depart from the conventional distinction between instrumental or this-worldly and expressive or other-worldly solutions to environmental problems.

I agree with Glock when he argues that there are sacred and secular solutions to deprivation (he distinguishes five types of deprivation—economic, social, organismic, ethical, and psychic), and when he says that sacred means will be used when either the cause of discomfort is "inaccurately perceived" or those experiencing the deprivation are not in a "position to deal with it directly." But I disagree with the proposition that "religious resolutions, then, are likely to compensate for feelings of deprivation rather than to eliminate its causes, and therefore also the feelings."[28] This statement implies that sacred solutions are essentially expressive. That is, they let off emotional steam but do not alter the conditions which generate the sense of deprivation. On substantive grounds I dissent from this view because Seventh-day Adventist ideology, as distinguished from their formal cosmological doctrines, which have decidedly fatalistic overtones, presses its adherents to adopt modes of action which are directly oriented to overcoming the secular sources of deprivation, and it does so in a realistic manner. It tells them how to become a "success" in this world and, more important, it treats these patterns of secular behavior as if they were absolutely essential for salvation. As we shall see, Pentecostal ideology is oriented to the same problem but is less effective because it in a sense evades the crucial issue: it holds that increased self-esteem in this society is not rooted in economic success. On a theoretical level, I hope to show that one of the primary elements of religious ideologies is oriented to shaping or controlling the secular world.[29]

28. Charles Glock, "The Role of Deprivation in the Origin and Evolution of Religious Groups," in *Religion and Social Conflict*, p. 29.
29. As Isidor Thorner observes, this does not hold true for all religious systems, especially mystical belief whose "affective and moral neutrality supports the traditional social order out of a basic indifference to the things of this world." "Prophetic and Mystic Experience:

The Seventh-day Adventist and Pentecostal sect members' feeling of status deprivation (the sense that one is valued by others less than one's behavior, demeanor, and attitudes warrant) is obviously related to their economic marginality and to their sensitivity to middle-class standards of social excellence. I do not treat social status as a unitary measure of both prestige and class position. Class refers to an individual's or group's objective ability to acquire and control economic opportunities and resources, the means with which socially valued ends are obtained. A person's class is defined by his life chances and is measured by his economic power—his ability to appropriate economic advantages in the marketplace. This follows Weber and more recently Goldthorpe and Lockwood.[30]

Whereas class systems are restricted to market-oriented societies which have a complex division of labor, status simply refers (when opposed to class and not merely taken as a position in a social structure to which certain rights and duties are attached) to the universal human tendency to judge oneself and others in terms of certain standards of social worth. Thus it is an inherently subjective phenomenon. A person's social status is determined by the amount of prestige he is allocated or can legitimately claim in light of certain images of accomplishment or admirability.[31]

Comparison and Consequences," *Journal for the Scientific Study of Religion* 5 (1965):9. It seems likely that religious ideologies are found only in those religious systems where salvation is somehow contingent on the believer's worldly activities.

30. John Goldthorpe and David Lockwood, "Affluence and the British Class Structure," *Sociological Review* 2 (1963).

31. Talcott Parsons holds that the very nature of social action implies stratification. Actors must discriminate between the utility and desirability of various means and ends, and this process of evaluating the units of social action results in a rank order or hierarchy of preferences which we commonly refer to as a system of stratification. These judgments are made in terms of a common set of values. For Parsons, "stratification in its *valuational aspect* then is the ranking of the units in a social system in accordance with the standards of the common value system." "A Revised Analytic Approach to the Theory of Social Stratification," in *Essays in Sociological Theory* (Glencoe, Ill.: Free Press, 1954), p. 338. Lloyd Fallers links Parsons's theoretical framework to the ways in which cultural definitions of the various properties and qualities of social roles and actions affect status judgments when he says that

If status and class are analytically independent dimensions of a stratification system, why should Seventh-day Adventists and Pentecostals suffer from status deprivation simply because of their economic marginality to the middle class? Weber points out that although status systems do not always occur with class systems, in contemporary Western societies the economic system forms the material basis of the status system: "Today the class situation is by far the predominant factor, for, of course, the possibility of a style of life expected for members of a status group is usually conditioned economically." [32] In this society, it is difficult to maintain one's sense of social honor and dignity without the means necessary to purchase those goods deemed essential for the good life, especially if the middle class is an individual's central reference group.

Although people do not need to occupy similar class positions to rank each other on a prestige scale, they must agree about the validity and applicability of at least one attribute or quality which confers status. This does not mean that they will necessarily agree on others. In his study of English clerks, Lockwood reports that both clerks and manual workers agree that education bestows prestige on its possessor, but they disagree about the prestige presumably inherent in manual as opposed to lower nonmanual or white-collar jobs.[33] Similarly, Seventh-day Adventists and Pentecostals openly admire the "solid citizen" element in the middle-class life style. But they deny that an affluent style of life is the proper basis for status assessments. I was struck by the ambivalence toward middle-class life styles expressed in sect sermons. Sect members refuse to accord "luxurious" modes of

---

"surely one of the fundamental bases for stratification phenomena everywhere is man's tendency to judge his fellows and himself as more or less worthy in the light of some moral standard. Thus a people's stratification system is rooted in its culture, and particularly in its culturally elaborated image of the 'admirable man,' the man whom everyone would like to be." "Equality, Modernity and Democracy in the New States," in *Old Societies and New States: The Quest for Modernity in Asia and Africa*, ed. Clifford Geertz (New York: Free Press, 1963), p. 162.

32. Weber, *From Max Weber*, p. 190.

33. David Lockwood, *The Blackcoated Worker: A Study in Class Consciousness* (London: Allen and Unwin, 1958).

living any great prestige value. Although they are sensitive to imputations that they are not quite "respectable," they nevertheless reject the idea that wealth and social worth are equivalent—that self-respect depends upon one's earning-power. Although they may long to be included among the "respectable" elements of the middle class rather than to exist along fringes of social acceptability, they will not admit (although among Seventh-day Adventists there is much more equivocation on this issue) that financial success is necessarily a great virtue. On the other hand, neither do they assert that it is a vice; it is what you do with your money and not how much you have or how you made it that counts! Sects simply believe that religious and moral qualifications rather than purely economic ones should govern judgments about who belongs to the "better" parts of society.

If Seventh-day Adventists and Pentecostals suffer from a depreciated sense of self-esteem, why should the former view their future secular fortunes with hope and the latter with dismay? At this point the concept of a religious ideology becomes the critical intervening variable between a sect member's status expectations and his secular behavior. I cannot account for a large part of the economic optimism of Seventh-day Adventism and the pessimism of Pentecostalism. But, taking these factors for granted, sect ideology not only reinforces the cognitive validity of these perceptions of prospects for upward mobility but also creates morally sanctioned modes of behavior which tend to transform them into self-fulfilling prophecies.

Religious Ideologies—The Link between Social Structure, Religious Doctrine, and Social Action

Intervening variables do not need to specify mathematical relationships between the independent variables and the dependent variables, nor must they postulate properties of these concepts which are amenable to operational definition. As an intervening variable between social structure and secular behavior, ideology is a theoretical construct. Koch, reviewing the contributions of psychologists to the notion of the links between independent and dependent variables, says that:

To take the specific instance of systematic independent variables, it is strongly stressed by these men [contributors to volume 3, *Psychology: A*

Study of a Science] that specification of the principal antecedent conditions for action for phyletically high order organisms involves a specification of their inferred *meaning* for the organism. Concepts put forward to meet such a requirement cannot be justly defined by "standard" operational procedures without liberalizing such procedures out of all recognition or identity.[34]

As an intervening variable, ideology specifies the meaningful connections between religious belief and social action. It mediates between an actor's position in the social structure and his status expectations, on the one hand, and his religious outlook, moral code, and secular behavior on the other. By conceiving of ideology in this manner, we can ask how objective social realities are translated into subjective religious experiences. In what ways do various amounts of wealth, prestige, and power transform an individual's perception of his immediate social situation into a religious vision of the good and proper life? And what prompts him to endow his secular activities with moral significance? That is, Why does he allow a religious ideology to govern his secular conduct, to legislate a comprehensive normative pattern for his entire life?

In more general terms, the problem focuses on the way in which a particular set of religious symbols creates a convincing model of reality and, at the same time, provides a "blueprint" for social action. Formal religious beliefs relate a complex series of natural and historical events to the motives and character of divine agents and unite partial visions of the nature of reality into a more comprehensive picture of the supernatural order which underlies the temporary flux of the perceptual world. In other words, a supernatural sphere encompasses apparently disconnected happenings in the disparate domains of human concern and understanding, and these cosmological doctrines supply both cognitive and moral support for a pattern of secular conduct. A supernaturally sanctioned moral ideology must take account of the external social pressures on its adherents as well as their own desires, aspirations, and goals.

This formulation of the nature of a religious ideology refers to the dual orientation of a religious belief system which has

34. Sigmund Koch, ed., *Psychology: A Study of a Science* (New York: McGraw-Hill, 1959), 3:747.

determinant consequences for social action. It codifies reality in metaphysical terms and yet provides a plan for acting upon it which is not oblivious to the adaptive requirements of a special natural and social environment.

I have borrowed and taken some liberty with Geertz's seminal distinction between the two kinds of religious models of reality.[35] Religious models *of* reality state the ways in which a person's conduct, feelings, and attitudes must be channeled or directed toward specific goals and must be governed by specific norms if social action is to conform to the intrinsic order of things.[36] As models of reality, the emphasis is on the molding of human impulses and desires to fit a cognitive (what the world really looks like) and an evaluative (what things are inherently good or evil, worthwhile or valueless) conception of the nature of the world. Thus, behavior must be in harmony with the structure of the universe if it is to be consonant with a religious world view.

Geertz's conception of religious models *for* reality emphasizes the capacity of religious ideas to outline the ways in which men can act to shape the world in the image of their desires.[37] This is very similar to what I mean by the ideological aspects of religious belief. Briefly, a religious ideology endows adaptive patterns of behavior with cognitive validity (the actor feels that these responses to the situation are both fitting and effective) and with moral validity (the actor feels that this is the right and proper way to go about getting things done). In a word, sect ideologies support and, to a certain extent, create social conduct

35. Clifford Geertz, "Religion as a Cultural System," in *Anthropological Approaches to the Study of Religion*, ed. Michael Banton, Association of Social Anthropologists Monographs, vol. 3 (London: Tavistock, 1966).

36. Geertz says that with respect to models "of," "what is stressed is the manipulation of symbol structures so as to bring them, more or less closely, into parallel with the pre-established non-symbolic system, as when we grasp how dams work by developing a theory of hydraulics or constructing a flow chart." Ibid., p. 7.

37. Geertz says that with respect to models "for," "what is stressed is the manipulation of the non-symbolic systems in terms of the relationships expressed in the symbolic, as when we construct a dam according to the specifications implied in an hydraulic theory or the conclusions drawn from a flow chart." Ibid., p. 7.

which has adaptive consequences for their adherents. More specifically, these ideologies serve as a means of formulating and dealing with status problems which are beyond immediate instrumental solutions, given the technical facilities available to the actor (which include his control over "scientific" knowledge). In fact, one of the most distinctive attributes of a religious ideology is that it states status problems in terms which enable actors to overcome, if in some cases only symbolically, obstacles to maintaining or increasing their self-respect which would otherwise appear insuperable to those with limited economic and social means.

This chapter will conclude with a few remarks about some of the more salient attributes of religious ideologies. Religious ideologies are grounded in sacred conceptions of time; ahistorical, supernatural world views are inimical to the formation of religious ideologies as I have defined them.

In the Christian tradition, this view of time places and evaluates events according to a teleological historical scheme. It contains the idea that it is possible to liberate man from the limitations imposed upon him by nature. Polak notes that this element of utopianism (the ability to imagine a future state of affairs when ideals, values, and aspirations will be fully realized) in religious belief is derived from conceptions of salvation:

> All of the images of the future which carry man out of and beyond himself also contain a time concept which is outside of and beyond existing time. This concept is often labeled eternity and as such is used in various ways by religion and philosophy . . . [and] the prototype of the image of the future—a story of salvation. The vision of salvation takes many diverse forms through history, but the keynote of the positive and idealistic image of the future is always triumphant over adverse forces.[38]

In the Seventh-day Adventist conception of history, a divinely instituted utopia in the here and now and not in some purely spiritual realm beyond the flux of human history occurs at a critical juncture in time. The present ceases and a new, harmonious era reserved exclusively for the righteous begins, to

38. F. L. Polak, *The Image of the Future* (New York: Oceana, 1961), pp. 30–33.

last forever on this earth. On the other hand, Pentecostals achieve immediate salvation through a transcendence of present time by spiritual aid. Their special form of religious experience takes them beyond the ordinary passage of time into the eternal spiritual realm of salvation. Nonetheless, Pentecostals envision a time when most men will be converted to their religious way of life, and the whole world will be revitalized by this collective effort to purify man's spiritual life. Thus, a particular conception of the special implications of the passage of time lies at the heart of their picture of spiritual transformation and rebirth.

As I use the term, religious ideologies are not separate evaluative and cognitive worlds which somehow stand opposed to the actor's perception of his immediate, concrete social and economic situation. Rather, the ideological component of an actor's orientation to his situation is an intrinsic aspect of the way in which he conceptualizes the meanings of external exigencies. Adaptive considerations become part of the moral dimension of the actor's view of the situation and thus have both a utopian and a compelling aspect.

The way I use the term divests ideology of its restricted reference to the perceptual limitations of a class perspective or to the distortions of political propaganda. I follow Polak when he argues that ideologies are not vague hopes for a better world in a distant future but consist of detailed normative prescriptions for action which are, in turn, based upon the firm belief that the world will be radically altered by forces which are beyond complete human control and direction. The nature of this agency distinguishes secular from sacred ideologies. Whatever their particular character—whether the transforming agency is in the impersonal forces of an economic system or in God's scheme for the salvation of man—ideologies demand that their adherents dedicate themselves to a set of values which implies the reorganization of conventional modes and patterns of action. This is why religious ideologies are conceptualized by their adherents as external forces which are not amenable to deliberate choice on rational, utilitarian grounds and which are not open to dispassionate inspection and investigation. According to the believer, men have only one alternative—to work in harmony with these forces—and thus one's goals must be defined in terms of these predetermined ends. In this respect, all ideologies are sacred rather than instrumental guides to action.

3 The Sect as a Sociological Construct

The Church-Sect Typology

In his classic study *The Social Teachings of the Christian Churches,* Ernst Troeltsch deals with the intellectual origins and institutional history of two antithetical sets of ecclesiastical values which scholars subsequently have referred to as the church-sect typology.[1] Perhaps no other concept has so greatly influenced research on religious groups in our society and yet, in my opinion, has suffered from such undeserved criticism for failure to provide theoretical services it was never designed to render. Although Troeltsch traces the origins of the church and the sect to opposing ideals expressed in the Gospels, the major thrust of his analysis concerns the ways in which these ideas about a Christian's proper relationship to God, to other believers, and to the means of salvation are institutionalized in ecclesiastical organizations whose norms not only prescribe very different modes of worship but also shape their members' attitudes toward

1. Ernst Troeltsch, *The Social Teaching of the Christian Churches,* trans. Olive Wyon, vols. 1 and 2 (London: Allen and Unwin, 1956).

numerous secular matters. The distinction between the church and the sect illuminates a complicated historical process: the post-Reformation growth of independent religious bodies which consciously separated themselves both from the Roman Catholic church and from the secular order.[2] These groups sought to recapture the spirit of primitive Christianity. Sects rely upon Scripture in dealings with temporal realities and stress the perfection of every believer rather than glorifying the ascetic virtuosos of the church, whose accomplishments were measured against "an average morality which is on relatively good terms with the world." [3]

The church provisionally accepts man's sinful nature and the "relative" laws of the social order.[4] It imposes a spiritual domain upon the mundane activities and interests of this world and thereby transcends man's original fallen state. The sect refuses to come to terms with the world as it is: "Grace does not mean the purification of nature and the ascent to supernature,

2. The church-sect typology systematizes and, to a certain extent, explains the unique social and theological consequences of this decisive breakthrough in Christian thought and organization. Troeltsch says that "it is also very important to understand this question thoroughly at this stage [late medieval times], since it explains the later development of Church history, in which the sect stands out ever more clearly alongside the Church. In the whole previous development of the Church this question was less vital, for during the early centuries the Church itself fluctuated a great deal between the sect and the Church-type; indeed, it only achieved the development of the Church-type with the development of sacerdotal and sacramental doctrine; precisely for that reason, in its process of development up to this time, the Church had only witnessed a sect development alongside of itself to a small extent, and the differences between them and the Church were still not clear." Ibid., p. 333.

3. Ibid., p. 332.

4. Troeltsch says that "in the case of the Church-type, its doctrine of sin facilitated the acceptance of the existing secular social order, whose merely relative non-Christian character is regarded as the result of sin; this social order, therefore, must be frankly accepted and tolerated. At the same time, 'grace' is regarded as the miraculous power which purifies these institutions, uses them as the basis of a higher structure, and subordinates them to a universal central authority. This authority is conceived in its essence as a wonderful supreme authority, transcending Nature in the graded structure of the entelechies of the universe." Ibid., p. 462.

rather it means pure and radical hostility to the whole principle of sin, expressed in a genuine Christian spirit, and in the Christian moral law."[5] The sect replaces the church's sacramental means of salvation with redemption through complete faith in and reliance upon the Word.

The church and the sect represent what might be best described as the conservative and radical viewpoints within Christianity, although the political analogy is somewhat strained. Historically, the radical approach characterizes the churches of the poor and socially disinherited whereas the conservative approach is typical of rich and powerful congregations. Troeltsch is not oblivious to the affinity between the outlook of the upper and lower classes and the theological viewpoints of the church and the sect, but he denies that these religious institutions are reflections of economic forces. The church and the sect are embedded in "fundamental impulses in the Gospels."[6]

According to ecclesiastical conservatives, the church is the rightful representative of Christ on earth and is the sole mediator between God and man. A person can reach the Divinity and offer his oblation for his sins only through its objective sacraments; consequently, a person outside the church is effectively cut off from God's saving grace. The church believes that it should incorporate all Christians into a religious organization which ideally is coterminous with the social order but which is not subservient to the purposes of the state. Although the church formally recognizes the limits of its spiritual authority, it also maintains that society should be governed by distinctively Christian standards of proper conduct. Thus, the church believes that the state ought to be guided by Christian ideals in both its domestic and its foreign policies. Troeltsch concludes that the church's view of the relationship between secular power and religious aims gives it a unique social character:

> The fully developed Church, however, utilizes the State and the ruling classes, and weaves these elements into her own life; she then becomes an integral part of the existing social order; from their standpoint, then,

5. Ibid.
6. Ibid., p. 342.

the Church both stabilizes and determines the social order; in doing so she becomes dependent upon the upper classes and upon their development.[7]

Arising out of opposition to the church, especially out of a reaction to its ritual formalism and its ethical compromises with the "powers that be," the sects embody the radical approach to the Gospels. Seeking to identify themselves with the original disciples, sects proclaim that the fellowship of the elect is the only legitimate form of Christian union. All believers are equal in the sight of God with respect to collective worship and prayer. Although someone may regularly preach the word of God and serve as the group's minister, no permanent religious status carries unequivocal doctrinal authority. But in practice sects recognize a past or present prophet or a similar sort of charismatic leader who focuses attention on the special aspects of their message to the wider Christian community.

Similarly, no one has the power to act as another's spiritual representative before God. Sect members allow that a person's friend or his minister may plead his case before God, asking for mercy and forgiveness in prayer. They also feel that it is a person's spiritual duty to point out the correct path to salvation to another who is in need of religious guidance. But the central tenet of sect dogma is that each man must face the Lord on his own merits; no spiritual emissary can release a Christian from this duty.

Sects reject the hierarchical structure of religious authority associated with the church. In their opinion, it stands between and alienates God and man. Since the most notable component of this structure is the priesthood, the sect minister is only the first among equals. Because of this emphasis on direct communication with God, sect members feel that the ornate religious garb and buildings associated with the church are nothing but meretricious obstacles to the Holy Spirit. These external signs of religious power are said to inhibit both free-flowing prayer and genuine spiritual introspection. Therefore the sect service does away with ritual which deflects or captures spiritual energies which otherwise would bring a believer closer to the "liv-

7. Ibid., p. 331.

ing" God. Troeltsch states that "the sect does not live on the miracles of the past, on the miraculous nature of the institutions but on the constantly renewed miracles of the Presence of Christ, and the subjective reality of individual mastery of life." [8]

The sect's social temper is defined by the norms of reciprocity and fraternal love. Sect members are supposed to aid their less fortunate brethern and to be hospitable to one another. Most important, they must rescue those who "backslide" from their previous religious commitments and face the dangers associated with descent into the "world." Obviously, these attitudes can flourish only in the intimate atmosphere of a small group. Sect solidarity, however, does not rest solely upon the sentiments produced by face-to-face contact; the sect is a special type of primary group. Although sect members usually call one another "brother" and "sister" and their relationships often have elements of familial solidarity and intimacy, the sect is not based upon common blood and residence. It does not rest upon primoridal ties. Of all Western religious organizations, the sect theoretically is least tied to a kinship base. Its ideology emphatically rejects the circumscribed perspective of religious groups which recruit their adherents primarily on the basis of particularistic social ties. Rather, sect ideology proclaims that ascriptive status relationships are impediments to salvation. For the sect member, a man's relationship to God transcends any loyalties he may have to any social unit (including his family) which is less universalistic than the Kingdom of God. Troeltsch says that "the sect is a voluntary community whose members join it of their own free will. The very life of the sect, therefore, depends upon actual service and co-operation." [9]

Sect cohesion is generated primarily by common ideological commitments. The members believe that only as a united group can they protect and promote their religious ideals, and that they enhance their own chance for salvation by working collectively to save others; that is, together they will hasten the day when either the whole world is converted to the truth or Christ will come to earth to purge the wicked from the Kingdom of

8. Ibid., p. 341.
9. Ibid., p. 338.

God. It is in the sect member's interest, therefore, to labor to save others from sin and ultimate damnation. And it is perfectly clear that a solitary person can hardly expect to extend this opportunity to many others on his own.

Sect solidarity, then, is buttressed by this desire to missionize the world. From what I have seen, truly committed sect members are almost obsessed with the idea that they must do all they can to reach everyone who has the slightest chance for salvation. They believe that they do this in a world which not only is antagonistic to their belief but also harbors hostile powers that are bent upon destroying the last vestige of religious truth. Sect members often say that God commands them to prevent the dark forces in the service of the Devil from extinguishing the light of religious truth. They conclude that only a unified group of people who believe in the righteousness of their cause can overcome the great odds set against them and kindle the spark of religious concern which dwells in the hearts of men.

In sum, Troeltsch saw the sect as a protest against the rigidities which crept into the early Christian church and were finally institutionalized in the ecclesiastical hierarchy of the Catholic church. For Troeltsch, church and sect are opposed but equally cogent conceptions of the role of dedicated Christians in the social order. According to the sect viewpoint, religious purposes are inevitably accommodated to secular interests and genuine religious experience is relegated to a secondary role within the church. From the church's standpoint, Christians ought to transform social institutions as well as infuse informal, face-to-face relationships with the light of Christian ideals. They must strive to influence and direct those who wield secular power if the entire social fabric is truly to experience the purifying effect of the Christian Logos. From the sect's perspective, true Christians should wait for the full realization of Christian social relationships in the kingdom established by God on this earth or in heaven. Until then, sect members feel impelled to gather the righteous into a Christian community which is not habitually contaminated by dealings with those who do not follow both the spirit and letter of the Law.

I indicated earlier that the church-sect typology has been

subjected to a good deal of criticism, not all of which is germane to the issues it raises. As a case in point, we might look closely at N. J. Demerath III's defense of his interpretation of the correlation between high and low social status and differing modes of participation in contemporary Protestant denominations as churchlike and sectlike orientations to religion.[10] Erich Goode argues that although this empirical finding is valid, Demerath's interpretation is spurious because the association between social status and religious participation merely reflects the organizational style of the middle class, which certainly is not restricted to religious settings.[11] Demerath retorts that he hoped that "in demonstrating the co-existence of church-like and sect-like parishioners within the same 'churchly' shells, I might sully the inherited ideal-type by faulting its assumptions of membership homogenity."[12] Putting aside for the moment the fact that the assumption of "membership homogenity" is Demerath's and not Troeltsch's, his final rejection of the church-sect typology typifies a common misperception of its intent. Demerath says that "the church-sect framework could stand replacement, and almost any alternative may be preferable so long as it is *not* theologically rooted or religious in its primary referent."[13]

Judging from Demerath's brief remarks about the sort of conceptual scheme he would like to see in its place, he prefers structural variables whose empirical referents are not tied to particular cultural contexts. He wants to discover something significant about organizations qua organizations through the study of religious groups rather than something about the nature of religious involvement in a specific sacred tradition. Of course, Demerath's program for the sociology of religious organization is legitimate, but it is alien to the purposes for which the church-sect typology was designed. Troeltsch used sociological constructs to unravel significant relationships between myr-

10. Nicholas J. Demerath III, "In a Sow's Ear: Reply to Erich Goode," *Journal for the Scientific Study of Religion* 6 (1967).
11. Erich Goode, "Some Critical Observations on the Church-Sect Dimension," *Journal for the Scientific Study of Religion* 6 (1967).
12. Demerath, "In a Sow's Ear," p. 84.
13. Ibid., p. 83.

iad institutional and ideological factors in a particular cultural-historical situation—that of Western Christianity. He had strong reservations about the applicability of these constructs outside the historical configuration from which they were derived, and the last thing Troeltsch was searching for was a culturally denatured theoretical vocabulary.[14] To use a distinction current in anthropological linguistics, Troeltsch sought an "emic" framework based upon the categories implicit in a religious tradition, whereas Demerath and others demand an "etic" paradigm constrained only by the investigator's analytic goals.[15]

In any event, it is strange indeed when sociologists presumably concerned with religious organizations feel that their paramount task is not to account for their distinctively religious character. Since this was Troeltsch's concern, perhaps we might reexamine the church-sect typology and then look at criticisms which expose some of its more substantial defects. Although Troeltsch was well aware of the role social and political factors played in the evolution of these two kinds of religious organizations, in his opinion theology was principally responsible for their genesis. Moreover, religious participation, for Troeltsch, is embedded in one's theological allegiances. Insofar as a believer is dedicated to either a churchlike or sectlike interpretation of the Gospels, he is constrained by the norms derived from these ideas to organize his relationships with other believers on a churchlike or sectlike basis. Here Troeltsch is concerned with the subjective values the believer imputes to religious activity and not with the frequency with which he attends church, the number of church offices he holds, the extent to which he finds his friends in the church, or similar measures of participation in church activities.

14. For an excellent discussion of Troeltsch's approach to the study of religion see the symposium, "Bibliographical Focus: Ernst Troeltsch," *Journal for the Scientific Study of Religion* 4 (1961).
15. For further explication of this distinction, see Kenneth L. Pike, "Towards a Theory of the Structure of Human Behavior," in *Language in Culture and Society*, ed. Dell Hymes (New York: Harper and Row, 1964), and William C. Sturtevant, "Studies in Ethnoscience," in *Transcultural Studies in Cognition*, ed. A. Kimball Rommney and Roy G. D'Andrade (part 2—*American Anthropologist* 66 [1964]).

In a very detailed discussion of the tendencies within Protestantism toward either the church or the sect type, Troeltsch observes that despite the willingness of Luther, Calvin, and others to use the power of the state to establish a territorial church, the Protestant emphasis on each believer's own interpretation of the Word as the fundament of his faith made these churches vulnerable to sectlike tendencies.[16] Except for the historically anomalous case of Anglicanism, Protestant churches lack an ideology which gives dogmatic authority to ecclesiastical institutions; thus, whatever political influence a Protestant church may have, it sits on an inherently precarious theological base. Commenting on Protestantism's unique fertility as a progenitor of genuine sect movements in Christianity, Troeltsch reveals the intellectual and, hence, theological foundations of the church and the sect type:

> In the last resort, however, the sect is a phenomenon which differs equally from the ecclesiastical spirit of Protestantism and of Catholicism. It is an independent branch of Christian thought; it is the complement of the Church-type, and it is based upon certain elements in the New Testament ideal. The great national churches represented both the idea of grace, and that of a common spirit which produces individual souls, and thus they also assimilated into their own life the presuppositions of civilization in general. For them the main question was this: how could they gain an influence over the masses? Salvation and grace are independent of the measure of subjective realization of strict ethical standards as they are pliable in adjusting themselves to the institutions of Natural Law, institutions which have become necessary through sin, which have a healing and disciplinary effect, but they certainly cannot really be called Christian. This adaptation to the institutions based on Natural Law turns the Christian ethic into a compromise which, in one way or another, accepts the world. Thus, from the point of view of their influence upon world history, the great national churches formed the main expression of Christian thought; they are great historic powers, under whose influence the Christian ethic has been carried forward and developed. They were the first great result of the world mission of the Primitive Church. Once they were firmly established, however, they provided both the material and the occasion for the play of forces, through which there was introduced the critical and hostile element of an individualistic form of Christian piety, severely ethical

16. Troeltsch, *Social Teaching of the Christian Churches*, pp. 695 ff.

in the Primitive Christian sense, which did not believe in a mass religion at all. This criticism, however, contained a fundamental element of the genuine ethic of Primitive Christianity. Under its influence there arose small groups of earnest souls who judged the life of the world by the high ethical standard of the Gospel. Their sociological expression naturally took the form of a society of persons united by a deep common personal conviction, who were entirely opposed to the ecclesiastical system, with its inclusive character, and its claim to be the sole depository of grace. This development took place within all the Christian churches, because in them all, along with the Bible, and the endowment of grace, the germ of the sect-type was latent. This seed of the sect-type developed along different lines within the different churches, but the end attained was the same. Within Catholicism its main form of expression was detachment from the world, realized in practice on the higher moral level of monasticism; within Protestantism it expressed itself in an individualistic and subjective method of interpreting the Scriptures, and its emphasis upon the attainment of salvation without priesthood or hierarchy. There is no doubt that Protestantism has proved the more fruitful soil for the growth of the sect-idea. The whole course of Protestant development has been accompanied by and carried through with the aid of a powerful sect-movement.[17]

From this statement I think it is possible to sense the historical depth Troeltsch attempts to encapsulate in the distinction between the church and the sect. To the extent that men still scrutinize the Scriptures for guidance in their worship, I suspect that this distinction will continue to illuminate the dialectic between purely religious values and the sociological consequences of their embodiment in a concrete form of church organization. Perhaps the most glaring omission in the church-sect typology is that it fails to take account of the denomination, which is undoubtedly the dominant form of contemporary Protestant church organization. Martin argues that the denomination is not merely a latter-day compromise between the church and sect type. He says that "sects generally succeed in maintaining their sectarian character, and many even reinforce it, and secondly that denominations have normally possessed their denominational character from their very beginnings."[18] In other words,

17. Ibid., p. 701.
18. D. A. Martin, "The Denomination," *British Journal of Sociology* 13 (1962):2.

denominations are not degenerate church organizations or the sect grown rich and successful and hence ready to compromise with the world. Martin, furthermore, thinks that the denomination has a fully independent theological character predicated upon the congregation's perception of its essence "as being a unity of experience rather than a unity of organization." [19] He says that "church, denomination and sect embody tensions and goals directly implicit in Christianity." [20]

The question whether the denomination is a truly independent form of Christian organization revolves, in large part, around its biblical sources. This raises an issue beyond my competence, but I suspect that the widespread dissatisfaction with the church-sect typology stems from the nature of denominational worship and not from its theoretical confusions or limitations. Briefly, theologically based characterizations of church organizations do not seem applicable to denominations because, as Bryan Wilson observes, there is a marked tendency for the clergy to buttress their position vis-a-vis an increasingly secularized laity by resorting to high-church ritualism.[21] Under the banner of ecumenicalism, Wilson claims that the clergy promotes ritualism as a means of protecting their tenuous professional identity when their other functions have been usurped or at least partially co-opted by better trained professionals in our society. Under these conditions, it is not hard to see why sociologists find the church-sect typology irrelevant, especially when the Gospels no longer create divergent yet deeply felt visions of doctrinally appropriate models of church organization for most Christians.

This situation does not hold for sectarian Christianity, and consequently studies of these groups use the sect type as a general organizational rubric. Among sects, people still take the model of apostolic Christian organization seriously, and disputes within a movement very frequently center on discrepant interpretations of the import of the Gospels for common worship.

19. Ibid., p. 5.
20. Ibid., p. 4.
21. Bryan Wilson, *Religion in Secular Society: A Sociological Comment* (Baltimore: Penguin Books, 1966).

This does not mean that the sect type alone is entirely adequate for the study of these groups. But most scholars still find it a useful point of departure for more sophisticated analyses of organizational dynamics. In fact, I will argue later that by treating evangelical, sectarian Christianity as an essentially undifferentiated ideological entity, with a cursory nod to a few theological embellishments here and there, we tend to overlook diverse latent functions of these groups which are generated by dissimilar theological premises.

Building upon Troeltsch's conception of the sect as a religious group which attracts social strata given to direct and often emotional worship, H. Richard Niebuhr puts the problem of sect affiliation in explicitly temporal terms.[22] According to Niebuhr, a person is born into a church but joins a sect; sect membership is not simply part of an individual's religious inheritance. In fact, sect ideology applauds a person's decision to break the ties to his religious past; the convert is the sect hero. Accordingly, sects deprecate religious affiliation based upon what they perceive as the sheer force of unthinking sacred custom and habit. Even a sect member whose parents belong to the group must go through the formal process of conversion. Niebuhr argues that in ordinary circumstances the members of the first and succeeding generations have dissimilar conversion experiences.

For the first-generation sect member, the sect is a refuge from an otherwise dreary and often intolerable world.[23] The sect reaffirms his social identity in the face of impersonal agencies

22. H. Richard Niebuhr, *The Social Sources of Denominationalism* (New York: Meridian Books, 1959).

23. Perhaps the most illuminating case study done in the framework proposed by Niebuhr is Liston Pope's *Millhands and Preachers* (New Haven, Conn.: Yale University Press, 1942). Pope noticed that the fundamentalist churches in a southern mill town expressed intense but unfocused resentment about their subordinate position in the local socioeconomic hierarchy. In a time of serious and open class conflict in the mills, this diffuse dissatisfaction with the prevailing distribution of economic power in the community was channeled by the fundamentalist churches into other-worldly forms of protest rather than into concrete political action. Pope concluded that the sects enabled the socially disinherited to "substitute religious status for social status" (p. 137).

which seem to reduce his already lowly social standing; sects enable the socially disinherited to assert their worth through the appropriate sacred symbols. The sect, then, counteracts the demoralizing frustrations and anxieties produced by overwhelming social and economic pressures.[24]

Niebuhr maintains that the conversion experiences of second-generation sect members can hardly avoid conventionality. Since second-generation members are born into the group, they naturally view its ideology as part of their family tradition; it is one of a number of familiar anchorages in their social milieu. Consequently, for the second generation conversion rarely entails radical changes in their social identities. It rather reaffirms family and group solidarity. Of course, ideally, second-generation members are supposed to become converts only after long introspection or in a moment of sudden religious inspiration. Practically, second-generation members have been subjected to a continuous stream of religious propaganda since childhood. The aim of religious socialization is to insure conformity to what is for the second-generation member received sacred opinion.

Niebuhr argues that the passage of time inevitably transforms the sect; it slowly becomes a denomination. An experience of being "born again"—a profound, sometimes cataclysmic, ecstatic religious upheaval which disengages a person from his previous commitments and demands a total reorientation of his life pattern—ceases to be the sole ground for entry into the sect. Doctrinal orthodoxy replaces enthusiasm as the accepted outward sign of a member in good standing. The second-generation sect member does not have to demonstrate the same forms of self-knowledge and self-control that the first generation member acquired with his new religious identity.

Niebuhr maintains that the sect members' probity almost invariably improves their economic circumstances. As the worldly fortunes of the sect improve, its members rarely resist

24. Niebuhr adds that intrinsically religious as well as secular motives prompt a person to join a sect: "It is quite unjustifiable, above all, to leave the religious factor out of account in dealing with religious movements. Only because the inspiration of such is religious do they develop the tremendous energy they display in history." *Social Sources of Denominationalism*, p. 27.

the temptation to indulge in status display. Now they can afford to make invidious comparisons with less prosperous groups. Niebuhr perceives a vicious circle from a Christian point of view. The sect now has moved away from a purifying and renewing impulse in Christianity: the desire to reject, from a standpoint of membership in the Kingdom of God, any social order which denigrates others. The group now emphasizes what Kenneth Burke aptly calls the "mysteries of hierarchy." Instead of fleeing a world which will not accept the equality of all men, the sect has become intrigued with the religious symbols for wealth, influence, and power. One of the fundamental Christian motives degenerates into a not too artfully concealed desire for secular recognition. According to Niebuhr, this interest in prestige is the distinguishing trait of the established denomination.

Contemporary Sociological Approaches to the Problem of Sect Affiliation

Although Troeltsch was mainly interested in how religious ideas and institutions developed along the church-sect axis, he was also quite sensitive to differences between sects. On an essentially ad hoc basis, he distinguished between aggressive (millenarian), passive (pietistic), and other-worldly (communistic) sects. Since then, others have devised more elaborate sect classifications which usually take as their point of departure the sect's response to the environing society.[25]

Classifications based on differences in sect belief emphasize the sect's ideological posture toward the larger society at the expense of its distinctive attributes as an integrated system of religious values and norms. For example, Bryan Wilson's recent typology tends to ignore the specific normative content of sect ideology and to concentrate instead on its "mission"—the sect's attitude toward societal values and standards.[26]

In this typology, sect ideologies are characterized as either antagonistic to, unconcerned with, or desiring to reform the

25. See Elmer T. Clark, *The Small Sects in America* (New York: Abingdon, 1949), who provided one of the earliest and most influential classifications of sects.
26. Bryan Wilson, "An Analysis of Sect Development," *American Sociological Review* 24 (1959).

established social order. They are also distinguished on the basis of the appeal they make or the warnings they give to the unconverted. Sect ideologies publicize the dangers outsiders are subject to or the blessings they are missing. Sect eschatology is significant for Wilson insofar as it reveals the group's underlying sentiments toward prevailing norms and dominant institutions. On the other hand, this typology overlooks those aspects of sect dogma and eschatology which are related to the member's ordinary social and economic conduct. His classification "rests essentially on the response of the sect to the values and relationships prevailing in the society." [27]

Wilson, then, examines sect ideologies for signs of alienation from, opposition to, or acceptance of societal values. Regardless of differences in doctrine, Wilson groups together all sects which share the same attitude toward the larger society. He claims that *Conversionist* sects are interested in changing and elevating moral behavior. *Introversionist* sects reject (although they normally do not attack) worldly values and replace them with transcendent spiritual ideals. *Gnostic* sects usually accept societal goals and search for the most effective supernatural means of achieving them. *Adventist* sects oppose the whole social order and eagerly await its destruction.

From a cultural point of view, one of the defects built into this kind of typology is that it tends to reduce the meaning of complex religious theologies to relatively simple social-psychological attitudes toward contemporary mores and conventional goals. An Adventist, for instance, is distinguished by his antipathy to current standards of success and to present systems of social rank and political power. The world view of an Adventist sect is collapsed into a "reaction-formation" to the life styles and the morals of the dominant social strata. The symbolism of Adventist belief is interpreted as a counterideology to the views of the wealthy and powerful.

This view of Adventist ideology neglects other, less obtrusive aspects of their belief and, consequently, misses some of the meanings hidden in the overt symbolism of antagonism. Seventh-day Adventist teachings on proper interpersonal behavior

27. Ibid., p. 5.

and economic conduct are quite similar to those Weber described for the Puritans, but this has been slighted in favor of their more spectacular apocalyptic doctrines. I hope to show that this modern-day version of the Protestant ethic is actually supported by this millennial eschatology. It provides an absolute moral sanction for a difficult course of action which is conducive to upward mobility. The dire Seventh-day Adventist predictions about the fate of those who fail to follow a rigid set of behavioral prescriptions are, in essence, an ideological support for persons who are trying to improve their socioeconomic status against formidable odds. However, this latent function of Adventist belief would never come to light if one took Wilson's description of Adventist orientations at their face value.

In sum, these sorts of typologies slight normative differences between sects which are not immediately related to societal values. For example, sociologists usually seem interested in only the gross similarities between the moral attitudes of various types of religious sects. Most studies will mention that sects proscribe smoking, drinking, gambling, and dancing and then let the matter rest. Seventh-day Adventists feel that smoking and similar personal indulgences are basic moral evils, whereas Pentecostals usually view such practices as wrong but as only relatively minor sins. As we shall see, Pentecostal and Seventh-day Adventist attitudes toward smoking and similar pleasures are symptomatic of their larger view of the bearing of secular behavior upon a person's preparation for salvation. Current sociological research glosses over some crucial ideological differences between religious sects because it often treats eschatological, cosmological, and ethical notions as disconnected traits, thereby relegating them to the status of variations on the same theme.

Ideological Consensus, Group Cohesion, and the Problem of Sect Affiliation

Yinger was among the first scholars who systematically challenged the idea that sects must, in time, become denominations.[28]

28. Milton Yinger, *Religion, Society and the Individual* (New York: Macmillan Co., 1957).

He noticed that sometimes the group's dogma and social teachings did not change substantially when its members' living standards rose. He suggested that if a sect retains its unique outlook for at least a few generations, we should call it an "established sect." In this sort of religious organization, most new members are recruited from among the children born into the group, even though the sect still tries to convert outsiders. Yinger pointed out that although some sects may adopt a more accommodating position on values that conflict with those of the larger society, this does not necessarily mean that they will automatically assume the conservative theological stance of a denomination. A growing body of evidence indicates that it is hazardous to make inferences about ideological changes from structural data. Isichei's historical study of Quakerism reminds us that slow organizational reform may mask the continuity of theological and ritual attitudes in a religious group, at least on the part of the more conservative elements of the movement.[29] Yinger's concept of an established sect underlies the necessity for treating sect organization and ideology as interdependent (in any concrete, historical context) but analytically independent variables.

Bryan Wilson enlarges the concept of an established sect.[30] In a detailed comparative study of the dynamics of sect organization, he shows that structural change does not always lead to doctrinal revision. Many ideological changes are responses to organizational necessities rather than shifts in fundamental religious attitudes. For example, if a sect wants to continue to increase its membership, it must adopt some sort of denominational form of organization. If it is to compete in the crowded fundamentalist market, the sect needs full-time administrators, missionaries, ministers, evangelists, and educators. Without these functionaries, the best it can hope to do is hold a small group of the faithful together. It is true, of course, that the emergent systems of authority which accompany functional specialization and formalized leadership tend to undermine a central sect value—the equality of all believers. Nevertheless, Wil-

29. Elizabeth Isichei, "From Sect to Church among English Quakers," *British Journal of Sociology* 15 (1964).
30. Bryan Wilson, *Sects and Society* (London: Heinemann, 1961).

son notes that these developments do not always affect many other aspects of the sect's ideology.

How do sects cohere over comparatively long periods of time when there is a great difference between the conversion experience of the first and succeeding generations of sect members? If, as Niebuhr indicates, the intensity and unique emotional flavor of a conversion experience diminishes rapidly with the passage of time, what attracts the children of the first generation and their children to the sect?

Sect solidarity is a consequence of the distinctive pattern of life which emerges from common ideological commitments. It is not, from a historical perspective, the product of intense religious feelings, which are easily dissipated after a revival meeting has run its course. Shared belief in the rightness of certain modes of knowing and acting, and not merely a common emotional experience, is the source of lasting sect solidarity.

All sect members, regardless of their generation, occupy a position in the larger society which is different from that of the members of the various denominations. All sect members must bear the same social disabilities in the outside world. The dedicated sect member's way of life is not acceptable in either conventional middle-class or working-class social circles. Consequently, the sect member subjects himself to subtle forms of social ostracism by virtue of his membership in the group; he rejects the "world" and it avoids him.

Most sects proscribe many of the ordinary forms of contemporary American entertainment such as smoking, dancing, drinking, innocent card playing as well as serious gambling, and, in some cases, movies, theater, and even television. Although my informants admitted that such leisure activities as bowling were intrinsically harmless, they held that these activities often occur in a deleterious atmosphere; for example, in these places people drink, smoke, and swear. Although they admit that it is a difficult and frustrating enterprise, sects feel that they must insulate their members against the insidious and corrupting influences of ostensibly innocuous forms of amusement. The watchword for the sect is avoidance of spiritual laxity rather than moral depravity.

Sect members are told to spend their free time in spiritually productive ways. Since the sect member's leisure is centered on prayer meetings and Bible-study classes, his friends tend to be persons who share his religious interests. The sect member is thereby shielded against seemingly harmless chance social contacts which might seduce him into acquiring a taste for worldly pleasures. At this level of religious commitment, the overt differences created by the sect's life style merely emphasize its members' removal from secular modes of relaxation and symbolically reveals their social distance from their more worldly contemporaries.

There are occasions when the values of the ordinary citizen and the sect member conflict. These disputes are not limited to general social issues such as the duty of every citizen to serve in the army (not all sects refuse to do military service). Tensions often arise in interpersonal relations. The dedicated sect member has a rather rigid code of social ethics and is very likely to withdraw from the social field when others violate it. For example, some of my informants vigorously denied that informal work norms should differ from the rules which constitute company policy. For example, they condemn petty theft, which some of their co-workers feel is part of their fringe benefits. Or sect members do not recognize covert collective work slowdowns ("goldbricking") as a legitimate means of resisting management's efforts to regulate the tempo of production. They told me that this violates one's right to give an honest day's work for an honest day's pay. For these and similar reasons, the sect member sometimes earns the enmity of his workmates. In general, there are few occasions when the sect member will bend his moral ideals to fit informal definitions of the situation. Thus, he often interrupts the normal flow of social interaction because he feels morally obliged to withhold his approval of practices which many others view as perfectly natural or, at least, as justifiable in the circumstances.

To add to this source of tension, the sect member is told to take any opportunity to proselytize. Whether or not he attempts to convert those he may already have offended, his propensity to see ethical implications in much routine social activity isolates him from a great deal of informal social intercourse. His attempts to convert his co-workers, acquaintances, and relatives often narrow the possible areas of common interest between them.

Regardless of generation, then, the dedicated sect member stands firmly against the grain of many contemporary mores. Therefore the dedicated third-generation sect member is no less attached to its ideology than the most recent convert. The sect's ideals are his ideals, its successes are his successes, and he ordinarily strives to extend its special point of view in the face of widespread outside derision and apathy.

We have seen that current theory in the sociology of religion is capable of explaining gross variations in the pattern of Protestant church affiliation. It tries to account for the attraction which sects have for the religiously inclined lower social strata and for the attractiveness of the denomination to the upper social strata, but its predictive power ends at this point. For instance, we do not know why some members of the lower social strata will join sects and others will ignore religion altogether.[31] Nor do we know why the very lowest social stratum, the urban "lumpen-proletariat," tends on the whole to avoid all religious involvement. Finally, sociological theory in this area does not explain why certain segments of the lower middle class will join sects rather than denominations.

But from my point of view the most important deficiency in the contemporary sociological theory of religious affiliation is that it tends to underestimate the significance of normative variations in sect ideologies. This is quite strange because, as I noted earlier, the sect is clearly identified by its distinctive beliefs and moral teachings, and schisms in sect movements usually take the form of ideological warfare. The sect member's religious identity also is directly tied to its ideology; he places

31. In an interesting study of this problem, Rodney Stark concludes, "I have tried to show that religion and radicalism both function in this manner [as solutions for status deprivation], and that the choice of one tends to preclude the other. I have offered no particular suggestions as to *why* some people adopt a religious solution, while others turn to radical politics, although this question surely merits careful investigation." "Class, Radicalism, and Religious Involvement," *American Sociological Review* 29 (1964):706.

his chance for salvation in the hands of its diagnosis of the proper way to reach this goal. Certainly there is much greater consensus on vital theological issues between Methodists and Baptists, for example, than between Pentecostals and Seventh-day Adventists.

In my opinion, one of the primary difficulties with current sociological approaches to the problem of differential sect affiliation is methodological. These approaches largely rely upon standard functional, institutional analysis. In short, sect membership is seen as the outgrowth of social and psychological needs which small, exclusive religious groups are able to satisfy in modern, industrial societies. These needs, in turn, are said to be created largely by the social structure. Owing to their lowly position in the class system, sect members are said to suffer from social discrimination and subordination, and consequently they are said to be searching for some sort of release from the frustrations and humiliation produced by material and social deprivation. From this perspective, the belief and worship of the sect act as a compensatory mechanism. Sect members, according to this theory, do not openly attack the status system or seriously disrupt the social order. At the same time, they are not totally immobilized by the seeming hopelessness of their present socioeconomic situation. Sect belief releases those feelings which might demoralize them or lead to open social conflict.

Bryan Wilson has recently widened this theory so that it can account for sect affiliation under the relative prosperity of the modern welfare state. He begins his study, as I do this one, by recognizing that there are fundamental ideological differences between Pentecostal (in this case, Elim) and Adventist (in this case, Christadelphian) sects; yet he immediately returns to the classic sociological position. He states that although "the eschatological ideas of Christadelphianism differ radically from those of Elim—functionally, the difference is less profound." [32]

Wilson argues that the social conditions which give rise to sects do not necessarily explain their persistence today: "The aetiology of origins is not, in such a case, the aetiology of

32. Wilson, *Sects and Society*, p. 318.

continuance."[33] He thinks that in an era of rising living standards and of a "limited" redistribution of wealth sects are able to hold on to many of their old members and recruit new ones because structural changes in the larger society have replaced one type of social marginality with another:

> The individual, although no longer economically disinherited, may be one of the culturally neglected, and the sect may now compensate for this lack of cultural status and *savior-faire*. Many members of the sect appear to suffer from a general inferiority feeling in regard to themselves and their religious organization; it reflects their awareness of educational, rather than economic deprivation.[34]

Wilson asserts that this social stratum experiences a strong sense of "social isolation." In his opinion, the sect offers these people a surrogate primary group. Wilson likens the sect to a psychodrama; he believes it functions as a therapeutic milieu for individuals exposed to the anomie which presumably pervades modern societies. Although Wilson has acutely uncovered one of the latent functions of the sect during periods of general prosperity and widespread social security (the study was done in England, where governmental social services protect much of the lower-class population against the worst vicissitudes of abject poverty), this brings us no closer to understanding the significance of ideological differences between various types of sects. The most one can say, in light of Wilson's theory, is that the reason a person decides to join a Pentecostal rather than an Adventist group or vice versa reflects his temperament, family background, and religious education.

Ideological differences between religious groups are secondary to the members of the denominations but not to the members of the sects. A person ordinarily joins a sect convinced that the religious viewpoint it espouses is of the utmost spiritual importance. He believes that this ideology, and no other, points out the correct road to salvation (the sects vocally dissent from the religious pluralism of the denominational world), and my informants were often quick to point out that other groups were

33. Ibid., p. 321.
34. Ibid.

likely to lead a person down the path to damnation. With this attitude toward the denominational ethos of religious tolerance, the sect member cannot afford to remain indifferent to the ideological differences between the various types of sects. He ignores them at his spiritual peril because he believes that his salvation depends upon the absolute validity of his religious belief.

One could argue that sect members are not the only people in this society who are deeply influenced by religious doctrines. However, I believe that they are perhaps the only groups in modern societies which accept a religious ideology as a cognitively complete and morally encompassing world view. It is true that many who belong to denominations subscribe wholeheartedly to the theological dogma and to the social teachings of their churches. Nevertheless, most of these people do not feel morally obligated, as sect members do, to follow religious precepts in every area of their personal lives. The sect member's conception of the proper role of sacred values in the regulation of human affairs differs basically from that of his more secularized contemporaries. He reveals a much stronger spiritual affinity to the medieval than to the modern view of the bearing of religious interests on worldly activities, as the latter is described by R. H. Tawney:

> Its essence is the secularization of social and economic philosophy. The synthesis is resolved into its elements—politics, business, and spiritual exercises; each assumes a separate and independent vitality and obeys laws of its own being. The social functions matured within the State, which in turn is idolized as the dispenser of prosperity and the guardian of civilization. The theory of a hierarchy of values, of which the apex is religion, is replaced by the conception of separate and parallel compartments, between which a due balance should be maintained, but which have no vital connection with each other.[35]

35. Richard H. Tawney, *Religion and the Rise of Capitalism* (New York: Mentor Books, 1954), p. 15.

4 Seventh-day Adventist Belief

Religious Belief and Ritual Action

Traditionally, anthropologists have viewed ritual—the collective and frequently dramatic enactment of personalized relationships between men and supernatural beings—as the crucial point at which metaphysical beliefs impinge on social action. The ritual domain provides the terrestrial location for transactions with the supernatural realm, and it provides the practical techniques for adjusting men to gods and gods to men. These negotiations with superior powers are predicated on the assumption that men and gods do not always have the same interests and that, at times, the gods resort to punitive measures to remind men of their ritual obligations. Gods, spirits, shades, and kindred beings are never willing to grant all that men ask of them, and, conversely, men can never render all the honor and obedience that the former demand. When men feel that their vital pursuits are frustrated by contingencies beyond their control, they become acutely aware of their moral improprieties and ritual malefactions. On these occasions communities ritually purge themselves of divisive motives and conflictive roles in an effort to restore the continuity between personal effort and material reward.

Under the aegis of a morally potent symbolism, ritual reconciles structural contradictions and ethical paradoxes. In a recent study of the ritual surrounding twinship in Ndembu society, Victor Turner says that

> Such symbols, then, unite the organic with the sociomoral order, proclaiming their ultimate religious unity, over and above conflicts between and within these orders. Powerful drives and emotions associated with human physiology, especially with the physiology of reproduction, are divested in the ritual process of their antisocial quality and attached to components of the normative order, energizing the latter with a borrowed vitality, and thus making the Durkheimian "obligatory" desirable. Symbols are both the resultants and the instigators of this process, and encapsulate its properties.[1]

Viewed this way, ritual acts as a master symbolic grid onto which a community maps the persistently problematic aspects of social experience. Ritual clarifies the intellectual and emotional grounds of that experience and thereby temporarily purifies the social structure of those dilemmas and oppositions that plague ordinary social existence. To quote Turner again, ritual symbolism "represents the whole cosmic and social order recognized by Ndembu in its harmony and balance, wherein all empirical contradictions are mystically resolved."[2]

It should be apparent that societies that support theological pluralism and that refuse to give credence to an overarching sacred cosmology are not in a position to profit from the communal therapy of collective rituals. This is to say not that ritual is unimportant in modern societies but rather that it no longer affords a universally satisfying explanation of suffering in the process of implementing a pragmatic remedy for it. Its healing action must be reserved for individuals and exclusive groups, and societies who need its services must look to what Robert Bellah calls the civil religion.

1. Victor Turner, *The Ritual Process: Structure and Anti-Structure* (Chicago: Aldine Publishing Co., 1969), p. 52.
2. Ibid., p. 85.

In modern societies ritual is not the principal action component of religious systems, at least not in a way that would make it analogous to the ritual systems of primitive and traditional societies. In our society, ritual does not specify the relationship between profane interests and sacred norms. Consequently, the member of a religious group who seeks to infuse his secular involvements with sacred meanings must bridge the gap between these two spheres of existence without the aid of the ritual prophylaxis of the disparities between them. In this cultural context, doctrine serves as the enduring repository of normative orientations to secular situations which, although revitalized and reinforced by common worship, are nonetheless not given public sanction by communal celebrations of societal values and purposes. To understand the connections between religious belief and social action, we must look at the secular implications of doctrinal commitments. And, in our society, it hardly needs to be said that these are not usually manifested in public acts of religious self-abnegation. Instead the believer tries to give his ordinary life a particular ethical cast. He cultivates a consistent, unspectacular piety by responding to prosaic choices and responsibilities in a fashion pleasing to God. He strives for religious justification "in the world."

Although rituals strengthen the sect member's resolve to remain faithful to the social teachings of his church, they do not delineate the situations in which his faith is likely to be tested. Rather, a religious ideology derived from theological postulates guides the believer through those areas of his life which affect his chance for salvation. Therefore, this account of Pentecostal and Seventh-day Adventist belief is notably devoid of detailed descriptions of church rituals except where, like the Pentecostal "speaking in tongues," they bear directly upon the genesis of a religious ideology. A religious ideology dwells on the critical relationship between a man's behavior and his standing on a scale of sacred merit. Here common worship does not attempt to manipulate or control supramundane forces as much as it tries to induce the believer to reorganize his elemental passions and desires into modes of action congruent with divine commands. The believer's life style becomes a vehicle for supplicating God, and it is a religious ideology rather than ritual per se that forms the model for his conduct.

Although many studies of non-Western religious behavior deal with belief as an explanatory variable, it is rarely accorded the same courtesy in comparable investigations of our society. The specific intellectual content of Christian theology is usually treated as a dependent variable and as one which deserves little more than cursory attention. The recent work of Bryan Wilson and other scholars has moved away from the mechanical procedure of briefly describing a sect's theology and then searching for conventional sociological and demographic variables which might explain the group's attractiveness to a particular social stratum.[3] Still there is little interest in the internal dynamics of belief systems: how major intellectual premises about the nature of the cosmos generate models of social reality which exert considerable influence on the believer's conduct.

In a sect, the believer must make some effort to learn a relatively recondite theological system or he must respond to the felt presence of God in ways which are hardly customary in American Protestantism. The sect member must do more than acknowledge the existence of God. He cannot formally assent to the group's doctrine and leave religious specialists to work out its implications for his daily life. The whole course of religious indoctrination sensitizes him to the pregnant consequences biblical revelation has for his temporal and eternal fate. In these circumstances, it seems reasonable to assume that sect belief has some bearing upon his conduct.

At an even more primary level, if a person believes that supernatural beings can materially affect his welfare, we might expect him to act in ways that will enhance his standing vis-à-vis these gods. To the extent that he believes that God scrutinizes his behavior and keeps a record of his spiritual successes and failures, the sect member is likely to accept normative constraints on his conduct, if only to protect his long-term interests in a place in the Kingdom of God. As a general principle, it

3. See *Patterns of Sectarianism: Organization and Ideology in Social and Religious Movements*, ed. Bryan Wilson (London: Heinemann, 1967).

seems reasonable to assume that religious beliefs will influence a person's behavior when he accepts them as veridical descriptions of reality.[4] Spiro states cogently the case for emphasizing the intellectual rather than the ritual aspects of religious systems:

> By "belief system" I shall mean "an enduring organization of cognitions about one or more aspects of the universe." I concentrate on belief systems, first, because of the relative neglect by anthropological (and especially functional) studies of religion of its cognitive, in favor of its ritual, aspects. Second, because I believe that its cognitive aspects are logically and psychologically, if not chronologically prior to its ritual aspects: any goal-oriented action—and for religion this means ritual action—is based on certain cognitive assumptions concerning the form, the meaning, the efficacy, etc., of the action. Rituals of whatever kind are instrumental to some end, and the performance of a ritual is predicated on the belief—a cognition—that for stipulated reasons, it is efficacious in achieving that end. Performance of ritual is inexplicable except in terms of these beliefs, and an investigation of their bases should, in my opinion, be one of the major tasks of religious research.[5]

The organization of this book follows Geertz's admonition that we must examine the intrinsic significance of religious ideas before we attempt to discern their functions in a particular social milieu. "The anthropological study of religion is therefore a two stage operation: First, an analysis of the system of meanings embodied in the symbols which make up the religion proper,

4. By veridical representations of reality I mean that the believer accepts these ideas as cognitively accurate and as compelling descriptions of his environment. To act on the basis of information about the contours of reality provided by these ideas strikes the believer as "natural," "sane," and "reasonable." To act otherwise strikes him as "mad" or "foolish." His willingness to arrange his affairs so that they do not contradict the disposition of supernatural agencies differs markedly from the situation of persons who simply accept these ideas as formal or specialized truths, that is, as true in certain contexts and not true in others. In modern societies, many treat religious ideas as poetic or metaphysical truths about reality which have no direct bearing on the course of human events. Hence, the knowledge derived from these ideas is not felt to be immediately applicable to the forces that presently affect their lives.

5. Melford Spiro, "Religion and the Irrational," in *Symposium on New Approaches to the Study of Religion*, ed. June Helm, Proceedings of the 1964 Annual Spring Meeting of the American Ethnological Society (Seattle: American Ethnological Society, 1964), p. 103.

and, second, the relating of these systems to social structural and psychological processes."[6] Before we examine Pentecostal and Seventh-day Adventist theologies, one question about the role of ritual in contemporary religious sects remains to be discussed.

As we have seen, in complex societies ritual does not create idealized models of the social structure which, at the same time, purify the residue of amoral and immoral experience of an entire community. Nevertheless ritual is a very salient feature of sect life. Its importance goes beyond its solidarity-generating function for the group and its emotionally cathartic function for the individual believer. The ritual process creates an experience of moral equality between men that is unencumbered by status considerations, and it thereby fulfills the sect's basic drive toward an association based upon principles uncontaminated by "worldly" criteria. Victor Turner associates this experience of "communitas" with rites of passage and especially with their "liminal" phase.[7] Here the segmentalized relationships predicated upon position in a social hierarchy are discarded and men confront one another as total human beings. Inasmuch as sect members are in transit from earthly to heavenly statuses or from lower to higher forms of spiritual understanding, they seem to qualify as "liminals." In any case, ritual enables the sect to offer its members an identity based upon qualities that derive exclusively from what they believe are generically human capacities and potentialities—love for Jesus, compassion for one's fellows. Although, as Turner points out, all enduring organizations cannot dispense with the kind of structure inimical to the experience of communitas, whatever hierarchy the sect develops within the group and in comparisons with other social categories (for example, with the unsaved) is periodically dissolved by ritual. At these times, sect members truly feel the equality of all believers before God and are emotionally prepared to accept

6. Clifford Geertz, "Religion as a Cultural System," in *Anthropological Approaches to the Study of Religion*, ed. Michael Banton, Association of Social Anthropologists Monographs, vol. 3 (London: Tavistock, 1966), p. 42.

7. Turner, *Ritual Process*.

men in their midst who otherwise might very well be repugnant to them.

Pentecostal and Seventh-day Adventist Belief and the Christian Tradition

In the next two chapters, I will discuss Pentecostal and Seventh-day Adventist religious doctrines. I will first outline their formal religious dogma, especially their cosmologies, eschatologies, and visions of the nature of religious experience. Then I will show how these views about the correct path to salvation promote and sanction certain moral codes and attitudes toward secular affairs. Before we look at these two religious systems in detail, something must be said about their connections to the larger body of Christian thought.

Not all Christian sects have either a Pentecostal or a Seventh-day Adventist theology, and there are many other types of esoteric religious belief in this society.[8] The distinction between a cult and a sect is relevant in this context.[9] Unlike sects, cults represent a decisive break with the cognitive and normative controls exercised by Christian theology over the activities of its followers. The cult searches for sources of mystical enlightenment among diverse religious traditions and recognizes charismatic leaders who cannot or will not demonstrate their connection to biblical prophecy. Moreover, any set of ethical routines and directives suggested by cult doctrines is optional in the sense that the believer is free to select those spiritual exercises most conducive to his quest for mystical knowledge and personal control over occult forces. In contrast to the openly syncretistic character of cults, sects strive to remain true to a pristine interpretation of the meaning of the sole source of divine revelation, the Bible. Although some cults try to establish some sort of

8. For a description of a wide range of cult belief see Charles Braden, *These Also Believe* (New York: Macmillan Co., 1949), and Arthur Fauset, *Black Gods of the Metropolis: Negro Religious Cults of the Urban North* (Philadelphia: University of Pennsylvania Press, 1944).
9. See Geoffrey K. Nelson, "The Spiritualist Movement: A Need for the Redefinition of the Concept of Cult," *Journal for the Scientific Study of Religion* 8 (1969).

intellectual link to orthodox Christian principles, they are at best, in my opinion, very tenuously and ambiguously related to systematic Christian thought.[10]

In contrast to basically non-Christian ideologies, Pentecostalism and Seventh-day Adventism represent "radical" theological tendencies which are not fully crystallized in many of the more eclectic fundamentalist groups.[11] Pentecostal and Seventh-day Adventist groups eschew all notions which would contradict Christian conceptions about the nature of the Divinity or the ways in which men reach him and, hence, remain in accord with Christianity's traditional historical world view and social teachings.[12]

The meaning of the term "radical" is undoubtedly ambiguous when used in a religious context. In my opinion, Pentecostal and Seventh-day Adventist religious ideologies are radical only in the sense that they select and emphasize certain ideas in the larger body of New Testament thought. They maintain that these notions above everything else contain the key to personal salvation.

One might argue that since Pentecostalism and Seventh-day Adventism are radical interpretations of the Gospels they invariably ignore important areas of theological inquiry. But this issue does not concern us. What is important, however, is that regardless of the "distortion" inherent in these two religious systems,

10. This is a historical judgment that holds true only for the later periods of Christianity, inasmuch as the earlier Gnostic tradition sustained visions of Christ which were closer to cultlike than to sectlike images of the Savior. Here Christ was merely a spiritual exemplar striving to escape from the bondage of all material, earthly, and heavenly realms to a state of being (i.e., genuine salvation) which was beyond time and outside the limits of the cosmos. See Hans Jonas, *The Gnostic Religion: The Message of the Alien God and the Beginnings of Christianity* (Boston: Beacon Press, 1958).

11. The term fundamentalism is often construed as opposition to theological "modernism" and as a literal approach to biblical interpretation. In my opinion, except for a thoroughgoing biblicism, fundamentalist thought is very fluid and embraces a number of distinct religious orientations. It is the "parent" culture from which the more definite Seventh-day Adventist and Pentecostal creeds developed.

12. For instance, unlike the Jehovah's Witnesses, another millenarian group, Seventh-day Adventists do not challenge the trinitarian constitution of the Godhead.

neither tampers with the basic symbolism of the primary Christian tradition. They do not deny the existence of the Trinity nor do they impute that Christ and God the Father are co-equal (i.e., synonyms for an impersonal creative force) rather than son and father, in the sense that the latter is conceived of as the principal creator of the universe and the former as his agent in the design for man's redemption and salvation. Seventh-day Adventists emphasize God's magisterial qualities and Pentecostals stress Christ's merciful qualities in ways which are not acceptable to orthodox denominations. Yet Seventh-day Adventists and Pentecostals do not claim, as many of the cults do, that Christ was merely an unusually gifted spiritual exemplar, that one can achieve salvation without first repenting for one's sins by accepting Christ's sacrifice on the cross, or that salvation ultimately depends upon the cultivation of unique spiritual abilities rather than on what happened at Calvary.

Although the members of the sects are urged not to attach themselves to the fleeting joys of social and political affairs, they are not encouraged to participate only minimally in the ordinary tasks of daily life. There is no discernible monastic impulse in Pentecostalism or Seventh-day Adventism. Their ideologies do, however, deny the spiritual relevance of the present distribution of power for those persons truly committed to Christ. For the dedicated sect member, spiritual growth consumes those energies others squander in the pursuit of power that, in the final analysis, will prove chimerical.[13] Although in this respect sects are truly other-worldly, it would be wrong, in my opinion, to conclude that they are similar to mystical, world-rejecting religious orders.

Neither Seventh-day Adventists nor Pentecostals turn their backs on worldly concerns. Members of both groups are expected to labor in this world and to take their jobs seriously. Seventh-day Adventists and Pentecostals do not allow religious

13. In the study of a Pentecostal group, Howard Elinson found that this sect is "conservative in the literal sense of that word. Allen people contribute to the status quo by refraining from worldly efforts to change it." "The Implications of Pentecostal Religion for Intellectualism, Politics, and Race Relations," *American Journal of Sociology* 70 (1965):414.

goals to interfere with the necessity of making a living. They are not urged to forsake their jobs to spread their religious message, and except for full-time, paid religious workers, proselytism is usually an avocation.

Most of the members of Pentecostal and Seventh-day Adventist sects do not envision a life spent in purely spiritual contemplation and devotion. Even religious action is never completely removed from the difficulties and distractions one encounters in the world. In the language of these groups, one overcomes but does not ignore external obstacles to salvation. Therefore few sect members rely upon others to provide them with the necessities of life while they extend the limits and depth of their spiritual experience. Unlike the true world-rejecting mystical groups, they do not sanction religious beggary in any form, nor do they encourage religious self-abnegation. In fact, sects do not demand ascetic regimes which go far beyond systematic avoidance of excessive luxury, ostentation, and self-indulgence. Although Pentecostals encourage their members to achieve mystical rapport with God, they nevertheless put great emphasis on the value of the tangible effects of ecstatic religious experiences. Here the benefits of this contact with God not only are evident in unique spiritual abilities such as healing but also are revealed by concrete changes in the believer's character. The man who has been "saved" is clearly recognizable as a certain kind of man in his ordinary as well as his religious activities.

Finally, unlike mystical religious ideologies, the sects do not preach indifference to the struggle for self-esteem and thereby approve of affective neutrality to all the nonsacred dimensions of interpersonal relations. In fact, both Seventh-day Adventists and Pentecostals are sensitive to their relative positions in societal status hierarchies and to the derogatory implications lowly social rank carries with it. The way in which these sects define moral excellence, those activities deemed to lead to spiritual superiority, is closely related to pragmatic and symbolic efforts to retrieve or gain the esteem they feel is rightfully theirs. These sects, then, are other-worldly only in a very qualified sense and remain well within the basic Protestant orientation to the world.

The Scope of This Treatment of Pentecostal and Seventh-day Adventist Theologies

This book does not present a complete account of all Pentecostal and Seventh-day Adventist religious beliefs, doctrines, and creeds. I have no intention of producing a theologically adequate discussion of the entire system of Pentecostal and Seventh-day Adventist thought. Consequently, I do not feel impelled to provide biblical support in the form of textual quotations for their various social, ethical, and religious teachings. Also I will ignore the controversial implications many Pentecostal and Seventh-day Adventist ideas have for the larger Protestant community.

This study has a much narrower compass. Specifically, I focus on those cosmological and eschatological ideas which bear upon the sect's conception of the correct path to salvation. These ideas about the significance of supernatural and natural events, about the course of human history, and about the fate of the individual soul coalesce to form a total view of the right way to achieve salvation. Even theologians find it difficult to separate these strands of thought.[14]

This is not the result of any intellectual deficiency in Protestantism, but rather is due to the overriding importance of personal salvation in this religious tradition. This concern with the ultimate fate of the self demands an evaluative response even from religious ideas which map out the boundaries and persona of the supernatural realm. In other words, ideas about the constitution of supernatural realities are invariably pressed into the service of the believer's desire to adapt his life to divine dictates and imperatives. In fact, the Christian, and especially the Protestant, notion of salvation not only refers to the "gracious act of God whereby man is delivered from his sinful selfhood into newness and fullness of life" but also "implies a

14. For instance, Paul Althaus says that "Christian eschatology is personal, universalistic, and cosmic at the same time. The fulfillment of persons, the goal of the history of mankind, and the renewal of the cosmos cannot be separated from one another." "Eschatology," in *A Handbook of Christian Theology*, ed. Arthur A. Cohen and Marvin Halverson (New York: Meridian Books, 1962), p. 102.

threat or danger to man from which he needs to be delivered."[15]

In the Christian tradition, then, religious ideas must define the proper ends of human endeavor and therefore specify the worthwhile areas of activity and striving. Incidentally, this is a particularly critical problem in Protestantism because it rejects the idea that good works and other gestures of goodwill can alleviate the burden of guilt which identifies man as a sinner. Man's propensity for good is said to flow from his capacity to accept and believe in God's unmediated mercy.[16] Nevertheless, these religious systems indicate the directions in which effort must be exerted if human actions are to fit into the enduring structure of the universe and if men are to present themselves as truly transformed by God's freely given grace. As I said before, the religious picture of the external world is always divided into worthwhile and worthless spheres of action; it is never a purely cognitive map or guide to the supernatural environment of the self or a set of instrumental techniques for the control of that environment.

Seventh-day Adventist Belief

Historical Background of the Seventh-day Adventist Movement

The Seventh-day Adventists trace their origin as a distinct religious movement to the Millerites of the nineteenth century. William Miller, a Baptist preacher, became convinced in 1831 that he had discovered the key to the more obscure prophetic, apocalyptic passages in both the Old and the New Testaments. In the official organ of the Millerite movement, the *Spirit of the Times,* Miller's predictions about the time for the Second Ad-

15. Roger Hazelton, "Salvation," Ibid., p. 336.
16. According to Truman B. Douglass, "The doctrine of justification by faith means the acceptance of Christ's work of reconciliation and redemption with radical and absolute seriousness. It resists any attempt to modify the efficacy of this work by ascribing to man some other capacity for good, or credit gained by good works, or virtue conferred by the sacraments of the Church. It asserts that such good works as man is able to perform are as much a gift of God's goodness as is the bestowal of forgiveness through Christ." "Protestantism," Ibid., p. 289.

vent were widely circulated among the members of various churches interested in such matters.

According to Miller, Christ was due to arrive between 21 March 1843 and 21 March 1844. After the Second Coming failed to materialize, Miller did not lose faith, and most of his followers remained convinced that the Second Advent was soon to occur. They agreed that a technical error was made in the calculations and Miller returned to correct his original estimate. Miller announced that 22 October 1844 was the day when Christ would appear. When this day also passed without noticeable signs of the earthly presence of Jesus, most Adventists concluded that it was impossible for men to set the exact time for Jesus' trip to earth. Nevertheless, they did not relinquish their belief in the *imminence* of the millennium; the end of the world was definitely in sight and only the moment of its destruction was in doubt.

Seventh-day Adventist Theology

After the "great disappointment" a small band of faithful Adventists pondered the discrepancy between their belief and reality. In order to resolve this "cognitive dissonance," they theorized that the reference in Heb. 8:1 to the high priest (i.e., Christ) who is "minister of the sanctuary and of the true tabernacle, which the Lord pitched" previously was misconstrued. The sanctuary was in heaven, and not on earth as they had presumed. Thus, the 1844 date only meant that at this time Christ entered the sanctuary to judge the sins of those living and dead. Seventh-day Adventists, following their "prophetess" Mrs. White, have further refined this idea. They believe that the Jewish sanctuary lost its function as the means of collective redemption for the "chosen people" when Christ died, and redemption continues on an individual basis in heaven.

This revision of the Adventist prediction not only reinforced their own belief in its general validity but introduced a new note of dramatic tension in the movement's theology. Seventh-day Adventists were still convinced that they were living in the critical period of the history of the world, and they remained certain that the final phase of human history had begun.

Shortly, they argued, Christ can no longer intercede for men before the divine court of justice. The doors of mercy will close forever. Men will have to make up their minds about which side in this conflict between the forces of good and evil they will align themselves with—there is no neutral ground. Christ could close the books in heaven at this very moment and living men, whatever their intentions, would be deprived of his company forever. This reinterpretation of the meaning of the 1844 date allowed Seventh-day Adventists to reaffirm the idea that the time was drawing near for the Second Coming. At the same time, they discovered a theologically satisfying reason for dispensing with attempts to fix the date of Christ's return, the results of which were damaging to the movement's prestige and morale.

A good deal of the formal codification of Seventh-day Adventist doctrine was the work of Ellen G. White, founder and prime mover of the religious organization. She was a dedicated Adventist who retained her orthodox denominational affiliation until her belief was attacked by church authorities after Christ failed to appear in 1844. Shortly thereafter Mrs. White experienced the first of many "visions" in which God gave her the correct answers to many theological and moral questions which agitated the Adventist movement. These issues, such as the proper day of the Sabbath—Saturday or Sunday—provided the ideological focus for schismatic groups which crystallized after the shock of the 1844 disappointment split the Millerite alliance.

Her writings still form the basis for scriptural interpretations in Seventh-day Adventist churches. In the group I studied, the pastor would support any argument about the meaning of a biblical passage with a reference to Mrs. White's writing on the subject; and dedicated sect members study her writings assiduously. Although Mrs. White introduced certain novel elements into Seventh-day Adventist doctrine, including the celebration of the seventh day of the week as the Sabbath, she did not claim unique spiritual abilities. She was an instrument of God who wanted Adventists to find the right path once again:

Although Mrs. White always refused to accept the designation "prophet" she did not deny prophetic inspiration. There is strong evidence to prove that God spoke through her, giving direction and, when necessary, reproof for the Advent Movement, otherwise known as the Seventh-day Adventist Church.[17]

For Seventh-day Adventists, her charisma resided in her ability to endow traditional Adventist beliefs with divine legitimacy during a period of intense spiritual doubt about the validity of their most cherished hopes. This is what Ramano V. aptly terms "renovative" rather than "innovative" charisma.[18] She revitalized and gave new credibility to these beliefs by placing them in a more comprehensive theological system. Mrs. White enabled Seventh-day Adventists to feel that their cognitive and moral judgments were right, especially in the vital matters of biblical prophecy. She brought them back from the edge of intellectual chaos. As Shils points out, the "charismatic propensity is a function of the need for order." [19]

Seventh-day Adventists do not approve of spontaneous, noninstitutionalized religious charisma. Displays of religious fervor are not sought outside the appropriate context (e.g., in a sermon), and the organization does not solicit extraordinary spiritual experiences from its members. Mrs. White is not endowed with any supramundane qualities beyond those accorded to a very dedicated member of the movement who had the good fortune to be the vessel through whom God revealed the meaning of passages of the Bible whose previous obscurity had impeded the development of Adventism.

Seventh-day Adventists do not believe that anyone now has the powers they attribute to Mrs. White. In sermons and informal discussions, they warn believers about "spiritualism," a term which covers any mystical phenomenon. One communicates with

17. *Seventh-day Adventist Information File* (Washington, D.C.: Bureau of Public Relations, General Conference of Seventh-day Adventists, n.d.), p. 7.
18. Octavio Ramano V., "Charismatic Medicine, Folk-Healing, and Folk-Sainthood," *American Anthropologist* 67 (1965).
19. Edward Shils, "Charisma, Order and Status," *American Sociological Review* 30 (1965):203.

God through prayer, but one knows his commands through the written text of the Bible. God does not ordinarily reveal himself through intermediaries, nor does he indulge in idiosyncratic advice on the way in which particular individuals should achieve salvation or carry out his work in this world. Seventh-day Adventists disparage any religious doctrine which encourages spiritual illumination through unconventional means, for example, seeking personal union with the ultimate source of spiritual enlightment.

Formal Doctrines

At the beginning of this section, I want to say that I have not digested the entire corpus of Seventh-day Adventist writings. Mrs. White's writings on theological topics alone could easily provide many months of intensive reading. My synthesis of Seventh-day Adventist theology is based on three types of data: official sect writings, sermons and Sabbath school talks given in the group I studied, and informal discussions with sect members. The agreement between these sources is striking; in almost every instance I found the opinions expressed in each complementary. There are few deviations from sect dogma. Those questions, such as the propriety of eating meat (Seventh-day Adventists are bound to treat the "body as the temple of the Holy Spirit" and to avoid all "unclean foods") are legitimately open to honest differences of opinion and in any case are relatively minor issues.

Seventh-day Adventists allow for a certain amount of latitude in the interpretation of some of their teachings. These areas of nonheretical disagreement are carefully established; the boundaries of acceptable theological dissent are explicit. Although any member who questioned the truth of major theological or ethical teachings would be forced to leave the movement, there are certain problems in biblical interpretation which involve the creative efforts of laymen and clergy. According to its adherents, Seventh-day Adventist belief evolves as God reveals more of his plan with the passage of time. For example, there is a good deal of discussion about the meaning of the 144,000 who are saved from annihilation in Rev. 7:4. There is no dogmatic interpretation of this passage because Seventh-day Adventists generally feel that there is not sufficient internal evidence in the Bible to arrive at an unequivocal statement about the nature and function of the 144,000.

Seventh-day Adventists, then, have a tradition of unwavering consensus on fundamental doctrines; consequently, I will rely principally upon Seventh-day Adventist writings in this presentation of their doctrines, adding observations drawn from sermons or conversations largely as corroboration. Incidentally, besides various devotional books and inspirational magazines, Seventh-day Adventists employ the *Sabbath School Lesson Quarterly* as a daily guide to spiritual development. The *Quarterly* provides the text for the discussion in Sabbath school classes in which all members, regardless of age, are supposed to participate before each Saturday service. In typical Seventh-day Adventist fashion, members are given a complete, detailed study plan for each day during the week, and there are questions after each short section in the *Quarterly* which the reader answers to prepare for class on Saturday.

Seventh-day Adventist theology discusses the relationship between Jewish ritual and the present constitution of the supernatural realm. They think that ancient Jewish customs reveal the disposition of God in our time:

> The whole worship of ancient Israel was a promise, in figures and symbols, of Christ; and it was not merely a promise, but an actual provision, designed by God to aid millions of people by lifting their thoughts to Him who was to manifest Himself to our world.[20]

They believe that the Jewish tabernacle was "patterned" after the heavenly sanctuary; it is a "type" (copy) which reveals both heavenly spatial arrangements and divine purposes. The conception of a heavenly sanctuary allows Seventh-day Adventists to account for the failure of Christ to arrive in 1844, and thus it legitimates their eschatology. Mrs. White says:

> The subject of the sanctuary was the key which unlocked the mystery of the disappointment of 1844: It opened to view a complete system of truth, connected and harmonious, showing that God's hand had directed the

20. *Sabbath School Quarterly*, no. 272 (1963), p. 5.

great advent movement and revealing present duty as it brought to light the position and work of His people.[21]

According to Mrs. White, Seventh-day Adventists previously were misinformed about the prophetic reference to the cleansing of the sanctuary in Dan. 8:14. She points out that

> In common with the rest of the Christian world, Adventists then held that the earth, or some portion of it, was the sanctuary. They understood that the cleansing of the sanctuary was the purification of the earth by the fires of the last great day, and that this would take place at the second advent. Hence the conclusion that Christ would return to the earth in 1844.[22]

The problem resided in the interpretation of the passage rather than in the calculation of 1844 as the date for the "cleansing of the sanctuary." The function of each compartment of the Jewish tabernacle presages one of the two distinct phases in the fulfillment of biblical prophecy. Seventh-day Adventists believe that the heavenly sanctuary, like its Jewish counterpart, is divided into two compartments: the holy place and the most holy place.

The first compartment of the Jewish tabernacle served as the arena for ritual sacrifice. Here the priest offered blood sacrifices for transgressions of the Law. Seventh-day Adventists stress the idea that salvation without blood is impossible:

> Many have expressed wonder that God demanded so many slain victims in the sacrificial offerings of the Jewish people; but it was to rivet in their minds the great truth that without the shedding of blood there is no remission of sins. . . . The sacrificial offerings were established by infinite wisdom to impress upon the fallen race the solemn truth that it was sin which caused death. Every time the life of a sacrificial offering was taken, they were reminded that if there had been no sin, there would have been no death.[23]

They believe that the only offering available to the Jewish priest who was a sinner like all other men was an unblemished

21. Ellen G. White, *The Great Controversy between Christ and Satan* (Washington, D.C.: Review and Herald Publishing Assn., 1950), p. 417.
22. Ibid., p. 403.
23. *Sabbath School Quarterly*, no. 272 (1963), p. 18.

and spotless creature, a lamb. According to Seventh-day Adventist theology, the Jewish sacrificial ritual is a first approximation to the ultimate sacrifice in God's plan to restore fallen man. They think that only Christ, who experienced temptation but not sin, could substitute for the Jewish lamb and thereby rescue men from their depravity. For Seventh-day Adventists, the relationship between sacrificial blood and sin is clear, and anyone who desires salvation must understand this elemental fact: the consequence of sin is eternal and everlasting death.

According to Mrs. White, the inner compartment of the Jewish sanctuary contained the ark which held the Ten Commandments. For Seventh-day Adventists the Ten Commandments represent the paramount sacred document. No other divine pronouncement so clearly reveals the standards which determine who is eligible for salvation, "the great rule of right by which all mankind are tested." [24]

Both of the sacrificial rituals performed in the inner and outer compartments "symbolized the transfer of the sin from the penitent to the sanctuary." [25] Ritual blood acts as the spiritual catalyst which removes the previously indelible stain of sin from the truly repentant believer. It is here, Mrs. White claims, that one can find the source of the vital phrase, the "cleansing of the sanctuary." After his resurrection and ascension, Christ is said to have begun his "work" in heaven which corresponds to the function of the outer compartment of the Jewish tabernacle. In his sacrificial capacity, as the "lamb" which bore the burden of man's sins, Christ acts as an intercessor before God the Father in the heavenly holy place. This phase of the redemptive process emphasizes the remission of sins.

Seventh-day Adventists think that although Christ actively strives to secure man's salvation, His efforts alone do not insure it. In essence, Christ's sacrifice at Calvary only created the preconditions under which sinful man has a chance to acquire divine forgiveness. Mrs. White argues that this part of Christ's mission ended decisively in 1844, and Christ then moved from the holy to the most holy place in heaven. This marked the

24. White, *Great Controversy*, p. 408.
25. Ibid., p. 412.

transition between the two great periods in the process of redemption and judgment of mankind.

In Seventh-day Adventism redemption and judgment are the result of discrete divine actions. Consequently, the dispensation of grace is a restricted opportunity, since it is definitely confined to a limited time period rather than an eternal possibility for man. It is bestowed until the time when God finally decides to execute the sentence reserved for the wicked. However, once a person has been judged, his fate is sealed; and if the findings are negative, punishment is inescapable. Only the exact moment for the final disposition of his case cannot be precisely determined.

The cleansing of the sanctuary, then, announces a critical moment in human history. Mrs. White describes the function of the stage which occurred in the heavenly sphere before 1844 in these terms:

> The ministration of the priest throughout the year in the first apartment of the sanctuary, "within the veil" which formed the door and separated the holy place from the outer court, represents the work of ministration upon which Christ entered at His ascension. It was the work of the priest in the daily ministration to present before God the blood of the sin offering, also the incense which ascended with the prayers of Israel. So did Christ plead His blood before the Father in behalf of sinners, and present before Him also, with the precious fragrance of his own righteousness, the prayers of penitent believers. Such was the work of ministration in the first apartment of the sanctuary in heaven. . . . For eighteen centuries this work of ministration continued in the first apartment of the sanctuary. The blood of Christ, pleaded in behalf of penitent believers, secured their pardon and acceptance with the Father, yet their sins still remained upon the books of record. As in the typical service there was the work of atonement at the close of the year, so before Christ's work for the redemption of men is completed there is work of atonement for the removal of sin from the sanctuary. This is the service which began when the 2300 days ended. At that time, as foretold by Daniel the prophet, our High Priest entered the most holy, to perform the last division of His solemn work—to cleanse the sanctuary.[26]

In short, the period of Christ's mediation, which lasted until 1844, is only the first step in the eventual return of Christ to

26. Ibid., p. 415.

earth and the establishment of the Kingdom of God on earth. Before this can happen, God must review the life of every man, living or dead, and only after he has decided who is to survive when the wicked are condemned can the sanctuary be cleansed. The sins of the truly deserving, forgiven believers will be transferred to those who bear the full responsibility for disobedience and evil.

The forces of evil play an active, causal role in this cosmology. They not only represent a deficiency of virtue but, more important, they are the product of a willing failure to comprehend and to obey the dictates of God. As in other Christian theological systems, disobedience acts as the formal cause which explains the origin of sin in the universe and accounts for the existence of death and suffering. But in Seventh-day Adventist theology the Devil and his followers play a very active, independent role in contemporary supernatural affairs. They not only compete with Christ for individual souls on more or less equal terms but also serve as the efficient cause of their own destruction and hence of the eradication of all evil from the world. This view of the independent role of evil in the universe fits the Seventh-day Adventist assumption that each man is responsible for his own decision to join the forces of either good or evil. The choice is clear-cut and requires personal commitment to one of two sets of mutually exclusive principles.

As we have seen, before Christ can return to earth to destroy finally all traces of sin, everyone must have been investigated. This process of investigation constitutes the first part of the second and contemporary period of human history. Although Seventh-day Adventists do not predict the exact moment for the conclusion of the investigation process, they believe that there is sufficient evidence to indicate that it will be soon indeed!

In the most holy place, Christ acts as an advocate rather than as an intercessor, and a person's fate depends upon the quality of the brief Christ can present before the divine tribunal of justice. Seventh-day Adventists describe the present period as a "crisis," not only because the entire universe is heading toward a showdown between the Devil and Christ in their struggle to shape the destiny of mankind but also because each person is under very close scrutiny in heaven. The lens of divine justice is said to be focused closely on even the most minute details of one's life and penetrates behind the ordinary facade of both public and private life. Seventh-day Adventists believe that they can determine their status in heaven by asking themselves whether they have increased or decreased their own moral endowment. Declarations of faith alone or membership in religious organizations, whatever their character, are of no avail without a substantial demonstration of positive ethical accomplishment:

> In the judgment the use made of every talent will be scrutinized. How have we employed the capital lent us in Heaven? Will the Lord at His coming receive His own usury? Have we improved the powers entrusted us, in hand and heart and brain, to the glory of God and the blessing of the world? How have we used our time, our pen, our voice, our money, our influence? What have we done for Christ, in the person of the poor, the afflicted, the orphan, or the widow? God has made us the depositaries of His holy word; what have we done with the light and truth given us to make men wise unto salvation? No value is attached to a mere profession of faith in Christ; only the love which is shown by works is counted genuine. . . . The work of preparation is an individual work. We are not saved in groups.[27]

The second phase of this process—the cleansing of the sanctuary—engages the personal interests of Seventh-day Adventists because their salvation depends upon the outcome of the "investigative process." No man, regardless of how spotless he believes his life has been, can be completely certain that God will not discover a serious fault in it. At the end of many sermons, the pastor in the group I studied would turn to a very common theme that nonetheless never lost its impact on his audience. He would relentlessly point out that no one can be certain that God will choose him as one of the elect, and he did not exempt himself from this warning. He often said quite sincerely that "if I don't see one of you [members of the congregation] in the Kingdom of God, I will ask what happened to you, and you should do the same for me if you don't see me there."

27. Ibid., pp. 481–84.

The interest at stake here is not simply the believer's relative status among the larger body of Christians. As far as salvation is concerned, it is a question of all or nothing; either one is selected for membership in what Seventh-day Adventists believe is the necessarily small group of the saved or he perishes forever in the fire which destroys the wicked. These concerns are apparent in rather free-flowing sermons like the following:

The pastor began the sermon, as he often does, by describing a scene (purported to be true) in which a ship was caught in a storm and "no one dared to ask, 'Is there hope?' " The captain is said to have stood motionless on the deck while the passengers screamed and then he looked at his watch; "Thank God, we are saved, the tide has turned. In one minute more, it would have been too late. We would have been smashed to bits on the rocks near the shore." From this abbreviated incident, the pastor concluded that "today is the crisis hour for this world—the door of mercy will soon be shut—the probation hour will soon be over—Jesus is soon to come and the end of the world is near. *Now* everyone can confess his sins. Soon this opportunity will pass, never to return. Soon destiny will be sealed for eternity." Matthew 7:13. (He often cites biblical passages without reading them; this one reads, "Therefore it is come to pass, that as he cried, and they would not hear; so they cried, and I would not hear, saith the Lord of hosts." He often goes into lengthy discussions of the Greek derivation of various translations, which I could not follow.) The pastor continued that "one must go in by the narrow gate and the hard road and only a few find it. If you do not change *now*, you will be left outside the Kingdom of God—the unsaved will be left outside; for the unsaved it will be too late to win heaven. Confess your sins or nothing will be left but eternal destruction. Each and every one of us must make everything right with God before the door swings shut! How can anyone indulge in impure thoughts and deeds! When the reward to be bestowed is so near our reach." He goes on to refer to a text by Mrs. White, who talks about fornicators and adulterers secretly working in iniquity "when we [Seventh-day Adventists] have the beautiful truths of the book of Revelation." And he says that "there will not be a second chance to be saved! And if you do not exercise eternal vigilance you may let down [your guard against temptation] and He will come at that time and then you will be left out [of the Kingdom]. And He is near—just about to come. I don't have to tell you and you don't have to tell me some of the sin we are indulging in—we must have a truly repentent attitude—it is in this life-time that you are saved, and not after you are dead." He concludes the sermon with two long stories, one from his own experience and one from the Bible, with the same moral: Frivolity and disbelief in the imminence of the millennium are symptoms of the same spiritual illness, an inability to commit oneself to the right way of life.

Quite obviously these injunctions are not intended simply to turn those with wicked inclinations toward righteousness or to convert the unsaved. Almost all of those at the service were regular members of the church who are not in immediate danger of succumbing to "depraved" modes of life. These warnings are meant to strengthen the believer against the ever present and usually fatal danger of falling into spiritual indolence; that is, the assumption that one does not have to constantly strive to keep his behavior within the proper moral boundaries. According to Seventh-day Adventist theology, people who feel that their place in heaven is reserved are likely to fall prey to the Devil's subtle temptations; sometimes, my informants added, without knowing it. Seventh-day Adventists are enjoined to avoid all doctrines that promise personal spiritual safety. This notion that life involves spiritual risk sustains many of their more specifically ideological orientations to practical matters. Seventh-day Adventists conclude that everyone is a sinner and must overcome his grave inborn spiritual defects through continuous effort to reach standards of conduct required by the Law. This requires constant control over one's impulses, and my informants often emphasized that a dedicated Seventh-day Adventist can ill afford even a temporary lapse. There is no such thing as moral relaxation in Seventh-day Adventist theology.

As we have seen, although Christ pleads for sinners, their sins remain on the books of record until the final disposition of their cases. In Seventh-day Adventist theology, the remission of sins involves a lifelong struggle by the believer to create the most favorable record possible, and consequently any misstep on his part can lead to permanent revocation of his status as one of the elect. One of the tenets of Seventh-day Adventist teaching is that although any unconfessed and unrepented serious transgression of the Law is undoubtedly enough to disqualify the believer, "minor" infractions, especially if they are many, may prevent him from joining the elect. This ambiguity about the import of "minor" deviations from the code of proper conduct is built into Seventh-day Adventist theology. Informants stress the idea that the only safe procedure is to follow religious behavioral prescriptions exactly. Any other course is likely to have disastrous consequences, even if it appears that slight slips are of little import. This is a point, incidentally, which is underscored in an almost infinite variety of ways in sermons and other discussions of sect belief. These themes are discernible in the following Sabbath school talk a member gave (informally) to his class:

> Each day's lesson [in the *Sabbath School Quarterly*] gives us a certificate to get into heaven; it tells us how to meet trials and temptations. The difficulty lies in being born again. Can we get rid of this fleshly nature? We are not certain whether we can get rid of this fleshly nature but when we are born again, [we discover] the old flesh is gone. If you find it hard to fight temptations, you are hanging on to the old nature—conversion is really a *complete* change in your way of life and your attitudes. There are two forces; one to serve God, the other to serve the Devil. In the first, you are brought into a new nature. The Devil injects desire for temptations, displays of personal feelings, or a taste of the world. How can we attain our divine nature? Perfect nature in Christ is achieved by believing in the promises of God. How does this change us? Belief in God's word is the center of Christian living; otherwise we have no power to resist temptation. [At this point, a member asked how Christ could save us if he didn't sin; the answer was that Christ loved us so much that he didn't sin, and the discussion leader added parenthetically that you don't find people like that in the world anymore.] Jesus puts his trust in God's word because even he could not argue with the Devil alone. How can you tell a change in Christ? There is joy, meekness, etc. A change in character.

The Seventh-day Adventist conception of the "investigative process" establishes the theological grounds for its ideology—those attitudes toward secular affairs which have ethical overtones and supernatural implications. Although Seventh-day Adventists often discriminate between greater and lesser evils, they nevertheless perceive only two ethical categories: one either is in the camp of the Devil or is a faithful follower of Christ. They see any evidence of theological or moral equivocation as a sign of a person's latent desire to join the Devil, and they think that anyone who would attack the absolute validity of the Ten Commandments as the standard for human action is obviously an ally of the Evil One.

These are not simply formal theological categories invoked in abstract religious thought and argument. Righteousness exists only so far as it is demonstrated in concrete behavior. Intentions, however virtuous they may be, are not enough for Seventh-day Adventists. For example, one of my informants asked in Sabbath school class whether the prayers of those who strive for (but do not always achieve) righteousness are answered. The leader replied that if our prayers were answered, we could break the commandments and excuse ourselves by saying we were striving. He continued:

> Only the Lord will determine who is righteous, but there is a rule to follow. If we are trying to keep his commandments to the best of our ability, our prayers will be answered; but there are just two classes of persons. The saved, who are righteous or who try to be righteous and confess their sins as soon as they commit them, and the wicked or unsaved—those who do not heed either the Law or the Word of God. The Law and the Word are one.

Although Seventh-day Adventists do not maintain that one slight slip condemns a man, they believe he must recognize every misdeed, confess his sins to God, and improve his behavior in the future. They believe that a truly converted member will manifest fewer and fewer "minor" deviations as time goes on, because his religious experience penetrates to the very core of his character.

The Sabbath school leader's response to this question reveals another aspect of their belief. Although he wanted to expose the fallacy of thinking that all that matters is seeking God's forgiveness in true sincerity, he also wanted to emphasize that the believer has clear, objective criteria before him which mark the line between those who go with Christ and the others who are to be destroyed in the fire. In other words, salvation is gained through a gradual process of behavioral reform and improvement, but the status of being saved admits of no degrees—one falls into one of two separate classes.

Seventh-day Adventists see powerful forces in the supernatural realm that move toward a final confrontation. Although the true followers of Christ must suffer intensified persecution in the "last days," the choice is clear: the supernatural rewards and punishments outweigh any temporal concerns or pleasures. The test which he must pass in the heavenly court is the Seventh-day Adventist's strongest theological inducement to maintain very high standards of proper conduct:

> Every man's work passes in review before God and is registered for faithfulness or unfaithfulness. Opposite each name in the books of heaven is entered with terrible exactness every wrong work, every selfish act, every unfilled duty, and every secret sin, with every artful dissembling. Heaven-sent warnings or reproofs neglected, wasted moments, unimproved opportunities, the influence exerted for good or for evil, with its far-reaching results, all are chronicled by the recording angel. The law of God is the standard by which the characters and the lives of men will be tested in the judgment.[28]

All this is, of course, the prelude to the central event in Seventh-day Adventist cosmology, the Second Coming of Christ and the establishment of the kingdom of the righteous on earth. The millennium is announced by a series of interrelated divine warnings. Seventh-day Adventists believe that the three angels' messages in Revelation contain a highly abbreviated key to the code of God's progressive revelation of his plans for man's salvation.

According to this condensed biblical time schedule, the first angel's message (Rev. 14:6, 7) has already been delivered; it tells men of the "approaching judgment." The "Fall of Babylon" is the image which pervades the second angel's message (Rev. 14:8), and this metaphor occurs in most Seventh-day Adventist sermons and writings in a variety of contexts. Its most encompassing meaning refers to the corruption and sin which lie behind the facades of worldly institutions, which, in their opinion, includes most churches.

On a more specific level, the Babylon image refers to what Seventh-day Adventists believe is the growing, corrupting influence of the Roman Catholic church over the civil government

28. Ibid., p. 476.

and over the Protestant religious establishment. For Seventh-day Adventists, the phrase "the mark of the beast" which is found in the apocalyptic passages of Revelation signifies Catholic depravity. They use this phrase as a metaphor for unmitigated evil, which they believe afflicts anyone who, knowingly or not, is subject to the Roman Catholic conspiracy. In their cosmology, the pope is the principal and conscious agent of the Devil. His attack on righteousness is concentrated on the distinctive emblem of Seventh-day Adventism; they celebrate the Sabbath on the seventh day of the week—Saturday—rather than on Sunday.[29] The pope is the primary force behind the various blue laws and similar legal campaigns to enforce Sunday as the day of rest.

Although Seventh-day Adventists do not think that the legal sanctions employed by the state are necessarily evil, the Devil often co-opts them. Civil laws which run counter to the commandments of God are among the Devil's most potent weapons in the design to undermine the faith and confidence of the true believer. To protect themselves from this external but nevertheless subtle evil force, Seventh-day Adventists emphasize the invariant and absolutely uncompromising character of their moral rules. As one of my informants put it, "God is manifested in the laws of nature—we cannot be wishy-washy about them." Anyone, therefore, who tampers with the literal meaning of the commandments, however slight his reinterpretations may be, is destined for damnation. This is the reason, Seventh-day Adventists explain, that the spiritual prognosis for those who ignore the "true" Sabbath (Saturday) is extremely dark even though such a violation of God's word may seem trivial to the outsider.

Seventh-day Adventist theology holds that the tempo of the war between those who strive to uphold and those who seek to subvert God's laws has intensified in recent times. This is a solid indication of the nearness of the Second Advent. They see a gradual but significant increase in war, civil disorders, natural

29. For the reasoning behind their claim that Saturday rather than Sunday is the correct day to observe the Sabbath see Arthur Lickey, *Highways to Truth* (Washington, D.C.: Review and Herald Publishing Assn., 1952).

catastrophes, and violence in Western history. All these ills spring from violations of the "true" source of moral authority; nations foolishly base their actions on "the traditions of men" rather than on divine law. They believe that the Catholic church actively substitutes pagan for divine traditions. As the apotheosis of worldly empires obsessed with the desire to dominate men's spiritual lives, its end will signal the end of this corrupt world:

> Quickly it dominated the scene, occupying the seat of the Caesars and exercising powers no emperor ever claimed. It was "diverse" from the others in that, while resembling a political organization, it assumed religious aspects, the resultant combination of church and state bringing upon the true saints of God the worst persecution known to man and stamping the era of its supremacy as the Dark Ages of history. . . . Sometimes it may seem as though God takes no notice of their blasphemies and cruelties. But He does. Every wicked word is recorded. So is every ugly deed. And when the books of heaven are opened there will be a heavy price to pay. . . . Such will be the fate of this monstrous religio-political despotism, and of all tyrannies, present and future. The judgment will decide against them. They shall be consumed and destroyed until there is nothing left of them, not even a memory.[30]

Incidentally, this rather virulent anti-Catholicism might appear atavistic; the mainstream of American Protestantism long ago ceased to regard Rome as the Devil's disciple. However, this anomalous attitude supports a basic theological premise. Seventh-day Adventists perceive the Catholic church as the institution which prevents men from scrutinizing the Scriptures on their own. This opposes their view that salvation is predicated upon intellectual free choice between "good" and "evil" interpretations of the Bible, and thus any religion which relies upon received spiritual opinion has a deadly effect upon the destiny of the believer. As we shall see in the following section on Seventh-day Adventist ideology, their attitudes toward secular affairs presuppose an actor who, through the sheer force of his will and his commitment to righteousness, constantly presses his behavior into a rigid mold despite continual temptations which threaten his moral course. In this sense, then, Catholicism,

30. Arthur Maxwell, *Courage for the Crisis* (Mountain View, Calif.: Pacific Publishing Assn., 1962), pp. 222–23.

which accepts the human propensity to sin and moral weakness among the vast majority of men and yet still holds out the promise of salvation, negates the fundamental moral symbolism of Seventh-day Adventist cosmology.

The third angel's message is actually the first step in the fulfillment of the prophesied event which, properly speaking, constitutes the enactment of the Second Advent. Before examining the series of events initiated by the third angel's message, I would like to dispose of a common misconception about the meaning of Seventh-day Adventists' version of the millennium. Adventist and millenarian movements are usually treated as a symbolic protest against the established secular order and, more particularly, against the domination of the wealthy and powerful over the poor and socially disfranchised. Wilson, for example, calls them "religiously inspired revolutionist movements" and claims that the common element in diverse movements is their "collectivist, this-worldly" orientation.[31] He explicitly includes Seventh-day Adventists in this category. This misconstrues the drift of their attitude toward the status quo, although Wilson notes that Seventh-day Adventists have no immediate and specifically *political* aspirations.

Those scholars who are convinced that religious millenarian ideologies are simply masks or disguises for revolutionary sentiments and who buttress their arguments by pointing to themes of role reversal between ruler and ruled and of supernatural retribution for exploitation ("the first shall be last and the last first," "the poor shall inherit the earth") assume that the manifest content of these ideologies all serves the same latent function.[32] This presupposition certainly does not hold true for Sev-

31. Bryan Wilson, "Millennialism in Comparative Perspective," *Comparative Studies in Society and History* 6 (1963).
32. For a case which seems to fit this model see Ernst Werner, "Popular Ideologies in Late Medieval Europe, *Comparative Studies in Society and History* 2 (1960). Also, Herbert S. Klein's fascinating study of a rebellion against the Spanish crown in eighteenth-century Mexico provides a detailed account of the development of a revolutionary peasant movement which had distinct millenarian overtones and a coherent military and political structure. "Peasant Communities in Revolt: The Tzeltal Republic of 1712," *Pacific Historical Review* 35 (1966).

enth-day Adventists, who definitely abhor any expression of truly secular revolutionary sentiment.[33]

In formal theological writings, in sermons, and in informal conversations, Seventh-day Adventists vented strong feelings against revolutionary movements other than the one led by Christ. In their comments on the passing political scene, Seventh-day Adventists often expressed intense dislike of any sort of political radicalism. The agencies of radical secular change were all thought to be devices controlled by the Devil for his own nefarious ends. They often cited the Cuban revolution as an outstanding instance of the evil inherent in all such developments. Their attitudes toward political revolutions are part of a more pervasive high regard for the legitimate exercise of duly constituted civil authority. They are antagonistic to any group which would "illegally" interfere with the operation of the government in order to achieve its own ends and would thereby stimulate civil disorder; for example, they are not favorably disposed to the techniques of "civil disobedience" employed by peace and civil-rights groups.

These attitudes are apparent even when Seventh-day Adventist moral prescriptions "conflict" with the rules of the secular order. In the case of blue laws and compulsory military service, Seventh-day Adventists prefer to reach a mutually acceptable compromise with the larger society rather than to resist obdurately its demands for conformity to its laws. Seventh-day Adventists operate a summer camp for boys likely to be inducted into the armed services in order to prepare them for active, noncombatant roles in medical and similar service units. They are very proud of army citations for the military excellence of their camp and invite ranking army officers to review its pro-

33. In a study whose thesis parallels this one's, E. U. Essien-Udom (*Black Nationalism: The Search for an Identity* [Chicago: University of Chicago Press, 1962]), argues that the radical, conflict-oriented, separatist, and apocalyptic beliefs of the Black Muslims obscure their abiding concern with upward mobility through conventional channels of social improvement. This supports the argument advanced here that Seventh-day Adventist eschatology conceals an essentially accommodative attitude toward the larger society *in those areas* which are instrumental for social and economic advancement.

gram and personnel each summer. They even tutor the boys in army drilling routines, albeit without using weapons. In this way, they satisfy both their desire to refrain from transgressing the commandment which prohibits killing and their commitment to the established political order.

Seventh-day Adventists also try to influence the "influentials" in their campaigns against blue laws and similar legislation forbidding work on Sundays. To do this, they send specially prepared literature to persons in the government and attempt to convince those whose aid would be strategic in repealing or preventing the passage of such legislation of the justice of their case. The pastor urges the members of the congregation to write to these persons, and leaders of the group testify before committees considering such legislation. In all of this, one can see the Seventh-day Adventists' preference for conventional political manipulation and pressure rather than for passive withdrawal from legal disputes. In short, they do not disobey secular rules they believe are wrong in a hostile or aggressive manner—they simply refuse to bend completely to those laws which contradict their religious teachings.

Seventh-day Adventists place great value on the preservation and restoration of civil order, even though they firmly believe that man-made and natural catastrophes will inevitably increase in frequency and severity. God uses these as a warning of the final disaster which will befall the sinful. Each Seventh-day Adventist church has a Dorcas society whose purpose is to aid those whose lives have been disrupted by natural catastrophes, and each regional headquarters maintains a fully equipped disaster unit.

Their antirevolutionary attitudes are apparent in theological writings on various historical topics. For example, Mrs. White asserts that the only valid revolutionary impact of the Reformation was theological and that the secular disturbances which accompanied it were illegitimate:

> The Reformers were solicitous that their cause should not be confounded with political questions; they felt that the Reformation should exercise no other influence than that which proceeds from the word of God. . . . One of the principles most firmly maintained by Luther was that there

should be no resort to secular power in support of the Reformation, and no appeal to arms for its defense.[34]

In fact, Seventh-day Adventists believe that spiritual corruption, particularly associated with the Catholic church, is a primary cause of revolutionary anarchy:

When France rejected the gift of heaven, she sowed the seeds of anarchy and ruin; and the inevitable outworking [*sic*] of cause and effect resulted in the Revolution and the Reign of Terror.[35]

Mrs. White identifies the political revolutionary as the prototype of the sinner: "He who obeys the Divine law will truly respect and obey the laws of his country. He who fears God will honor the king in the exercise of all just and legitimate authority."[36] And conversely:

Those who refuse to submit to the government of God are wholly unfitted to govern themselves. Through their pernicious teachings the spirit of insubordination is implanted in the hearts of children and youth, who are naturally impatient of control; and a lawless, licentious state of society results. . . . Those who teach the people to regard lightly the commandments of God sow disobedience to reap disobedience. Let the restraint imposed by the divine law be wholly cast aside, and human laws would soon be disregarded.[37]

The reforms for which the French Revolution strove can be realized only by strict adherence to biblical commandments and by *respect* for the civil authorities, whatever the justification for their power. In general, they believe that class conflict creates greater wrongs than it can possibly right. In the final analysis, Seventh-day Adventists hold that discrepancies in material power and wealth are of little significance, because a man's spiritual worth is not necessarily correlated with his socioeconomic status. In this religious movement, then, there is no disguised appeal to oppressed strata to overthrow those who exploit them. Quite the contrary, Seventh-day Adventists divest

34. White, *Great Controversy*, pp. 193–95.
35. Ibid., p. 217.
36. Ibid., p. 267.
37. Ibid., p. 578.

their religious message of explicit class bias; they implore rich and poor alike to give up "luxurious" modes of life which destroy strict adherence to the routines prescribed by their ideology. They reject *all* life styles oriented to immediate gratification of sensual impulses, regardless of whether this desire to indulge hedonistic desires is found among the working or the middle classes.

As I pointed out earlier, the Second Advent is set in motion by the end of the "investigative process" in heaven, that is, when God judges the last living person on his list. "The doors of mercy" are finally closed; it is too late to change one's ways and thus sins unrepented stigmatize a person as a sinner. Seventh-day Adventists explain that the reason for the apparent delay in Christ's return to this planet is threefold. First, it gives men more time to mend their ways and, at the same time, indicates the depth of God's compassion for man. Second, it proves to the angels and the residents of other planets that God was originally justified in expelling the Devil and his band of fallen angels from heaven. According to their cosmology, these other worlds are inhabited by rational, sentient beings who have never been infected by the virus of sin. These beings are the audience for the struggle between Christ and Satan, and therefore they must be convinced that the Devil really intends to destroy the human race:

> Why did God not blot out Satan when he first sinned? I think you see why. There was only one way to handle the situation. Lucifer must be given every chance—until he reached the point of no return and until the watching universe understood all the issues involved.[38]

Finally, this postponement allows those who keep God's commandments only out of a surface, hypocritical piety to reveal their true nature.

Just before Christ arrives in the clouds above the earth, the persecution of the faithful will become very intense and violent, and they will be forced to flee in small groups to refuge far away from the city (here again we see the influence of the

38. George Vandeman, *Planet in Rebellion* (Nashville: Southern Publishing Assn., 1960), p. 40.

Babylon image—urban areas are seen as the focus of corruption and depravity):

> When He leaves the sanctuary, darkness covers the inhabitants of the earth. In that fearful time the righteous must live in the sight of a holy God without an intercessor. The restraint which has been upon the wicked is removed, and Satan has entire control of the finally impenitent. God's long-suffering has ended. The world has rejected His mercy, despised His love, and trampled upon His law. The wicked have passed the boundary of their probation; the Spirit of God, persistently resisted, has been at last withdrawn. Unsheltered by divine grace, they have no protection from the wicked one. Satan will then plunge the inhabitants of the earth into one great, final trouble.[39]

They predict that those who follow God's laws, particularly those concerning the Sabbath, will be accused of causing the misfortunes that will occur during this period. Then, just before the faithful are murdered by the civil-religious conspiracy directed by the Devil, unusual and frightening natural phenomena such as tidal waves and earthquakes will prevent the execution of the faithful. People will be paralyzed by these ominous signs of impending disaster. These events will set the stage for what is to follow: the bestowal of the gift of eternal life on the righteous and the execution of the wicked.

Seventh-day Adventists assert that hell, with its supposed indeterminate suffering and consciousness after death, is not consonant with the idea of a just and merciful God. On the other hand, they believe that an ethereal, other-worldly heaven exists, but point out that God's promises to the faithful were tangible —an earthly kingdom in the here and now. Divine rewards and punishments are things that man can experience and observe; they have a direct, material character. Men will be given the opportunity to live forever as they do now and not in some disembodied form in a vague hereafter. They will reside in a community on earth which will be free of conflict and scarcity; their bodies and minds will no longer suffer pain or ignorance. Sinners will be excluded from this paradise; they will be returned to the dust from which they were created.

39. White, *Great Controversy*, pp. 607–8.

Let us return to the sequence of events which constitutes the millennium proper. God intervenes just before the "evil multitude" kills the righteous. A dark mist falls over the earth, and

> then a rainbow, shining with glory from the throne of God, spans the heavens and seems to encircle each praying company. The angry multitudes are suddenly arrested. Their mocking cries die away. The objects of their murderous rage are forgotten. With fearful forebodings they gaze upon the symbol of God's covenant and long to be shielded from its overpowering brightness.[40]

Christ raises the living righteous ones into the clouds and takes them into heaven with him while all the wicked inhabitants of the earth are destroyed by natural phenomena. Except for the Devil, the earth remains desolate and uninhabited for the next thousand years. During this time its infamous occupant can survey the visible results of his futile battle against Christ, and he is invested with the entire burden of the sins previously committed by those who truly repented and changed their behavior (this is the Devil's scapegoat function).

After a thousand years pass, Christ returns to earth with his followers and raises both the righteous and the wicked dead to life. The wicked quickly join forces with the Devil to make one last stand against Christ. They attack Christ and the faithful, who now occupy the New Jerusalem, the site of the new kingdom. As the wicked prepare to storm the city's gate, Christ appears in the air above the city with the faithful grouped around him. Then the major events in Christ's life are flashed in the sky in a "panoramic view"—the final sentence is pronounced upon the wicked, and they are totally destroyed by fire. The planet is physically transformed into a garden paradise and men are suddenly cured of all their infirmities.

Seventh-day Adventists interpret supernatural events, directives and promises in very concrete terms. This tendency to give abstract theological ideas specific visual content and to attach particular mood states to these pictorial images fits their orientation to social reality—they select alternative approaches to secu-

40. Ibid., p. 627.

lar situations in terms of their immediate tangible effects. That is, they approve or disapprove of various courses of action according to the results they can *see*. In passing it is worth noting that the metaphoric content of this mass of minute pictorial detail—Seventh-day Adventist books are full of very detailed monochrome and color pictures—is highly consistent. The contrast between lightness and darkness pervades their treatment of particular issues and occurrences. Evil, wickedness, sickness, corruption, and depravity are modes or attributes of the darkness principle personified by Satan. Purity, harmony, wholesomeness, radiance, beauty, and health are modes or attributes of the lightness principle personified by Christ.

The entire drama of Seventh-day Adventist cosmology and eschatology is largely created by the progressive movement from pristine lightness to deepening shades of darkness, and then, just before all light is extinguished, a single highly condensed ray of light breaks through the darkness to reestablish the complete hegemony of the forces of light over the universe. This imagery, then, encapsulates the dialectic between good and evil in the history of the world.

> The whole earth appears like a desolate wilderness. The ruins of cities and villages destroyed by the earthquake, uprooted trees, ragged rocks thrown out of the sea or torn out by the earth itself, are scattered over its surface, while vast caverns mark the spot where the mountains have been rent from their foundations. . . . And as the scapegoat was sent away into a land not inhabited, so Satan will be banished to the desolate earth, an uninhabited and dreary wilderness. . . . At the coming of Christ the wicked are blotted from the face of the whole earth—consumed with the spirit of His mouth and destroyed by the brightness of His glory.[41]

In summary, Seventh-day Adventist cosmology and eschatology stress the decisive struggle between the forces of good and evil which involve the interests and destiny of all sentient creatures in the universe. The Second Coming of Christ, the subsequent destruction of the Devil and his followers, and the creation of a new Kingdom of God on earth are inevitable consequences of this cosmic confrontation. The retributive as-

41. Ibid., p. 648.

pects of the millennium, the annihilation of those who fail to heed God's warning, are but one act in a larger drama. These supernatural incidents do not mask revolutionary sentiments. Rather, the special character of the Seventh-day Adventist conception of the judgment and punishment of the wicked arises from an entire set of presuppositions about the relationship between ordinary behavior and salvation. Seventh-day Adventist ideology, as a distinct subsystem of Adventist religious belief, emerges at the point where general injunctions to strengthen one's resolve to resist temptations and escape the clutches of the tempter are adjusted to social reality. This supernatural vision of the millennium generates rules which regulate ordinary conduct—an actor's "natural" inclinations are transformed by the specifically religious sanctions attached to different courses of action. From a cosmological perspective, the forces of evil have a single purpose regardless of the many deceptions they set before man. The Devil wants man to renounce his commitment to God's law.

There is a distinct Manichaean cast to Adventist thought. Evil is an independent and active principle and not simply a deficiency or the absence of virtue. This idea plays a critical role in the genesis of Seventh-day Adventist ideology because they assume that salvation is contingent upon a believer's free choice between two alternatives. Those who opt for evil do so not out of ignorance or oversight but out of a desire to follow this mode of existence.

Seventh-day Adventist Ideology

In this section, I hope to show that the drift of Seventh-day Adventist ideology is very much in the direction of a present-day version of the Protestant ethic. Attitudes toward the ethical implications of work are ingrained in the personality of the elect.

Like Calvinists, Seventh-day Adventists assume that the saved are placed upon earth to labor in ways that are pleasing to God regardless of whether men find them onerous. Mrs. White says that "men are instruments in the hand of God, employed by Him to accomplish His purposes of grace and mercy."[42]

42. Ibid., p. 337.

This idea is elaborated more concretely in terms of the meaning of prayer. According to Seventh-day Adventist teachings, prayer strengthens one's resolve to obey God's commandments. Prayer does not inform him of our needs; he knows them already. Since all spiritual and material blessings depend upon conformity to his demands, prayer is seen as the most effective way of increasing the probability that a believer will act in the morally proper manner and receive the rewards promised to the faithful. "Prayer is not to work any change in God, it is to bring us into harmony with God." [43]

Seventh-day Adventists consider prayer the best way to protect oneself from the temptations the Devil constantly sets in the path of the righteous. They think that a person is powerless to resist degrading desires when he relies solely upon his own emotional resources. Prayer, then, supports the struggle against the emotional excesses the Devil tries to incite in the mind of the believer. However—and this is a very important tenet of Seventh-day Adventist theology—the effectiveness of prayer, as of all action, depends upon prior compliance with God's rules for proper behavior, that is, "with the conditions under which it is possible for Him to answer prayer." [44]

Each person, then, must make an *enduring* commitment to a righteous way of life before he can expect God to help him battle the Devil:

> Everything depends on the right action of the will. The power of choice God has given to men; it is theirs to exercise. You cannot change your heart, you cannot of yourself give to God its affections; but you can *choose* to serve Him. You can give Him your will; He will then work in you to will and to do according to His good pleasure. . . . Desires for goodness and holiness are right as far as they go; but if you stop here, they will avail nothing. Many will be lost while hoping and desiring to be Christians. They do not come to the point of yielding the will to God. They do not not *choose* to be Christians.[45]

Seventh-day Adventist ideology asserts that salvation is contingent on a change in one's total personality. Minor alterations in

43. *Sabbath School Quarterly*, no. 271 (1963), p. 25.
44. Ibid., no. 270 (1962), p. 35.
45. Ibid., p. 44.

superficial habits do not shape one's inner life in the right direction:

There are many who have not a correct knowledge of what constitutes a Christian character, and their lives are a reproach to the cause of truth. . . . Many feel well pleased with themselves; they think that a nominal observance of the divine law is sufficient, while they are unacquainted with the grace of Christ. . . . It is not enough to believe the theory of truth. It is not enough to make a profession of faith in Christ and have our names registered on the church roll. . . . Whatever our profession, it amounts to nothing unless Christ is revealed in works of righteousness.[46]

And they mean "character" in the sense of probity in all secular dealings:

The Christian in his business life is to represent to the world the manner in which our Lord would conduct business enterprises. In every transaction he is to make it manifest that God is his teacher. "Holiness unto the Lord" is to be written upon daybooks and ledgers, on deeds, receipts, and bills of exchange. Those who profess to be followers of Christ and who deal in an unrighteous manner are bearing false witness against the character of a holy, just, and merciful God.[47]

Seventh-day Adventist ideology rests upon a premise about the nature of the relationship between human volition and moral responsibility. In their grammar of motives, choice between good and evil is predicated on "free will." The decision to opt for a life of righteousness or wickedness is the unmoved mover of Seventh-day Adventist ideology.

Seventh-day Adventist ideology equates reason with righteousness and impulse with wickedness. It exalts the dominance of reason over impulse, of temperance over indulgence, of self-control over spontaneity. These distinctions are encompassed in an overriding conceptual dichotomy between two primary modalities of an actor's orientation to a social situation: circumspect analysis versus immediate emotional response to social situations.[48] In more practical terms, Seventh-day Adventists hold

46. Ibid., pp. 17–18.
47. Ibid., no. 271 (1963), p. 18.
48. Those familiar with Talcott Parsons's theory of action will recognize this dilemma as one of the pattern variables: affectivity vs. affective neutrality. Affective neutrality is a cardinal principle of Seventh-day Adventist doctrine.

that although every man suffers from continual inner desires to yield to temptation, only the saved can summon the necessary willpower to fend off these pernicious impulses:

This brings us face to face with a very familiar word—*temptation*. Surprising as it may seem, temptation is not sin. Temptation will be with us at all times. For as long as we have body and brain, temptation will attempt to reach us through both. We carry it with us like germs. . . . If we mistakenly believe that temptation is sin, we will blame ourselves for suggestions of evil even while we detest them. This will bring a sense of condemnation and discouragement. And discouragement, if continued in, ends at last in actual sin. We fall often from the very fear of having fallen. The enemy of mankind stands ready to make the best of any situation. . . . You see, the great point is that the enemy can never overcome a man until he has the co-operation of the man himself. There is no sin until by thought, word, or deed we encourage the tempter. Temptations may allure. They may create an atmosphere in which it is mighty hard to breathe. But they cannot contaminate without an act of your will. They cannot triumph over you without your consent. It takes two to make a successful temptation.[49]

The notion that "only man, by casting in the weight of his own personal choice, may decide which way the scale beam moves and what power shall be dominant in his life" is accompanied by a more concrete corollary:[50] Seventh-day Adventists are told not to mistake a vague sense of guilt with the reality of sin. If one equated sin with sinful wishes, he would find it impossible to realistically assess the moral implications of his behavior. For a similar reason, Seventh-day Adventists emphatically deny that a man's conduct is sometimes determined by forces beyond his control. According to their ideology, this means that every man must try to achieve something worthwhile during his stay on this earth, whatever the objective, material limitations on his aspirations:

A very dear friend of mine was so unfortunate as to be reared in an orphanage. He knew nothing about his father or mother. Many thousands of boys and girls have been reared in similar institutions, but in spite of this handicap they have developed healthy bodies, good minds, and strong personalities. They have become worthy citizens and achieved distinction,

49. Vandeman, *Planet in Rebellion*, p. 168.
50. Lickey, *Highways to Truth*, p. 91.

standing out from the crowd in blessing to their fellow men. . . . Whatever our lot, here we are. Even if we don't like our surroundings, there is no honorable way of getting out of this world. What are we going to do about it? . . . At times it may seem that we have come into a hard old world, that we have not had a fair deal, that there is not much use in our trying, that others have all the breaks, and things are against us. In spite of occasional forbidding circumstances, however, there are always encouraging factors if we look for them. . . . Although we cannot change the background or circumstances under which we came into the world, we can decide where we are going and what we shall be and do.[51]

In sum, the saved perceive the right course of action and pursue it regardless of obstacles. This ability to follow a consistent life plan depends upon an individual's ability to master his lower passions. In turn, this resolve to subdue one's desires which corrupt ultimately derives from commitment to the Law.

In the congregation I studied, sermons repeated the theme that good intentions do not count when God looks at a man's life record. One of my informants said that as far as good intentions are concerned "being a Christian is the easiest thing in the world"; but he quickly added that only those who live according to Seventh-day Adventist precepts will be saved. He went on to point out that his father is a "chronic alcoholic" who refuses to give up drink despite urging to follow the path of righteousness. Although he did not relish the idea that his father will soon be destroyed along with the others who refuse to heed God's law, he felt this fate was only just.

These sentiments about each man's moral responsibility for choosing between good and evil and not some supposedly revolutionary animus toward the upper classes give Seventh-day Adventist ideology its harsh overtones:

If you should see an unfortunate specimen of humanity lying in the gutter, would you accuse his mother of giving birth to a derelict of society? Of course not. When that man was a baby, he was as pure and sweet as any other baby. As he grew to manhood, he chose to do evil. He made a derelict out of himself.[52]

51. C. L. Paddock, *Highways to Happiness* (Washington, D.C.: Review and Herald Publishing Assn., 1950), pp. 11–15.
52. Vandeman, *Planet in Rebellion*, p. 36.

Although this idea reinforces their unswerving dedication to probity in all secular transactions, it nevertheless causes them some concern. The image of one's friends and relatives who do not belong to the church burned in the fire of the Last Judgment is not pleasant; consequently, the pastor urges the members of the congregation not to give up trying to convert their relatives. Besides, he adds, certainly one of the greatest pleasures imaginable is meeting your friends and relatives at Jesus' side in Heaven.

Their attitudes toward the problem of self-control are evident in the following talk given in a Sabbath school class. The speaker asked two rhetorical questions: "What do we say about a born-again Christian who has blown his top? What takes place inside that leads to discouragement?" He answered by saying that "the Devil does not care whether you lose control—the Devil is after the emotional strain inside. You go down to the bottom [although the explicit reference here is to emotional depression, this statement has strong connotations of social descent as well] where the Devil wants to keep you." A member of the class interjected that although a person who loses control all the time certainly will not be saved, if he does so once in a while, he may be saved. To this comment the speaker replied:

> Mrs. White said that we are not saved by an individual act but by the tenor of our life—a Christian realizes his sin. The man who feels righteous is the man you better watch, because the mark of a Christian is a person who knows he is a sinner. Temptations come from the Devil; you are led away by your own lust [i.e., any unholy desire]. The Devil cannot force you to sin but he can give you the thought. If you dwell on the idea, then you are more susceptible to temptation. Temptations are good for us in the sense that they work on our patience. There is joy in being victorious over temptation; every temptation is a contest with the Devil: overcoming temptations are the only real joys in life. God made a promise to the entire universe that sin will not rise up a second time—God has to have *dependable* people to take into heaven and every temptation must be rooted out. Our life must be completely filled with Christ. God permits just the right degree of temptation that each one of us can bear.

Like many evangelical, fundamentalist churches, Seventh-day Adventists proscribe dancing, drinking, smoking, going to most commercial movies, wearing makeup and jewelry and other "frivolities." They believe that anyone who engages in these and similar illicit activities is beyond redemption *whatever* his degree of involvement in them. His only chance for salvation lies in the immediate elimination of these forbidden pleasures from his life.

For instance, a former smoker or drinker must demonstrate that he has given up these intemperate ways before he can present himself as a candidate for baptism. "Backsliding" is almost tantamount to damnation. Seventh-day Adventists willingly accept a "fallen" member back into the fold if he has proved that he has abandoned his worldly vices. But he has taken enormous risks with his eternal fate; there are very few second chances in this lifetime.

Seventh-day Adventists are also enjoined to exercise "carefulness in deportment, and modesty and simplicity in dress." The significance of their attitudes toward what are usually treated as minor vices by the larger society is evident in the following quote from Mrs. White:

> The apostle James declares that the wisdom from above is "first pure." Had he encountered those who take the precious name of Jesus upon lips defiled by tobacco, those whose breath and person are contaminated by its foul odor, and who pollute the air of Heaven and force all about them to inhale the poison—had the apostle come into contact with a practice so opposed to the purity of the gospel, would he not have denounced it as "earthly, sensual, devilish?"[53]

Thus far I have tried to show that Seventh-day Adventist ideology outlines a general moral posture toward secular affairs and, at the same time, presses its adherents to avoid certain kinds of secular attitudes and activities. But this ideology has a positive as well as a negative thrust. It tries to instill comprehensive orientations toward practical matters in its adherents. In other words, it holds that a person who is saved not only lacks certain vices but also displays certain virtues.

This ideology provides its adherents with a set of guidelines for decisions in ordinary life. Advice on the proper approach to

53. White, *Great Controversy*, p. 496.

practical matters is not presented as an optional feature of Seventh-day Adventist ideology. This program for self-improvement has crucial spiritual consequences, and thus social and economic advancement becomes morally binding. A person must try to "better" himself or he reveals, in Seventh-day Adventist opinion, a character which refuses to heed God's dictates on the kind of life which is proper for Christians.

Seventh-day Adventist ideology asserts that an individual's spiritual worthiness is not simply the result of his overt adherence to the standards of proper behavior. This ideology fosters a state of mind which rejects certain courses of action automatically; the believer knows they are wrong because they are suggested by the wrong motives. Deviations from this ethical code which exist solely in the feelings of the believer are censored, because the Seventh-day Adventist thinks that God constantly scrutinizes his thoughts:

> Secret sins of the heart, such as pride, envy, hatred and covetousness, which may escape the view of man, are seen by God and are especially hateful in His eyes. The Scriptures are scheduled to reveal, as an X-ray, this inner trouble. . . . The Bible will reveal the crooked and misshapen bones of doctrine, and bring to view the selfish and evil thought. Thus does the Word of God become a reprover of sin, whether that sin be in a believer or unbeliever. It is no respecter of persons. Anyone who searches the Scriptures with honesty of heart will find that he will be reproved. Evil unreproved is dangerous. Correction follows reproof. Mere reproof would be of little value if no change for the better could be effected. The Scriptures not only set up great beliefs, they not only reprove us individually for individual sins, but tend to correct the evil pointed out, to effect an amendment of life and to keep us on the right path.[54]

Seventh-day Adventists occasionally remark that these modes of determining which behavioral alternatives are right also promote their economic welfare. As far as they are concerned, the purpose of their social teachings is to develop a moral character responsive to internal signals of an impending departure from either the spirit or the letter of the Law. Therefore, although the effects of their ideology upon their material well-being are not entirely latent, most of my informants pointed to them as an

54. Lickey, *Highways to Truth*, p. 68.

afterthought. Certainly, from their vantage point, the basic aim of a righteous life is not to produce great successes in the business world; but my informants often added that they are never surprised when it does. Many of the members of this congregation testified that a religious life always has some beneficial, practical consequences.

Seventh-day Adventist ideology talks about the dangers of subjective interpretations of God's directive to man; a person who transgresses one aspect of the Law reveals his contempt for the whole:

> Every commandment to God is, of course, a test whether it be a command to do a certain thing, or not to do it. And since God's law is a law of love, the willful violation of any one command of God violates our love and loyalty to the God who gave the whole law.[55]

When a person embraces a righteous mode of life, his actions fit into an overall life plan approved by the central values of Seventh-day Adventist ideology—continuous striving to achieve something in the "serious" pursuits of this life; that is, in business and religion. Anyone who strays from this path is likely to fall into dangerous straits:

> My course of action was not paying off. I knew deep in my soul, as does any man who has tried it, that "the way of the transgressor is hard." I do not mean that there is no pleasure in sin. There is. But it satisfies only an impulse. It does not satisfy life. And the price is too big to pay. . . . I set out at once to reconstruct my life, thinking this to be my duty. And I did it with the meticulous care of a civil engineer. Vigorously I attempted to set my house in order. . . . No wonder I had made so little progress in overcoming evil habits. How could it be otherwise, so long as my fundamental nature was unchanged? I had attempted to cover conflict and defeat by outward discipline. I had been content to keep my unholy traits of character, while I grasped frantically for grace and poise and personality to cover them up. . . . It is one thing for an employer to be courteous to a bungling workman, a blundering customer, when influence and reputation are at stake—though all the while hate burns in his heart. But it is quite another thing to have a power inside that will take away the hate and the burning! . . . Thank God that the Christian life is not simply a modification or improvement of the old! Instead, it is a transformation of a man's nature that brings every promise of God within

55. Ibid.

> his reach. . . . For without the transforming process that comes alone through divine power, the original tendencies to sin are left in the heart in all their strength, there to forge new chains and impose a new slavery that the power of man can never break.[56]

Seventh-day Adventist ideology does not attempt to construct a complete map of the correct approaches to all situational contingencies. Rather, at all levels of abstraction, discussions of what a person should do in a given situation are meant to create a certain kind of personality. In other words, it attempts to engender a stable and enduring set of character traits which the actors define as moral dispositions essential for salvation.

In essence, Seventh-day Adventist ideology attempts to create the religious equivalent of the character type which David Riesman called "inner-directed." That is, a person who will not renounce his allegiance to certain invariant standards of accomplishment and propriety despite the opinions of others and who will not pursue short-term advantages which run counter to his long-term ideals and goals. My informants often talked about this crucial aspect of the morally sound personality in terms of the idiom of "sincerity." One informant told me that we must be earnest in both our actions and our thoughts or our prayers mean nothing. On other occasions, the members of the congregation urged that if a person does not get what he wants he should examine his motives, and then if he finds that he has not violated God's law, he should not passively accept the disappointment but should rededicate himself to the task at hand. The pastor expressed a similar idea when he said "that you have to choose what God wants *before* he comes into your life. We die daily to our mistakes; we must never feel that we can't be perfect on this earth and we must do this through Christ."

It may seem that this ideology creates the kind of person who rigidly conforms to inflexible moral rules and who fails to act unless clear guidelines are set out in advance. However, Seventh-day Adventists consider the most efficient approaches to practical problems as long as the solution does not contradict their image of the righteous life. One can discern this pragmatic but not mercenary attitude toward economic affairs in their

56. Vandeman, *Planet in Rebellion*, p. 156.

discussions of professional careers. To a certain extent, their desire for upward mobility for either their children or themselves accounts for their high evaluation of professional occupations. But they also value the freedom from external control that professionals have in dealing with the problems they confront, and they admire the knowledge and skill associated with a professional status. Judging from informal talks with sect members, the popular folk hero for this group is the missionary doctor who shows great inventiveness and resourcefulness in overcoming the physical and material limitations of healing people in remote corners of the world. In numerous contexts, Seventh-day Adventists remarked how wonderful it must be to be one's own boss and hence responsible for one's own successes and failures. They value the occupational role in terms of its *intrinsic* rewards and view its financial benefits as important but as *morally* incidental aspects of its desirability.

Perhaps the basic Seventh-day Adventist moral dictum is that a person should persevere in the face of obstacles and, concomitantly, should clearly define his goals long before he attacks specific problems. According to one author, the key to success is ambition; an early decision about one's career and the ability to set all secondary diversions aside leads a person upward in this world. He tells a story about a twelve-year-old shoeshine boy who told him that he wanted to be a doctor and had already saved eight-hundred dollars for his medical education. The author comments:

> Here was a boy of twelve who knew where he was going. He had a goal in mind and, young as he was, he was working to that end. Who wouldn't like to help a boy like that along the way to his goal! Statisticians tell us that 10 per cent of the people have some definite aim in mind, and are working to that end; and the other 90 per cent are just drifting, they know not where. This is sad to contemplate. In the 10 per cent class are the leaders of men, the salt of the earth, the Daniels, Esthers, Lincolns, Moodys, Edisons, Fanny Crosbys, Pasteurs, and others. When but a youth Daniel, who later became one of the greatest prophets of the Bible, was carried away from his home and country into the court of old Babylon. Though he was surrounded by the luxury and temptations of a heathen nation, the Bible recorded of him "Daniel purposed in his heart that he would not define himself with the portion of the King's meat," or with the drinking

and other customs of the court. He had a goal in mind and he was determined to be true.[57]

The author related another success story, this time emphasizing the necessity of being able to visualize the end result of a long chain of intermediate actions and personal sacrifices:

There was a considerable elapse of time between the boy's resolution to fly around the world and the fulfilling of his dreams and ambitions. We can only imagine some of the sacrifices he made, the hours and weeks and months of study and practice it cost him, before he felt capable of starting on a round-the-world flight. He had ambitions, he dreamed dreams, and he made those dreams come true. He had a goal, and he reached it. He knew where he was going, and let nothing turn him aside.[58]

Seventh-day Adventists never seem to tire of Horatio Alger sagas:

Whenever I go through Flagstaff, Arizona, I always recall the story of a little boy who lived there. One day a teacher in the Flagstaff school was walking up and down the aisles of her schoolroom checking on the work of her pupils. She noticed one little fellow writing on the flyleaf of his book, and she quietly stood and read over his shoulder, "Henry F. Ashurst, Senator from Arizona." He was in grade school and not very old, but he had decided that someday he would represent his State in the Senate. He traveled a long hard road to reach his goal. He was a clerk in a store, a lumberjack, a lawyer, and finally a Senator. While just a boy he decided where he was going, and he finally got there.[59]

And:

Chalmers was employed as a janitor in a large Ohio factory. He had an aim, however, which did not savor of janitorship as a lifework. He studied shorthand in night school, and some time later, when the firm needed a stenographer, the young man applied for the position. "What do you know about shorthand?" the manager asked. "Haven't you been janitor here?" "Yes," answered young Chalmers, "but I have been studying shorthand at night school, and I believe I can do the work." He made good as a stenographer, but he went on studying. He wanted to be a salesman, and studied salesmanship after working hours in the office. One noon when he

57. Paddock, *Highways to Happiness*, pp. 20–21.
58. Ibid., p. 23.
59. Ibid., pp. 23–24.

was alone a customer called, and young Chalmers sold him a cash register, much to the surprise of his superiors. They put him on the road as a salesman, and at twenty-three he became sales manager. At twenty-eight he became general manager of the firm, at a salary of fifty thousand dollars a year. Purpose did it.[60]

The author concludes:

If you want to reach a place of achievement, you will first of all have to decide upon a goal. . . . Someday we must give an account of our stewardship; we must stand before the Judge of the earth. How many of us are making preparation for this journey, this accounting, this judgment? We would not work for a firm all year, and go to another establishment at the end of the twelve-month period to ask for our pay, would we? But many of us say by our actions that we feel sure we can serve the Devil all our lives and then offer God the last few minutes of our conscious existence, and all will be well. . . . Aren't we foolish to think we can lie and steal and swear and drink and live for ourselves alone, disregarding all the commandments of the Bible, ignoring the perfect pattern left us by the Master, until we face death, and then expect to reap the reward of right-doing? [61]

Achievement, then, requires dedication to specific career goals, and therefore success rests upon a much more substantial motivational base than a diffuse desire to improve oneself. Yet even though a person may know exactly what he wants and may work unceasingly to reach this end, he may find that his progress has been minimal or that his efforts have been of no avail. Seventh-day Adventism makes a special point of eliminating "defeatism" and "pessimism" from its adherents' attitudes toward advancement in the secular world despite the difficulties they may encounter:

The ability to stay through, to persevere, to go on in the face of discouragement, may make the difference between success and failure. How often the difference between success and failure is just a matter of time! . . . Maybe you have spent long years in preparation for your lifework and have found no opening, no place to use your talents. Perhaps you have set a goal for yourself and have been struggling and working to reach it, yet find yourself a long, long way from the destination of your

60. Ibid., p. 24.
61. Ibid., p. 23.

dreams. Maybe your plans have been upset time and time again. Maybe relatives or friends have told you that you might as well give up. Perchance you have been overcome by temptations and have stumbled and fallen. . . . Do not let some physical handicap hold you back, or discourage you from trying. Not many men who gained eminence were born with the proverbial "silver spoon" in their mouths. . . . Poverty is no handicap. It has so often proved a real blessing. . . . No matter where you live somewhere near you will be some crapehanger, some pessimist, some kill-joy, to discourage you, to tell you that you can never reach the goal you have set for yourself. . . . When satanic suggestion whispers to you, "Surrender," God sends along a message of hope: "Don't give up; I'm coming." So hold on, fight on. Heaven will send help just when we need it.[62]

According to Seventh-day Adventist ideology, giving in to despair is one of the first observable steps to damnation. Despair encourages the believer to relax his grip in the continuous inner struggle against divisive emotions, weakens his willpower, and thereby eventually leads him to indulge in worldly pleasure.

The dire predictions about the destruction of "earthly kingdoms" of Seventh-day Adventist theology has led many students of these movements to conclude that they are predicated upon withdrawal from the ordinary concerns of everyday life. Why struggle to achieve something in this world when God will soon destroy it and institute one in which the righteous will get their just rewards? For instance, Clark insists that Adventists are antagonistic to the present social order:

Adventism is the typical cult of the disinherited and suffering poor. Its peculiar world views reflects the psychology of a distressed class in despair of obtaining the benefits it seeks through the present social order and seeking escape through divine intervention and a cosmic cataclysm, which will destroy the world and the "worldly" classes and elevate "the saints" to the position they could not attain through social processes.[63]

He stresses their passivity about economic striving: "They are profoundly pessimistic. . . . The doctrine inevitably operates to prevent efforts for social betterment on the part of those whose dearest dreams are set on the second advent." [64]

62. Ibid., pp. 80–87.
63. Elmer T. Clark, *The Small Sects in America* (New York: Abingdon Press, 1949), p. 25.
64. Ibid., p. 26.

On the other hand, I have tried to show that Seventh-day Adventists feel that life is worth living actively and purposively. They feel that a person's activities should emerge out of a complete design for living, and consequently that long-range goals should organize various momentary interests into a coherent life plan. This, in turn, is related to their dominant emphasis on the economic basis of one's future happiness, and they attach great significance to systematic saving. Their discussions about the proper use of time are permeated with achievement imagery, and in place of immediate gratification they stress remote, abstract goals:

> People who are highly motivated for achievement think more often in anticipatory and generalized terms. They are concerned with general and vague life-goals. They want to relate the "now" to the "then," to see the connection between what they are studying and what they want to do later.[65]

The final part of this section looks briefly at some of the advice contained in stories and columns of the *Youth's Instructor*, a Seventh-day Adventist magazine published largely for internal consumption. These articles are concerned with the character traits Seventh-day Adventists would like to develop in their children and, hence, they reveal their conceptions of those practical virtues intimately associated with moral excellence.

One theme which occurs frequently is the fallacy of the short-cut; that is, a job worth doing is worth doing right. For instance, a story about the failure to inspect an airplane cylinder carefully, which cost thirty lives in a subsequent crash, tells the reader: "As your own inspector, scrutinize yourself for the following defects, particularly if you are a college or academy [the private secondary schools run by Seventh-day Adventists] student."[66] This article admonishes the reader not to accept convenient subterfuges for disguising cheating on examinations, and it tells the student to develop the proper respect for school property. Finally, the author asserts that the decision not to take

65. David McClelland, quoted in Josephine Klein, *Samples from English Cultures* (London: Routledge and Kegan Paul, 1965), p. 511.
66. *Youth's Instructor*, 26 March 1963, p. 3.

an active role in school activities is tantamount to "becoming the school's leading fifth columnist, the school-spirit saboteur supreme." The article ends on the note that even the seemingly most minor fault is the first sign of general character deterioration: "It goes without saying that the stress brought about by character faults will eventually cause the human cylinder to crack under the strain. The result? An influence that may well cause the loss of eternal life to many an innocent person." [67]

In general, the *Youth's Instructor* tells its readers to create their own opportunities rather than waiting for fortune to smile upon them. The writer of one article strongly approves of the slogan "Don't think. Work!" because "it would help keep us from lying, so to speak, on our faces, waiting for better opportunity instead of getting up and facing the day with courage and a willingness to operate vigorously." [68] He then returns to the central theme of Seventh-day Adventist ideology. All lasting improvements in one's outward character and habits depend upon a radical transformation of one's underlying ethical personality:

> We step before God to congratulate ourselves instead of to ask whether a cleansing work ought to be done. Our personality, our habits, our character, need to be overhauled. This takes work, more than it does self-satisfied withdrawal . . . wrong attitudes, wrong emotions, wrong actions—they must be eradicated from our lives; otherwise they will cause nothing but trouble. We cannot play on both sides of the fence and still expect the blessing of God. We must look beyond our failures to the causes for these failures. Then we must go to work. . . . None of us ever will have genuine success in life until he does the same—that is, brings the hidden wrongs out of his unconscious and lays them honestly before God.[69]

To illustrate his point, the author tells how he recently paid back to his sister *with interest* a dime he had stolen from her many years before. He gives similar examples of rectitude in seemingly the most trivial matters.

Seventh-day Adventist advice columns perceive the conjugal pair as the unit responsible for success or failure in the economic

67. Ibid., p. 4.
68. Ibid., 2 April 1963, p. 3.
69. Ibid., pp. 4–15.

world. One author asks prospective spouses a number of questions which reveal a markedly pragmatic rather than romantic attitude toward marriage. This writer declares that marriages should be timed correctly; they should not interrupt a person's education. He suggests that potential partners should carefully estimate their collective financial liabilities and assets before entering into a binding contract. Before a woman marries, she should distinguish probable resources the family will immediately control from dreams of future advancement:

> I tried to help the young woman to see that she was taking too great a risk in planning to marry a man whose assets were promises for the future. Were he the responsible type, he would have had savings or equity in property or an established vocational skill to offer as evidence of his realization that marriage carries both privileges and obligations![70]

These writers also emphasize the importance of a stable moral character reflected in *consistently* proper behavior:

> True, the Christian code requires a willingness to forgive. But the genuineness of repentance cannot be safely judged on the basis of a mere promise to turn over a new leaf. Only as part of the miracle of conversion does it become possible for a person to turn his old habits of conduct and have a better life in the future. The proof of conversion is not by words spoken, but by a demonstration over many months of a new way of life.[71]

In these magazines there are many stories about ambitious Seventh-day Adventist youths who work their way through school selling religious literature—the role of a colporteur allows one to make a profit from what is essentially an evangelical activity. One student who worked as a religious book salesman in a rural area needed his car to return to college, but at the end of the summer's work he sold the car to pay the previous year's tuition. After a number of trading transactions—such as books for old cars—he still found that he did not have enough money to get home but *refused to borrow it* because "Sister White says we should shun debt as we should leprosy."[72] Of course, he

70. Ibid., 9 April 1963, p. 10.
71. Ibid.
72. Ibid., 5 March 1963, p. 8.

finally triumphs over adversity, as do all the heroes and heroines in these moral epics. These youths are rewarded because they do not waste their time in "harmless pursuits" and recognize that "there is no tomorrow designated for what we believe, for understanding that time is our greatest personal responsibility, and that how we invest it today will determine whether we stand or fall when all that can be shaken will be shaken." [73] And these youths do not undermine their "Christian stewardship by spending more than necessary for any item, regardless of your affluence." [74]

It is possible to multiply such stories, but the moral lesson is always the same. Aspirations to move up in the social class system are not only legitimate but desirable: "not all social class distinctions are morally and ethically bad, for there are as a matter of fact, distinctions made necessary by the developing civilization and technology in which the world finds itself." [75] Rationality should govern a person's relationships and activities in all spheres of life:

> In speaking of this rule of temperance, we are not referring merely to the need for abstaining from the use of intoxicating drinks. We are using the word "temperance" in its broad sense to refer to a rational plan of living by which a person takes his work and his play in stride without abusing his physical powers and without burning the candle of life's resources at both ends.[76]

Good business practices are fundamental signs of a good moral character: "A true Christian in all business dealings must be at least as prudent as a nonbeliever" and must know "something about the business in which he invests, its prospects and the general economic climate of the time." [77] Sermons and these stories warn those young people who might squander their inheritance on a "good time" that they waste not only their money but also their chance for salvation.

In general, my informants were very concerned about the

73. Ibid., 4 June 1963, p. 5.
74. Ibid., 9 April 1963, p. 5.
75. Ibid., 16 July 1963, p. 18.
76. Ibid., 30 July 1963, p. 20.
77. Ibid., 13 August 1963, p. 23.

attitudes and practices which will increase a person's chances for success in the marketplace. They often tell their children that employees should not "cheat" their boss; for example, a person should not extend a fifteen-minute coffee break just because the boss is not looking. The leader of the young people's Sabbath school class pressed the theme that success in the business world is based upon a person's reliability and conscientiousness. One should work very hard regardless of what the rest of the office regards as a normal day's work.

Some Seventh-day Adventist writers are even more specific. For example, cheerfulness "is a habit trait that should be cultivated for the sake of clear thinking and pleasant social and business relationships" and "courtesy pays in satisfaction to all concerned. I believe it pays in dollars and cents too." [78] Even the minor aspects of etiquette are often very important, because

> sometimes a seemingly trivial habit may hinder a person's progress. I know a man who siphons his food into his mouth. It is an acquired table manner; and although it may seem a small thing, such a disgusting habit may keep a man down all his life, hindering his progress and raising a barrier between him and success.[79]

In concluding this section, I will examine the basic social implications of Seventh-day Adventist ideology. Of course, any attempt to specify the meaning of religious symbols involves a certain amount of inference on the observer's part, particularly when the interpretation is based upon semantic and contextual analysis. However, the anthropologist has an advantage over the humanist scholar, who is confined largely to written texts. I found that informal discussions with my informants, often about topics apparently unrelated to the significance of belief, gave me the best clues as to which portions of this religious system were incorporated into the believer's action system. In the next chapter I hope to show that data on the socioeconomic aspirations of some of my informants makes this interpretation plausible.

In the first place, the expressive symbolism of Seventh-day Adventist ideology is characterized by a dominant fear and a

78. Paddock, *Highways to Happiness*, p. 146.
79. Ibid., p. 147.

dominant hope. The fear of falling in the status system accounts for the supernaturally sanctioned injunction to stay out of "trouble"—to avoid drinking, adultery, and the other patterns of what they perceive as a "lower" mode of life which inevitably drags a person down into the gutter. The hope of rising in the status system supports their moral code, which enjoins mobilizing one's social and economic resources for the express purpose of occupational advancement—thus the emphasis on hard work, saving, careful expenditure. Both this hope and this fear are adaptive means of improving one's opportunities for upward mobility, but the dominant success image which underlies this ideology may be somewhat out of date. These people see the independent entrepreneur and the self-employed professional or businessman rather than the corporate executive or technician as the model for success in this world. They value self-reliance and hard work rather than a specialized education and organizational savoir faire. In this context, the ambivalent attitude of most of my informants toward labor unions is explicable. Unions provide a financial platform (comparatively high wages, job security) for social advancement but do not allow for the individualistic distinction on the job which Seventh-day Adventists feel will ultimately raise a person above the ordinary worker.

This ideology also has significance in a slightly different dimension—the contrast between those who are socially "upright" and those who fall below the standards of morally acceptable behavior. This corresponds to what my informants perceived as the crucial difference between the middle and lower classes. They constantly refer to profanity, loud talk, a lack of manners, and disinterest in the "finer" things of life as characteristic of those "classes" of people who also fornicate, drink, smoke, and so forth. In essence, they associate righteousness with socially acceptable (middle-class) life styles and wickedness with sensual (lower-class) life styles. In this context, they use the term "lower" class in the morally pejorative sense of people whose behavior excludes them from "proper" society; that is, they separate the "respectable" from the "degraded" elements of the community. Finally, I would like to point out that this ideology conceives of the human career as a series of discrete steps in a progressive movement toward sacred and secular success. It holds that those who remain faithful to a strict ethical code will inevitably reach the highest status accorded to man—membership in the Kingdom of God. It further implies that those who refuse to prepare themselves for this difficult climb upward toward the ideal of moral purity or who squander their ethical gains in escapades of self-indulgence will not find real satisfaction in this world or in the one shortly to come. In brief, each man must make a fateful decision early in his life and then never deviate from the straight and narrow path if he expects to be rewarded by God. Seventh-day Adventists perceive the human career in unilinear terms. One moves progressively toward either salvation or damnation; it is extremely difficult to change from the latter track to the former and is extremely easy to fall from the former track into the latter.

5 Pentecostal Belief

Pentecostal and Holiness Belief

Pentecostalism is the perfect foil for Seventh-day Adventism; the imagery of the two religious systems differs markedly. The dominant metaphors of Seventh-day Adventist theological argument are dark and foreboding. Seventh-day Adventists not only announce the dreadful fate of this world but are also very pessimistic about the slim chance a person has of escaping from the dismal destiny of most men. On the other hand, the surface metaphors of Pentecostalism stress joy and optimism. The way to great personal spiritual rewards is open to anyone who is willing to love Jesus unreservedly. Those who fall from grace can return to his favor if they admit their sin and have faith in his ability to carry them through life's difficulties.

In the previous section, I tried to show that the eschatological doctrines of Seventh-day Adventism obscured the fundamental optimism of their ideology; they not only hope but expect to improve their position in this world. In this section, we will see that the optimistic theology of Pentecostalism masks the fundamental pessimism of Pentecostal ideology. Pentecostals may hope but do not expect to advance in worldly status systems.

All evangelical, fundamentalist churches are interested in justification and sanctification. The former is concerned with the repentance that secures the remission of sins and the latter is concerned with internal changes in the believer that purify his soul. Seventh-day Adventist theology is much less interested in the confessional nature of justification than in the manifestations of sanctification in social behavior. Once a Seventh-day Adventist has admitted his guilt, he refuses to dwell on this theme. In contrast, Pentecostals are absorbed by the intricacies of justification. In their theology, the core of religious experience and hence of salvation inheres in the process of seeking divine forgiveness of one's sins. Sanctification is a product of sincere repentance and love for Jesus.

Pentecostal doctrine focuses upon the way an individual gains access to the supreme religious experience available to man: salvation through "baptism of the Holy Spirit." The Holy Ghost is thought to actually enter into the mind and body of the believer and not only to remove the taint of sin but also to endow the believer for these moments with spiritual powers not otherwise accessible to mankind. Pentecostal theology, then, largely concentrates on the nature and benefits of this distinctive emotional-spiritual experience.

In contrast to the dispassionate, intellectual tone of Seventh-day Adventist sermons, Pentecostal sermons have a dramatic, passionate character. Pentecostal sermons attempt to "spontaneously" arouse feelings in the believer conducive to the "in-filling" of the Holy Ghost. The sermons rely upon an elementary rhetorical device; the speaker continually repeats the same themes in slightly varied contexts. The "outpouring of the Spirit" is inherently unpredictable and is said to often strike its beneficiaries in unexpected ways. Thus, the excitement builds until it reaches an intense climax when "the gifts of the Spirit" are in evidence. This is the overriding aim of all ritual activity. "The avowed object of all services is the experiencing of the power of God by members. A successful service is one at which the Spirit is present and manifest." [1]

I shall argue that Pentecostalism, unlike Seventh-day Adventism, strives to create a pervasive sense of spiritual security in its adherents. Whatever the source of his suffering, Pentecostal belief holds that a person will strengthen his sense of personal worth and dignity through union with the Holy Ghost. Pentecostalism urges the believer to turn his back on his secular problems and to make himself completely dependent upon God.

At this point, I shall examine some of the implications of the idea that salvation depends upon one's ability to release himself from all his ordinary cares and to depend totally upon Jesus. This means that one should recognize that he is an unregenerate sinner and that his unaided efforts to expiate his sin are worthless. Only through Christ can he overcome his guilt for Christ's death. Therefore redemption depends upon his capacity to express his love for Jesus in unqualified terms—to let Jesus "move" him and influence his life in any way that He so chooses. According to this theology, the believer not only should be uninterested in worldly affairs but also should not be overly concerned with specifying the ethical implications of religious belief in great detail. Unlike Holiness groups, Pentecostals do not spend a great deal of energy elaborating codes for proper behavior. On the other hand, they are absolutely convinced that the "in-filling" of the Holy Ghost cannot fail eventually to fill their lives with holiness. Intimate contact with Jesus purifies. Otherwise, Pentecostals argue, how can one account for the special spiritual "gifts" which are given only to them?

These groups are not antinomian. They recognize that sin implies violations of the Law but choose to deal with the generic rather than the specific aspects of sin. In other words, the Pentecostal typically links his individual contravention of the Law to the suffering which unites all sinners as suppliants before Christ. Holiness movements are concerned with the "spiritual taint" of sin and with internal spiritual purification. Like Pente-

1. Malcom Calley, *God's People: West Indian Pentecostal Sects in England* (London: Oxford University Press, 1965), p. 85.

costals, they perceive excessive guilt as the principal impediment to salvation; that is, it prevents them from experiencing the full cleansing effect of God's mercy. However, Holiness groups place a much greater importance upon outward behavior as a valid sign of inner holiness than do Pentecostals. They are more concerned with "proper" behavior than Pentecostal groups, who place the "baptism of the Holy Ghost" before all other considerations. Pentecostals, according to their theology, would follow the dictates of the Spirit regardless of its effect upon the external conduct, whereas Holiness groups try to contain the influence of the Spirit to clearly defined and circumscribed ritual contexts. From the Pentecostal perspective, critical indicators of spiritual transformation are primarily emotional rather than moral. For Pentecostals, God intervenes in the believer's life in unpredictable ways and at unpredictable times. Hence, my informants argued that there is no single pattern of ordinary behavior which is an unmistakable sign of salvation.

Although the sermons in the Pentecostal groups I observed continually pressed the listener to work toward spiritual purity and perfection, my informants readily admitted that those who attain it can lose it, and then regain it again, almost ad infinitum. This is not true for Holiness groups, where repeated lapses into "worldliness" lead to disfellowship.[2] In fact, almost every one of my informants and many Pentecostals I knew more casually mentioned that they had had at least one serious episode of "falling away from" the church. Their return to the group was seen as a great victory for both the individual and the church, and the return was always a very poignant moment. In one Pentecostal group, everyone both laughed and cried when someone came back from the "world." There were a few persons who continually joined and left the group, and the members never lost hope that the next time they returned, their conversions would be lasting ones.

It is difficult to neatly circumscribe the belief systems of evangelical sects that accept inner spiritual illumination as the fundament of their faith. Although the cognitive boundaries

2. See Val Clear, "The Church of God: A Study in Social Adaptation" (Ph.D. diss.: University of Chicago, 1953).

between such groups are not necessarily imprecise, there is always a certain amount of reciprocal influence between churches that ground their worship in the believer's emotional receptivity to Jesus. In these religious circles, it is commonly recognized that the vagaries of an individual's spiritual development may make him responsive to different forms of worship at various stages of his religious career. Persons attracted to these sects are not converted to particular theological doctrines as much as they are satisfied by beliefs consistent with their personal experience. These groups do not impose complex intellectual schemata upon religious activity. Instead they elicit and ratify those aspects of the believer's experience consonant with beliefs laden with distinctively Christian expressive symbolism. For instance, the emotional significance of conversion is often conveyed in terms of the concrete symbol of love, suffering and sacrifice, the blood of Jesus. It is constantly invoked to remind the believer of his complicity in the crucifixion and of the magnitude of Christ's compassion for mankind. It fuses the powerful feelings of guilt and gratitude into the fundamental Christian motive, love for one's brethern through love for Christ. Unlike groups with tightly constructed systems of thought, such as Seventh-day Adventism, these sects do not strive to encapsulate the believer in a complete theological structure and thereby specify the correct interpretation of his spiritual situation in minute detail. For the members of these sects, a person's ability to grasp the implications of metaphysical notions is considerably less important than the personal meaning he derives from his conversion to Christ.

Although the cognitive boundaries between Holiness and Pentecostal groups are not rigid, there are substantial theological differences between them. These differences inhere in ideological proclivities that do not always correspond to organizational boundaries. By this I mean that one can find churches formally identified with the Pentecostal movement that adhere to a Holiness ideology. To the extent that the members of a Pentecostal group value ritual decorum over spiritual virtuosity they will move in the direction of Holiness worship. This tendency is often quite visible in the services of Pentecostal churches that adopt a denominational outlook. Here the service is sedate. Ecstatic religious experience such as "speaking in tongues" is relegated to special occasions when only those who specifically demand it are present. It is no longer the central focus of common worship. Holiness churches, then, place much greater emphasis on the outward appearances of their services. And the greater formality of worship introduces a note of ritualism inimical to the Pentecostal creed of complete freedom to move "in the Spirit."

Until recently, sociologists have tended to lump Holiness and Pentecostal groups into the same theological category, which has created a good deal of confusion about the functions these groups perform for their members. In an influential paper, Benton Johnson argues persuasively that Holiness groups socialize lower middle class persons into a way of life congruent with the values of the dominant social strata. He observes that these groups are quick to punish departures from rather stringent rules of personal conduct: "First, whereas an individual believer is only required to experience the initial stage of grace, that is, of conversion itself, *all* members are required to abide by the set of rules that calls forth strong negative sanctions on the part of the congregation." [3] Holiness worship helps its adherents assimilate life styles consistent with the norms of "polite" society by leveling supernatural sanctions against violations of these codes. This makes the dedicated Holiness person an unlikely candidate for participation in Pentecostal activities. It is hard indeed to define oneself as a religious enthusiast who is searching for very unconventional spiritual powers and, at the same time, to adopt the muted social demeanor of the middle classes.

Despite the fact that Holiness and Pentecostal groups spring from a common religious milieu, the Wesleyan tradition, Warburton shows that their theologies lead the believer in very different directions.[4] The Holiness church remains well within the pale of Protestant orthodoxy, whereas the Pentecostal

3. Benton Johnson, "Do Holiness Sects Socialize in Dominant Values?" *Social Forces* 39 (1961):314.
4. T. R. Warburton, "Holiness Religion: An Anomaly of Sectarian Typologies," *Journal for the Scientific Study of Religion* 8 (1969).

church contravenes the injunction against the laity's experimenting with what is essentially a magical as well as a mystical phenomenon. The central tenet of Holiness worship concerns the second blessing—sanctification. This experience is purely subjective and inward; it has no public manifestations. Whether it is acquired suddenly or gradually, sanctification merely refers to an increase in the believer's spiritual purity. It does not bestow any special powers upon him or elevate him above other sincere Christians. Pentecostals claim to have discovered a third blessing, Spirit baptism, which not only strikes Protestant orthodoxy as theologically suspect but leads to forms of overt religious behavior that are undecorous to say the least. As Warburton observes, Pentecostals stand far to the "left" of Holiness groups in the Protestant community. Their worship separates them decisively from an orthodoxy that will not recognize the laity's control over charismata not in evidence elsewhere in the church.

Pentecostal Theology

In a general way, Pentecostal churches in this country can trace their origins to the Great Awakening in 1734, which roughly paralleled the Wesleyan movement in England. The most concrete historical tie between the contemporary multitude of independent Pentecostal groups and earlier religious developments is the Kentucky Revival of 1799.[5] This period of intense revivalism set the tone for future demonstrations of religious enthusiasm in this country.[6]

The Pentecostal groups I studied had no ties to any larger religious organization. This is a distinctive characteristic of religious groups which try to induce spiritual possession at every

5. For a historical description of American revivalism see Bernard Weisberger, *They Gathered at the River* (New York: Little, Brown and Co., 1958).

6. M. T. Kelsey (*Tongue Speaking: An Experiment in Spiritual Experience* [Garden City, N.Y.: Doubleday, 1964]) traces the origins of the Pentecostal movement in this country to the Azusa Mission which was founded in Los Angeles in 1906. Nils Bloch-Hoell (*The Pentecostal Movement* [London: Allen and Unwin, 1964]) discovered some midwestern precursors of the Azusa Mission, but both scholars agree that the Pentecostal movement emerged when the Spirit baptism and "speaking in tongues" became the central focus of the believer's religious activity.

opportunity. As they see it, formal organization of any sort ultimately interferes with the emotional efficacy of the service, and the "gifts" of the Spirit are thus rarely evidenced. Furthermore, unlike Seventh-day Adventism, the Pentecostal movement in this country does not have a superordinate organization whose functionaries are charged with extending their point of view and with keeping doctrinal statements of local churches consistent with the movement's dogmatic precepts. In fact, Pentecostals do not subscribe to a definitive creedal statement, partly because each member always has recourse to the Spirit in matters of scriptural interpretation. In addition, every Pentecostal minister or revivalist likes to develop his own unique style in the pulpit and therefore adds his own embellishments to the generally accepted core of Pentecostal theology. A student of Pentecostalism goes so far as to declare that "the Pentecostal Movement has no common creed and no real theological literature. The Movement is markedly subjective, and it will to a certain extent be difficult to record precisely its dogmatic outlines."[7] The following statement of Pentecostal theology relies much more heavily upon verbal rather than written data than in the Seventh-day Adventist case. I will depart briefly from my plan to discuss sect organization separately in the next chapter so that the reader can appreciate the sorts of local congregations from which my information is drawn.

I worked in two somewhat different church settings—in a small storefront church and in a large church. The small Pentecostal church had no intention of establishing any ties which would inhibit its theological and ritual freedom. In fact, the minister often claimed that other Pentecostal churches frequently asked him to affiliate with them but that he would never join any group which placed any restrictions whatsoever upon his freedom and obligation to "move" in whatever direction the Spirit saw fit to take. He refused to accept the idea that any service or meeting should not be governed by spontaneous reactions to the emanations of the Spirit. The entire group would often confirm their suspicions that other groups restricted the

7. Bloch-Hoell, *Pentecostal Movement*, p. 3.

free movement of the Spirit by deciding to visit them en masse. Characteristically, they would do so on the spur of the moment.

The larger Pentecostal church—a revival center actually is a more appropriate term for this congregation—was a splinter group from a large, independent Pentecostal church which had adopted more conventional theological attitudes. I visited this group regularly because the smaller group had only about eight or nine members, and I wanted to be sure that its theological orientation was not substantially different from the rest of the Pentecostal movement. Both groups had very similar theologies and modes of worship.

As Wilson notes, though most Pentecostals formally acknowledge the trinitarian constitution of the Divinity, they are "unmitigatedly Jesucentric." Pentecostals do not always see Jesus as the immediate source of all spiritual blessings. Rather, Jesus is the principal source of divine mercy, and the believer must absolve himself before the Lord if his guilt is not to interfere with his inward spiritual development. One informant raised in a strict religious home told me that she had never done anything overtly sinful but that before she could be saved she had to discover that she too was a sinner. Then, she said, it was possible for her to move on to become perfect in Christ; this meant the growth of inner holiness through repeated contact with the Holy Spirit. The minister of the small Pentecostal group constantly stressed that the results of this experience were immediate and perceptible: revelation or prophecy, divine healing, and "speaking in tongues."

It was often difficult to decide when a religious speaker was making a judgment about the future on his own and when he was acting as the agent of the Holy Spirit. Unlike "speaking in tongues," not all prophetic utterances were rooted in spiritual possession. Rather, the minister often termed as prophecy a more attenuated experience of religious illumination, and consequently the group could often discuss their own feelings about each other and about their destiny as a separate religious organization in a prophetic idiom.

In general, Pentecostals perceive two major sources of "static" in direct communications from God. One is the machinations of the Devil, who tries to mislead and confuse the believer. The believer can exorcise this unwanted influence through personal rededication to Christ. In the Pentecostal congregations I observed, ministers and revivalists often told those who had difficulties in the area of "gifts" to allow only Jesus' influence in their life.

Conflict between members of the congregation was the other source of spiritual contamination. Although these groups prescribe fraternal solidarity, their theology promotes religious individualism. Each person seeks his own consummation of a feeling of oneness with Jesus. He does not engage in collective ritual to bring the "in-filling" of the Spirit to others except incidentally; he wants these benefits for himself. This was most evident in the larger group, where most of the members came to services in search of specific results and did not remain with the group unless they regularly found them. They might return when a very famous revivalist or healer spoke, but, on the whole, their loyalty was weak even though they might make a large donation when they attended services. In fact, there is a great deal of movement between these kinds of churches because Pentecostals think there is nothing wrong with "shopping around" for the most suitable congregation. Their decision about the congregation is undoubtedly biased by the relatively unpredictable and short-lived quality of their experiences during its services. A couple who had been members of the smaller congregation, and at the time of the study were members of the larger congregation, saw this as a natural and inevitable process. Even though they were personal friends of the minister of the smaller group, they felt that the larger congregation fit their present spiritual mood but that perhaps they someday would be "moved" to return to the smaller group.

The members of the smaller group were genuinely concerned about each other's spiritual fate. But since each member wanted to achieve spiritual distinction and saw his relationship with the minister as a sign of his religious status, they often were jealous of one another. The minister often pointed to these latent hostilities as the cause of their inability at times to move freely in the Spirit. He used the prophetic idiom "thus saith the Lord" to buttress his usually successful attempts to force them to discuss openly their grievances and negative feelings. In this instance, prophecy was used to reveal sentiments which reduced rapport and, in Pentecostal theory, damaged the believers' capacity to receive the Holy Spirit.

Pentecostals constantly prophesy, but they lack a prophetic tradition. Unlike Seventh-day Adventists, Pentecostals do not try to build a theory about the universe which is committed to a unified interpretation of the meaning of human events. Rather, there is a profusion of often contradictory declarations about all sorts of matters. One day the minister will say that God has told him the group will miraculously receive a large sum of money next week; if this prediction does not materialize, he extends the time limit or forgets the matter. In the strict sense of the term, Seventh-day Adventists do not prophesy, but use an already established exegesis of prophetic texts to orient themselves to the world. On the other hand, prophecy for Pentecostals involves the sudden intrusion of divine power; they search for signs of this extraordinary supernatural efficacy in the events which impinge upon their lives.

Unlike religious systems where the believer induces divinities through offerings and entreaties to use their miraculous powers on his behalf, Pentecostalism lacks any ritual which might coerce Jesus to dispense practical benefits for the suppliant even though the members practice spiritual healing. In theory, only through God's freely given grace and the believer's love for and faith in Christ can the believer become a candidate for the unusual spiritual "gifts." My informants told me that although there are a number of ways to make oneself receptive to the Holy Spirit (principally by intense prayer and introspection), there is no way to compel the Spirit's arrival. In fact, many informants had tried to receive the Holy Spirit for months before becoming successfully possessed, and they claimed that it sometimes happened when they least expected it. Furthermore, one seeks the experience for its intrinsic meaning and not simply for its tangible benefits. In practice, however, many people come to services looking for a solution to immediate and pressing personal problems, for example, illness or emotional disorders.

From what I saw, dedicated sect members tried to convince these people that although it was surely possible to apply divine healing powers to their ills, they ought to try to forget their problems and seek the entire personal transformation which comes from union with the Holy Spirit. In time, the healing power of divine contact would solve their problems.

According to Pentecostal doctrine, the Holy Spirit is more than "the life-giving breath of our God."[8] Although there is some obscurity on this point, Jesus provides access to the Holy Spirit, but the latter has a separate existence outside the manifestations of Christ's redeeming qualities. In the Pentecostal churches I studied, the Holy Spirit has a discrete identity and its own special function in the redemptive process. For Pentecostals, the Holy Spirit is as much a distinct and whole divinity as God-the-Father or Jesus; the Holy Ghost acts on its own and in distinctive ways.

The Holy Ghost stands at the center of Pentecostal thought and is not merely a modality of Jesus. This view differs somewhat from Wilson, who says that in the Pentecostal group he studied (Elim, Foursquare Gospel) Jesus is the

> arch-symbol of faith, the repository of ideals, values and aspirations. . . . He is the savior who redeems men from their sin, and assures them of eternal life; He is the healer who fulfills scriptural promise to cure all manner of illnesses; He is the baptizer in the Holy Ghost; and He is the coming King.[9]

Wilson ties Christ's crucial "cathartic role" to "the core of all evangelical teaching—an emphasis on man's sinful state, Jesus's worthiness, His sacrifice and atonement and the redemption of all who, by believing in the efficacy of His atonement, accept it and Him."[10]

Although this is an admirable statement of the theological ground that unites diverse fundamentalist churches who have a

8. Stanley Hopper, "Spirit," in *A Handbook of Christian Theology*, ed. Arthur Cohen and Marvin Halverson (New York: Meridian Books, 1962), p. 171.
9. Bryan Wilson, *Sects and Society* (London: Heinemann, 1961), p. 16.
10. Ibid.

decidedly redemptive orientation, it does not differentiate Pentecostals from Holiness groups and other churches which seek inner spiritual purification through admission of guilt for Christ's death and a willingness to achieve salvation through his blood. Although Wilson is certainly correct that Pentecostals gain the "spiritual baptism" and its attendant "gifts" through Jesus, I think he underestimates the theological focus on the Holy Spirit qua Holy Spirit in these groups. Of course, there are "Jesus only" Pentecostal groups who formally acknowledge the trinitarian structure of the Godhead but focus almost exclusively upon the attributes and qualities of Jesus, and Wilson may refer to such churches. But in the groups I studied not one informant ever ascribed the all-important spiritual charismata such as the ability to "speak in tongues" to Jesus. According to my informants, Jesus is the one who releases the believer's inner potentialities for this experience, but the Holy Ghost alone is able to actualize it. Many of the sermons in both the large and the small congregations monotonously hammered at the theme that those present should be "seized" by the Spirit and "touched" by the Spirit, and that the whole world should be "shaken" by the Spirit. They also claim that one should not miss a meeting because you never can tell when there will be a great "outpouring of gifts." This contrasts markedly with their attitude toward Jesus, who they firmly maintain is always available and is always ready to offer solace and comfort to those who seek him.

I have pressed this distinction between the qualities attributable to Jesus and those attributable to the Holy Spirit much further than any Pentecostal would wish to do because it is important to underline the reality of the Holy Spirit as an independent divinity for these believers. In sum, the Holy Spirit is not simply a religious metaphor for Jesus' ability to penetrate into the depths of a person's inner being and to endow him with supernatural abilities; the Spirit is a reality sui generis.

Of all the nine gifts of the Spirit (wisdom, knowledge, faith, healing, miracles, prophecy, discernment, tongues, and interpretation), "speaking in tongues" is clearly the most prominent in Pentecostal worship and the most sought after by its adherents.[11] It not only is the most tangible sign of salvation but is said to also bring the greatest personal happiness one can imagine. Here we can see the basic Pentecostal orientation to the world: it is the reality of the sensate experience of physical and emotional contact with God and not the intellectual knowledge of his abstract attributes that matters.

Of course Pentecostals engage in biblical exegesis, although sermons rarely concentrate on the intellectual substance of the text. In general, Pentecostals are not overly concerned about varying interpretations of biblical texts as long as a particular theological tract does not contradict their distinctive teachings or denigrate their approach to God. Seventh-day Adventists, on the other hand, are very sensitive to the discrepancy between their interpretations of key biblical passages and the views of other churches. They spend a good deal of theological energy on point-by-point refutations of positions which conflict with their view of scriptural truth. Pentecostals often urged me to read a wide range of popular evangelical literature that did not espouse or defend their special emphasis on spiritual baptism but that did not attack it either.

The minister of the smaller group did not reject such literature, but he felt very strongly that his congregation could "get into" the Word only under very specific conditions. He gave private Bible classes to members of his congregation, which he termed was their "discipleship." They had to write very detailed reports on selected biblical passages and he would correct any misinterpretations. He further maintained that without divine inspiration assiduous Bible study was almost worthless. The emphasis in Pentecostal belief is always on worship which brings

11. Kelsey says that "they believe that tongues is the evidence of being filled with the Holy Spirit; even more important, they believe that this is the only experience a Christian needs in order to have the fullness of Christian life. The gift of tongues is not had by holiness in personal life nor does it come on the heels of any gift of sanctification. Desiring the experience and waiting upon God (tarrying) for it are the real essentials. This experience of baptism in the Holy Ghost is known as finished work, the beginning and end of Christian experience. Once received, the experience only has to be retained and applied to life. It becomes the foundation upon which Christian life is built, the essential Christian experience." *Tongue Speaking*, p. 77.

the believer into a closer and more intimate relationship with God.

I do not think that the primary purpose of the Bible study sessions was to construct a systematic theology. Pentecostals, of course, are vitally interested in the veracity of biblical interpretation, but they do not erect an elaborate cognitive structure such as I described for Seventh-day Adventism to validate their perceptions of religious reality. On the surface, these discussions of the Bible were intended to convince the members of the group that the minister's insight into the Bible was truly inspired by his special relationship with God. He often described his role as a kind of "prophethood" but always pointed out that this was not an exclusive status and that others with his guidance could move into these elevated spiritual realms.

The essential function of these Bible classes was to create an appreciation for the mystery of the Word. The minister always pointed out that each passage in the Bible contains many layers of meaning, and that one cannot rely upon ordinary scholarship and logic to resolve apparent inconsistencies and ambiguities. In his opinion, biblical paradox was an entry into the mind of God if only the reader would seek the Holy Ghost as the source of enlightenment. True understanding in Pentecostal doctrine always derives from intimate contact with God; rational analysis is always a weak and faulty tool when the analyst relies solely upon his own natural intellectual powers.

In this religious tradition, cognitive activity should serve an essentially affective end. It should strengthen the believer's feeling of the reality of the "living" God and of the immediacy of his Word. Through the Word, the Pentecostal is convinced that God talks directly to him, in a language he often can comprehend.

Pentecostals do not hold that "baptism of the Holy Ghost" and the display of spiritual "gifts" are absolutely necessary for salvation. But they assert that those who devalue or ridicule this experience are most likely unsaved. They further believe, though not with the same force, that this experience usually follows conversion if the latter is genuine, that is, if there is a real desire to seek Jesus' aid and comfort and a complete willingness to place one's fate in Jesus' hands. The "in-filling" of the Holy Spirit is the most significant sign of one's membership in the elect—those with whom God has a special relationship and who constitute the vanguard in his plan to save mankind.

The literature on spiritual baptism and "speaking in tongues" often treats these phenomena as some form of collective psychological aberration or as symptoms of individual personality disorders.[12] There are some excellent discussions of the limitations of purely psychiatric explanations of behavior embedded in roles which express the norms of a religious system,[13] and consequently I shall limit the following discussion to the cultural meaning of possession by the Holy Ghost.

The "in-filling of the Holy Ghost" is revealed by motor behavior which involves intense physiological stress and is revealed by shaking, tremors, and so forth. There is considerable variation in response to this experience, and in some people it is revealed only by deep inner concentration and oblivion to most external stimuli. However, I have not seen a "trance" state where the possessed person becomes oblivious to communications from at least some of those who surround him and where he cannot recall what occurred during this state. Although there are conventional formulas for reporting this experience, there is also considerable latitude for ascribing various forms of knowledge and feeling to it. From what I have seen, most Pentecostals talk about the happiness it brings them or how it changed their lives (renewed or purified them). Unlike adherents of

12. For an analysis of this sort see Ari Kiev, "Psychotherapeutic Aspects of Pentecostal Sects among West Indian Immigrants to England," *British Journal of Sociology* 15 (1964). Kiev recognizes that religious affiliation is shaped by social class and further believes that various emotional disorders are correlated with position in the class structure. In his opinion, these emotional disorders often take the form of compensatory religious behavior, and therefore a person is attracted to a sect because its belief and worship are compatible with his neuroses. Sect ideology is treated as an overt symptom of an underlying emotional disturbance.

13. For an incisive critique of the direct application of psychiatric diagnostic categories to entire systems of belief and worship see Alexander Alland, "Possession in a Revivalistic Negro Church," *Journal for the Scientific Study of Religion* 1 (1962).

other mystical traditions, they do not attribute consistent imagery to these states of possession, nor do they claim to have perceived clearly defined aspects of the cosmos. In this respect, they differ from the institutionalized mystical revelation of Seventh-day Adventism or the early Jewish mystics who expanded their vision of the structure of the cosmos and who lent new or deeper interpretation to the meaning of biblical prophecy.[14] In my opinion, the absence of specific intellectual content is a function of the essentially emotional bias of their theology.

Spiritual baptism often occurs during Pentecostal prayer meetings or services, particularly when the believer is in need of spiritual assistance with any of the myriad of difficulties which afflict his life. Pentecostals enjoy recounting the "suffering" they endured before they became "born again" Christians. Most of my informants felt there was a decisive change in the amount of distress they were subjected to after they underwent spiritual baptism. They testified frequently about the great burdens this experience had removed from their minds. However, no one claimed that suffering was totally eliminated from his life. This is consistent with their theological assumption that sin is part of the human condition, and that therefore even the most saintly person cannot entirely escape its deleterious influence. Sin gives rise to guilt, and hence inner distress is often perceived as an indication that they need to renew themselves in the spiritual baptism.

According to my informants, the most meaningful contact with the Holy Spirit often occurs in moments of solitary meditation and prayer. This vitiates explanations of spiritual baptism which invoke some variant of the crowd psychology thesis, that is, that something happens to the normal emotional controls of people when they are thrown into a volatile group situation.[15] In

14. Gershom Scholem says that "the earliest Jewish mysticism is throne-mysticism. Its essence is not absorbed contemplation of God's true nature, but perception of His appearance on the throne, as described by Ezekiel, and cognition of the mysteries of the celestial throne-world." *Major Trends in Jewish Mysticism* (New York: Schocken Books, 1965), p. 44.

15. For a statement of his thesis see Elmer T. Clark, *The Small Sects in America* (New York: Abingdon Press, 1949).

fact, the formal cultural definitions of spiritual possession stress the emergence of new and more potent forms of self-control often absent in ordinary existence.

From the instances of spiritual baptism I have seen, it appears that the believer possesses cognitive criteria which clearly distinguish experiences with God from "counterfeit" experiences which are the Devil's way of misleading the faithful. For example, the phenomenon of "speaking in tongues" has the same phonetic and phonemic structure as English and, although I am not a trained linguist, it also seems to have the same stress and intonation pattern. Furthermore, certain phonemic combinations seem to have a rudimentary morphemic organization: conventional meanings are assigned to certain phrases although not to their constituents. Certain combinations of English syllables recur in phrases spoken by members of the larger church who are possessed by the Holy Spirit, and those endowed with the "gift of interpretation" assign what appears to an untrained ear as the same meaning to the same segment of the Spirit language. When a person is possessed by the Devil, he speaks gibberish; he cannot articulate anything above a complex series of grunts and cries. When a person speaks in the Spirit language he does not lose control of his motor processes, although his body and gestures certainly reflect an unusual presence.

A woman who repeatedly had great difficulty experiencing the genuine "in-filling" of the Holy Spirit exhibited certain symptoms. My informants pointed out that she somehow could not disentangle the Spirit from whatever was holding her back. In their opinion, this accounted for the gutteral, blurred quality of her voice. Further, they noted that what I perceived as an almost total inability to control her body (she literally needed physical support) was due to inner distress and unhappiness. Interestingly enough, the minister diagnosed her case as one where interference by the Devil was actually a symptom rather than a basic cause of her inability to allow the Holy Spirit to enter her soul. He pointed out that her peculiar religious background was an important source of her spiritual difficulties. She was originally a member of a snake-handling Pentecostal church in West Virginia, and he felt that these practices inhibited her spiritual enlightenment. He went on to say that there were certain irregularities in her life (from what I was able to infer these were largely sexual) which stunted her spiritual freedom. But (and this is an important point) he felt that these moral deficiencies were not absolute barriers to spiritual renewal in the Holy Ghost. Moral impurities reduce the probability of divine contact, but many sinful persons have been saved and renewed by spiritual baptism.

To recapitulate, the critical feature of the baptism of the Holy Ghost from the believer's perspective is the acquisition of extraordinary forms of insight, power, and control. True, they talk about the necessity of relaxing inner constraints to receive the Holy Spirit, but they surrender themselves to the Holy Ghost because they are convinced that in return they are endowed with supernatural talents denied to even the most pious and dedicated who are not "born again" Christians.[16] Although admission to this status is temporary (no Pentecostal retains these powers in undiminished intensity outside the context of supernatural possession), the Pentecostal feels that he is the beneficiary of a pervasive and enduring change in the position he occupies in society. He now is uniquely qualified to interpret God to man and has, so to speak, the divine seal of approval. God has chosen him as the human vehicle through which he heals the sick, interprets his messages to mankind, and reveals the future.

Thus, the Pentecostal is not an entirely passive agent of the Holy Spirit. His innate spiritual capacities are mixed with those given him by the Holy Spirit, and the product is a new identity. Unlike Haitian spiritual possession, where the possessed person is so completely taken over by the divinity that he does not remember the experience, the Pentecostal never completely

16. Kelsey says that "the Christian who receives spiritual baptism and speaks in tongues then enters into a charismatic life in which he is open to receive all the gifts of the Spirit. He will manifest the gifts of healing and discernment of spirits, of knowledge and wisdom, of faith and miraculous powers, of prophecy and also the continued use of tongues with a different significance. They believe that the fruits of love and compassion and brotherhood also flow from the Spirit as one receives it in an experience of tongues." *Tongue Speaking*, p. 78.

loses his contribution to the process.[17] He knows what is happening to him and is able to describe it after the experience is over.

Pentecostals assert that during these moments they become the center of the universe; God reaches down and, by touching them, distinguishes them from all other men. And as we shall see, this contrasts with their ordinary social obscurity and anonymity. The Pentecostal typically does not claim unusual secular merit but directs those he meets to view him in light of his spiritual achievements. His status assertions rest upon more than a life filled with religious purity and holiness. His accomplishments are tangible and demonstrable, and they are of undoubted worth and rarity. Not everyone can say that God has come to him and filled his very being with His light. In a study of the Pentecostal movement in Brazil and Chile, Willems observes that "if he was a 'nobody' before his conversion, he is a 'somebody' now—a person who has become a recipient of special supernatural powers, who belongs to a 'chosen' people."[18]

This experience confirms the believer's perception of his own worth. It lessens the impact of all those external forces which reduce his self-esteem. Spiritual baptism provides the believer with a valued personal identity because he knows and feels that his personal contact with God transcends the boundaries of ordinary human knowledge and understanding. This experience not only enables him to solve some of his problems but also places his present worldly difficulties in a new, less confining perspective. According to dedicated "born again" Christians, secular exigencies are inherently trivial because God will remedy any defect in the believer's life; God will provide for those who maintain their faith in the face of serious doubt and uncertainty. This is one of the principal points of tension in this belief system, because it demands certain changes in reality which it cannot always produce. For example, one woman obviously suffering from a severe visual deficiency was promised

17. See Erika Bourguignon, "The Self, the Behavioral Environment, and the Theory of Spirit Possession," in *Context and Meaning in Cultural Anthropology*, ed. Melford Spiro (New York: Free Press, 1965).

18. Emilio Willems, *Followers of the New Faith: Culture Change and the Rise of Protestantism in Brazil and Chile* (Nashville: Vanderbilt University Press, 1967), p. 144.

that the Holy Spirit would heal her eyesight so that she could see without her thick glasses. Removing her glasses, she stumbled over a chair after being healed and was extremely upset and agitated.

In sum, spiritual possession enables the believer to dramatize his unique talents and thus place his personal dignity and integrity beyond the pale of those who rely upon worldly criteria for their status judgments. Spiritual baptism symbolizes feelings and ideas which enhance rather than detract from one's self-image, and the function of spiritual possession may be independent of the specific content of the theology which supports and encourages it:

> Yet in the Haitian examples cited above, the self-serving nature of the supposedly "dissociated" wishes and desires is perhaps their most notable aspect. I should like to argue that ritualized dissociation provides the self with an inventory of roles, in which unfulfilled desires, "unrealistic" in the context of the workaday world, get a second chance at fulfillment, a fulfillment which is surely not merely vicarious because the glory goes to the possessing spirit rather than to the "horse.". . . In a world of poverty, disease, and frustrations, ritual possession, rather than destroying the integrity of the self, provides increased scope for fulfillment.[19]

Although the Pentecostal does not suffer from the same afflictions as the Haitian peasant, he too not only desires to escape from a world with few prospects for radical improvement but also wants to prove that his claims to special esteem are justified. Supernatural validation is an effective means of convincing those already prepared to accept the reality of such occurrences that the person who is possessed stands in a special relationship to the force which determines the very movements of the universe and shapes the destiny of men.

Perhaps the best way to understand the meaning of this experience is to examine the Pentecostal's encounter with the Holy Spirit in the context of his conversion. The following is the story of the conversion of the minister of the small group, who has no formal theological training and seeks none. He

19. Bourguignon, "The Self, the Behavioral Environment, and the Theory of Spirit Possession," p. 57.

insisted on the primacy of the Word and the Spirit in everyday affairs and religious matters. His sacred authority rested partly on his power to say what God would have members choose, do, or say in almost every sphere of their lives. This required enormous spiritual self-confidence, which the minister exuded, and yet he never was arrogant or overly authoritarian.

Nonetheless, I should note that the group had great difficulty recruiting and retaining new members. It moved back and forth between Chicago and California in search of a stable home base. The minister demanded total commitment to a life filled with the Holy Spirit but did not establish unrealistic moral standards. Quite the contrary, he expected everyone to periodically suffer moral lapses and he did not exclude himself. He expected every member of his congregation to attempt constantly to realize the ideal of total love for Jesus and for each other and to achieve this through the agency of the Spirit. On these points there was no compromise; he would say that "this is no Mickey Mouse group." In other Pentecostal groups I visited, the ministers would encourage those present to come up to testify and to get filled with the Spirit, but they allowed those who did not feel moved to do so to remain in the background. The minister of the small group castigated those who did not demonstrably "move" with the group.

The minister's insistence that the members of his congregation live according to this radical version of the ethic of Christian love was the primary source of his charismatic qualities. At first this looks like a dubious proposition. The small size of the congregation scarcely attests to his personal magnetism. Nevertheless, I shall argue that the leader's charisma arises out of the ethically uncompromising character of the demands he makes on his followers, and out of his followers' perception of benign intentions behind his call for a complete reformation of their lives.

According to this view, charismatic leaders are not identified by the size and power of the movements they inspire. That is a function of the historical situation in which they experience a prophetic call to their special vocation. Their particular message to mankind may go unheeded for a variety of reasons, and circumstances may catapult a previously obscure leader into great prominence. Finally, I think that the very qualities that constitute a charismatic personality are sometimes responsible for restricted attractiveness to potential converts. A man who makes great demands upon followers is capable of mobilizing powerful energies in the service of his cause, especially when his followers sense his absolute dedication to the movement's goals. On the other hand, unless the convert's circumstances are dire, it is usually more comfortable to seek salvation in a more diluted and less rigorous form.

In a careful reanalysis of the concept of charismatic leadership, Tucker points out that the leader's influence over his followers depends upon a talent for persuasive argument and upon the ability to imagine new responses to stressful situations. But, more than that, "whatever the particular social setting (religion, politics, and so forth), charismatic leadership rejects old rules and issues a demand for change. It preaches or creates *new* obligations."[20] And the demands the charismatic leader makes upon his followers aim at a transformation of the convert's entire way of life:

> Briefly, the charismatic leader is one in whom, by virtue of unusual personal qualities, the promise or hope of salvation—deliverance from distress—appears to be embodied. He is a leader who convincingly offers himself to a group of people in distress as one peculiarly qualified to lead them out of their predicament. He is in essence a savior, or one who is so perceived by his followers. *Charismatic leadership is specifically salvationist or messanic in nature.*[21]

Pentecostals formally subscribe to the idea of complete openness before God. But many ministers are quite skilled in the public relations of religious self-disclosure. The minister of the small Pentecostal group refused to accede to these role stratagems. He regarded such devices for protecting one's motives from public scrutiny and for hiding potentially embarrassing feelings as deceitful—part of the sham that plagues the Pentecostal movement. In an atmosphere that requires critical public

20. Robert C. Tucker, "The Theory of Charismatic Leadership," *Daedalus* 97 (1968):737.
21. Ibid., p. 742.

self-examination, one must trust the intentions of those who control this process. To obtain this trust, the minister had to convince the members of the congregation that he desired above all else to help them attain a state of spiritual well-being without using this accomplishment for his own aggrandizement. This task requires great sensitivity to the individual convert's psychological makeup combined with a strenuous effort to nurture those qualities that strengthen his rapport with God and to eradicate those qualities that interfere with his communion with the Holy Ghost.

Charisma, then, depends in large measure on the potential convert's perceptions of the intentions of a leader who implores or commands him to change his life pattern and to adopt new values. The convert must feel that such a person has *his* best interests at heart and, moreover, that the leader genuinely understands his problems and can offer a viable solution to them. Charismatic authority flows from the convert's feeling that the leader genuinely wants him to achieve a highly valuable goal, in this case the Spirit baptism, and that this effort will have positive ramifications in other areas of his life. Here the love of Jesus was said to be the agency through which salvation, in the widest meaning of the word, becomes possible for man—salvation which restructures one's feelings about others and about oneself and provides material blessings and spiritual security. I suspect that the convert must also feel that the leader provides his "last hope" before he will commit himself completely to a radical social ethic, and that the absence of a widespread feeling of "spiritual crisis" perhaps accounts for this leader's difficulties in attracting new converts to his church.

In the minister's opinion, his life story and how he came to accept his religious calling are inextricably intertwined. His early religious training was confined to sporadic attendance at a local Gospel church Sunday school. He and his sister were sent there by his parents, who wanted them out of the house and who rarely went to church, and then never to a specific church. His father, whom he described as a minor hoodlum with some vague connection with the syndicate, and his mother were always fighting, breaking up, and then reconciling when he was a child. One day he came home and found that the apartment was bare; all the furniture was gone and there were no notes telling him where everyone had gone. At the age of fourteen he was on his own. But even before this time he had lived on the streets. He was a "very tough kid," a "true" delinquent. After this experience, he got much "harder." He became extremely hostile and aggressive; he was a person who loved only "old ladies and little kids." "If a guy would give him a hard look, he would go right up and nail him."

He then showed me a picture taken on his wedding day. At the moment the picture was taken he said he was thinking about killing his (first) wife's brother, whom he hated—along with everyone else. Until the time he was saved, when he started to go to church with his (present) wife, he was always in fights and brawls. He showed me his air force discharge papers, which diagnosed him as incurable and with highly aggressive tendencies.

He then told me that he used to carry a loaded forty-five (pistol) around with him at all times. He said that he made so many enemies when he was in the Air Force that he thought the whole world was after him—his buddies, the air force, the people in the black market to whom he was selling stolen goods, and the "commies." He says that half of this fear may have been due to his "complex" but that the other half was true because he was so generally hated. Even before joining the air force he started to "go down." He got an English girl "in trouble" while he was in service and after he was discharged, they came back to Chicago. The marriage did not last because he was so "mean," the "meanest" person he could think of; so after he beat her she left him and found another man.

When he was processed by air force psychologists before his discharge, he said that he begged them "with tears running down my face" to help him, as he felt that "I was going further and further down and nothing I could do could stop it." But he said they could do nothing for him. And he asserted they were "the best men" (i.e., competent doctors) but he thought that psychiatry could not deal with a problem like his—it was just too complex for men to heal. In retrospect, he says that he could see that even then God was using his life for a purpose; he now knows that everything fitted into a larger plan which he could not perceive at that time.

After the episode with his first wife in Chicago, he drifted and finally moved to Los Angeles, where he fell in with a group of "arabs"—petty criminals. He led a dissolute life, working sporadically and living with one "arab" with whom he shared his money. Then he was in a horrible car accident and was seriously injured. The doctors told him he would never walk again, and for three months he was on pain killers with only unemployment compensation to keep himself going. His roommate left him in the room for three days without food or money, and after that, all he could think of was killing him. He planned to blow his foot off first and then a year or so later to "blow his brains out." He said that this desire consumed him, and that whenever he saw his roommate this was all he could think about. However, once he was saved, his hatred turned to love. After he was saved, he went to his apartment, where his "arab" friend had a "dope ring." There were four girls there who said they were innocent and showed him some heroin. He called the police and told his friend that he must come home with him (he had moved to a boardinghouse) or he would turn him over to the police. Of course the friend chose the former alternative and was made comfortable with the minister, but after a week he disappeared and he never saw him again.

His landlady, who was an old woman, had been urging him to attend a Foursquare Gospel meeting and he went to accommodate her. At first the service made no noticeable impression upon him. It was after he met his (present) wife that he found religion. He met her at a drive-in where he "picked her up." He asked her for a date and she went out with him because she said she was curious about how mean a person could be. Her parents were religious (fundamentalist) and were opposed to him, and he said that he would feel the same way if his daughter went out with someone just a tenth as bad as he was.

At this time, he was hopelessly crippled and was resigned to walking on crutches for the rest of his life. Then one night at church with his wife he did not know what came over him, but tears started rolling down his face. Then the woman preacher (Foursquare Gospel) began the altar call and his landlady, who was standing behind him, nudged him to go up and he went. He stayed at the altar for three and a half hours, pouring out his heart to God. Right there he gave his life to the Lord. His leg was miraculously healed, and his former "arab" friends were upset by the change in his character but could not "put down" the fact that his leg had healed. He got some of them to come to the Foursquare service with him, but the woman preacher was put off by their experience (their criminal occupations) and he felt that they were lost to Christ because she did not know how to deal with them. He added that women in general do not make good preachers.

After this "cleansing" experience, he immediately became passionately interested in studying and preaching. He said he "ran through" what the Foursquare Gospel church had to offer in six months. In fact, he remarked that when he was (religiously) naive, he went to the church and told the woman that he wanted the Holy Spirit, as if "it were something they kept in a box"; and they took him to various rooms and left him alone to pray (after trying to put him in the proper frame of mind), but nothing happened.

One night when he was lying in bed (he had married his second wife by this time), he got the Holy Spirit. First he sensed a "presence" in the room. He had been seeking it "all over the place" but at this time he was just lying in bed thinking about nothing in particular when it came. After he experienced the presence, he started praying; his wife was asleep. All of a sudden it was just as if an unseen hand had taken hold of him. He spoke in tongues. He was so deliriously happy that he tried to call his wife's parents, who had been praying for him (he was living in their house when this occurred) but he could speak only in tongues. His soul "broke like a floodgate when he got saved" but this was an even greater experience. The Holy Spirit had full control of his faculties; thoughts went through his mind in English and came out in tongues. He had full possession of his reason and control over his behavior. There was an especial clarity to his mind and yet he could speak only in tongues.

He told me that his ministerial training came from a pastor of a nondenominational Full Gospel church under whom he studied. He worked part time and studied eight hours a day. He had plenty of opportunity to preach and was often preaching before he reached the altar. Now he studies, preaches, and ministers to the needs of his flock (his wife works and his congregation, which forms an extended family with the minister as the center patriarchal figure, contributes to his support).

He mentioned that he used no denominational literature, just the Greek and archaic versions of the Bible along with the standard English translation; he has no faith in "sect" literature (although he does not stop any member of his congregation from reading other religious literature, he rather ruthlessly castigates them in public if he discerns a point of view in their testimonials which does not accord with this theological bias). His evangelical contacts are as the Spirit moves him, and he does not believe in or encourage indiscriminate evangelical activity, for example, door to door. Since "God is dealing with certain people," evangelical activity which is indiscriminate is like "digging for treasure without a map." On the other hand, when the Spirit prompted him, he has walked up to people on the street and they received him without trouble because they knew the Lord wanted him to do it, and they thanked him for his help.

He believes one is justified by faith in Christ—not in what one does. If you are in Christ and he is in you, then you are naturally righteous. If he is in you, then the tendencies toward righteousness will grow in you. No prohibitions or penalties will make you righteous. He adds that television is superior to the movies because you can't choose your company in the movie house. He saved his two sisters and ultimately his father. "Christianity is true because it works!" "It transforms rotten lives." "You have the authority in Christ to have a new nature; you grow and these things develop in you."

Although there are undoubtedly many intrapersonal aspects

to conversion experiences, I shall limit my comments to the cultural implications of rebirth through spiritual possession. Most of my informants said that they sought rebirth in the Holy Spirit because they felt their lives were "going down the drain." They feared falling into states of moral depravity or spiritual vacuity.[22] Pentecostal converts wanted to escape from an inner state over which each could exercise little control and which entailed sinking to a level lower than he felt his better self should be.

These themes of falling into a highly undesirable mode of existence embody the pivotal symbolic link with the status system of the environing society. In my opinion, the Pentecostal sees himself in an ambiguous position in the status system of the larger society. Although he feels there are no real similarities between his own life style and moral ideals and those of "ordinary" working-class people, he knows that objectively he has about the same standard of living as they do. And his command over vital social resources gives him little hope of escape from his present status dilemma. Incidentally, Walter Miller's description of the focal concerns of lower-class culture represents the antithesis of the "respectable" status image Pentecostals try to create for themselves.[23]

In his study of the Pentecostal movement in Chile and Brazil, Willems noticed that most converts came from the upper segments of the lower class and from the lower middle class. Characteristically, "all subjects expressed dissatisfaction with their life before conversion." [24] Willems observes that a crucial motive underlying conversion involves a deep and pervasive identification with middle-class respectability:

> Surely enough, the convert sheds his "vices," but *as he does he carefully rids himself of forms of behavior which the society at large holds in*

22. Although some of my informants claimed to have led dissolute lives before their conversion, those who revealed the exact nature of their former immorality did not suffer from a complete ethical breakdown. Fornication, drunkenness, and such were the principal evils from which they sought to free themselves.
23. Walter Miller, "Lower-Class Culture as a Generating Milieu of Gang Delinquency," *Journal of Social Issues* 14 (1958).
24. Willems, *Followers of the New Faith*, p. 129.

> *disrepute.* Drunken bouts, tavern brawls, wife-beating, illegitimacy, neglect of children and a disorganized home life, personal appearance suggesting neglect and uncleanliness, failure to improve poor housing conditions, and similar traits are often held against the lower classes. One may say, they are identified with lower class behavior and therefore looked upon with a mixture of moral indignation and amused contempt. It seems that the Protestant convert is particularly sensitive to such criticism, for henceforward he carefully avoids "disreputable" forms of behavior.[25]

This identification with the middle class is not confined to attitudes toward lower-class behavior. The convert desires the material symbols of middle-class life; "A major aspiration of every *roto chileno* become Pentecostal is to purchase, at the earliest possible opportunity, a dark woolen suit, black or preferably dark blue, colors which, in his mind, symbolize middle class status. . . . These sects very definitely convey an air of petit bourgeois respectability."[26]

This intense concern with being rescued and rescuing others from ways of life which are degrading arises from a fear of losing a rather precarious status advantage. Once a person is saved, he places himself in a position morally superior to those people addicted to activities which either involve no special spiritual merit or deserve spiritual demerits (e.g., drinking). Sermons often dwell upon the evils of dope, sex, and alcohol, which presumably are the principal forms of illicit excitement of the "lower" classes. After describing the horrible effects of drink, dope, and so forth, the speaker almost invariably urges the members of the congregation to go out to save these people from their worst instincts. Pentecostals think that those whose lives are rooted in vice or spiritual sloth constitute the "prime mission fields."

Since Pentecostals follow the lead of the Spirit rather than any set of theological traditions, they rely, by and large, on spoken rather than written guides to religious understanding. The former not only have greater immediacy but also imply closer contact with the source of divine inspiration. This sort of religious practice is not bound by the "restrictive" canons of established truths stated in propositional form. Rather, paradox

25. Ibid., p. 130.
26. Ibid., p. 131.

and ambiguity are sought as the way to reach higher levels of religious being. They accept a few theological dogmas as a platform from which to proceed to more intimate communication with God. Sometimes "speaking in tongues" is translatable into ordinary language by those endowed with this "gift." However this is often impossible, and these untranslatable communications are the apotheosis of the personal contact with the Divinity.

Formally, Pentecostals believe in a premillenarian version of the Second Advent but espouse this doctrine without passion and certainly do not inject a good deal of specific theological content into this general notion of the final days and the Last Judgment. They interpret this doctrine in ways which mitigate its apocalyptic, catastrophic overtones. Instead of the vision of a cataclysmic conflagration which will consume the wicked, Pentecostals perceive the last days in relatively neutral tones. According to the sermons I heard, God will one day rid the earth of its remaining evil-doers. However, Pentecostals add that the primary force that will renew mankind is the spiritual elect—those "born again" Christians who carry Christ's message of redemption to the world. The world will be purified not by the Adventist fire but by the hope inherent in the Word. For many Pentecostal groups, the revival service is the principal weapon in the battle against widespread religious indifference and against the forces of the Devil. According to many Pentecostals, the Devil uses communism to attack "true" Christianity. In the words of one revivalist:

It is important to realize that the end of the world is soon to come, but this should not be our primary concern. We should be doing the work of winning and saving souls for Christ. During the Second World War they thought at first that Mussolini, and then Hitler, and finally that Stalin was the Anti-Christ who was to appear in the last days. The moral of all this is that we should be less concerned with our position in this situation of the last days but rather with the work that must be done, according to Christ's order to his disciples that these days are yet to come. [She then ridicules those who want to know the exact date because it is just not that crucial]; what is crucial is the visitation of the Spirit right here among us. The Bible says that the confrontation will be among two forces and that nation will rise against nation—this applies to the present inasmuch as the real enemy is not Russia but Communism. In this sense we are in the last days but we should go out and win the world for Christ—convert the masses. Our desire is a spiritual reawakening and revival, first in this neighborhood and in the city and then in the world.

Pentecostals, then, adhere to a very diluted form of Adventism. Almost invariably, mention of the Second Coming stimulates Pentecostals to restate their commitment to work unceasingly to convert *all* sinners before Christ returns to earth. Although they realize that this ideal cannot be completely achieved in their lifetime, they believe that they eventually can transform the world through evangelical activity.

Most of my informants hoped to become "missionaries" who would lead revivals in this country and abroad. They argue that a missionary should emphasize the positive, benign, hopeful aspects of Christ's message. They rarely warn those who fail to respond to their point of view that sinners are destined to be destroyed by God. The Second Advent is not an imminent reality.

Unlike Seventh-day Adventists, Pentecostals accept the conventional, orthodox Christian vision of heaven and hell:

Movements which accept the likelihood of an early second advent, and admit this to the forefront of their stated beliefs, sometimes deny, or at least ignore, the ordinary eschatological teachings of more orthodox Christianity. They tend to rely on the advent and the subsequent resurrection of believers to provide them with an eschatology. Elim stands in a more orthodox position, and preaches both Heaven and Hell as definite locations where men receive their just deserts for their earthly belief or unbelief.[27]

Although Pentecostals believe in heaven as a reward and hell as a punishment in the afterlife, they are much more interested in the spiritual equivalents of heaven and hell on earth. Briefly, heaven is the same as salvation in the present: a oneness with Jesus realized in the spiritual baptism in all its dimensions. Hell or damnation is equivalent to a feeling of separation from Jesus and distance from the Holy Spirit.

In summary, Pentecostal theology focuses on the experience of spiritual love for Jesus and through him salvation for all

27. Wilson, *Sects and Society*, p. 19.

men. This intense, personal relationship with God is consummated in the Spirit baptism. Although Pentecostals recognize the universality of human depravity, they also believe that through Christ man can escape the limitations of his sinful flesh. The "natural man" becomes "perfect" in Christ. Thus Spirit baptism assumes central theological significance in this religious system because the attendant spiritual "gifts" constitute the most concrete demonstration of the believer's relationship with God. This accounts not only for the emotional orientation of this religious system but also for its tendency to employ doctrine as an instrument which mobilizes the believer's desire to overcome any inner reluctance to seek God completely—to put himself in a totally submissive and responsive position in his relationship with God:

> The ordinary member is less concerned with the doctrine than with subjective experience—the conviction of, sorrow for, confession of, atonement for, and redemption from, sin. And this is to be achieved by belief on Jesus and His sacrifice. . . . It is in terms of the experience of conversion, Holy Ghost baptism, and the exercise of spiritual gifts that Elimites understand their adherence, rather than in terms of specific doctrines which are prescribed or proscribed.[28]

Pentecostal Ideology

I have already discussed some of the ideological aspects of Pentecostal belief in the section devoted to theology; however, the distinction between theology and ideology is analytic. The ideological aspects of religious belief emerge when assumptions about man's relationship to supernatural forces are adjusted to nonsacred realities. That is, a religious ideology consists of those sacred beliefs which define the salient aspects of the social environment and, to a certain extent, enable its adherents to shape it. One cannot easily sort religious notions into metaphysical and ideological categories without considerable overlap, because they are not discrete, bounded cognitive (metaphysical) and evaluative (ideological) statements. Following Parsons, I think that they are distinguished by the relative emphasis placed upon either of these dimensions. The following examination of

28. Ibid., p. 28.

Pentecostal ideology expands certain themes already evident in the foregoing discussion of their theology.

Unlike Seventh-day Adventism, Pentecostalism does not provide its followers with unequivocal ethical imperatives for salvation which, at the same time, tell them what it takes to become a "success" in this world. Pentecostal ideology consists of a positive status assertion coupled with an implicit status denial. It is concerned with those personal qualities which mark this group off from the rest of humanity. Pentecostal ideology says that a person's spiritual abilities rather than his economic accomplishments should determine his fundamental worth. Furthermore, it subtly denies that its adherents share devalued social qualities with those among the "lower" classes who do not cultivate special religious virtues.

For Seventh-day Adventist ideology, the ethical implications of a person's "works" establish the principal point of articulation between formal theology and secular attitudes. The essential meaning of Pentecostal ideology lies in its negation of the relevance of a person's "works" for his salvation. This accounts for the paucity of moral prescriptions in Pentecostal ideology. Of course, Pentecostals are supposed to avoid all worldly entanglements which would work against the efficacy of the Spirit baptism. But they do so because they see secular interests as distractions from truly valuable spiritual concerns and not because they see most worldly distractions as evil.

For example, the members and the minister of the small congregation discussed the relative merits and the spiritual risks of various forms of recreation and entertainment. They were quite receptive to television and would watch most programs except those which were markedly sexual or violent. Their attitudes toward most innocuous forms of recreation were similar; they did not feel compelled to spend all their leisure time in spiritually profitable ways.

Pentecostal ideology does not point to the believer's moral habits as the crucial sign of his spiritual status. Pentecostals believe that as long as a person's conduct remains within the normal boundaries of propriety, it has an insignificant bearing upon his candidacy for salvation. What matters, Pentecostal preachers constantly tell their congregations, is the believer's efforts to strengthen and improve his natural receptivity to Jesus and hence to the Holy Spirit. Thus, according to Pentecostal ideology, a person who truly desires salvation does not need to worry about immediately reforming his minor vices, and he can even postpone resolving major moral deficiencies in his life until well after the Holy Spirit has had a chance to change his character.

Pentecostals in the congregations I studied felt that the intrinsic meaning of the multitude of concrete sins was the same: separation from God. The minister in the small congregation once ran down a list of venial sins, pointing out that in each instance the thought which lies behind the deed is detestable regardless of whether or not one commits the sinful act. In his opinion, wrong feelings and behavior disrupt "the body of Christ" and thereby render worship ineffective. In this list of sins he included such emotions as anger and jealousy, because they tended to inhibit the spiritual capacities of the believer as well as interfere with the group's access to the Spirit. He concluded that the gravest sin is "to think what you want. It is what He wants; it is Jesus in you that is your only chance to get to the Lord."

Unlike Seventh-day Adventists, Pentecostals do not feel that vices, such as smoking, are intimately associated with the principle of wickedness, the Devil, or that anyone who practices one of these vices is necessarily aligned with the forces of evil. Consequently, the groups I studied accepted persons who still led lives marred by some sort of moral irregularity. For instance, the minister of the small congregation once anticipated what he thought would be my negative response to a member of his congregation who smoked in his house. He said that one of the things which comes from "moving in the Spirit" is understanding and love for others, and he felt that in time this member would give up smoking owing to the cumulative effect of the holiness inherent in spiritual baptism. But, he added, even if he does not forsake this habit, it is a trivial matter when placed against the issue of salvation through faith in and openness to Jesus. A few of my informants in the larger group confided that they led very "depraved" lives when they first joined the group and were extremely relieved when the leader did not demand instant reform. Instead, they were warmly greeted by other members of the group who talked about the positive aspects of their worship rather than the negative consequences of sin. One of my informants could not entirely give up his sinful inclinations but nevertheless was not excluded from the group. He suffered from what he felt was his unworthiness and sought to complete the process of change which identifies a "born again" Christian.

This material illustrates a Pentecostal attitude which is expressed in diverse ways. Despite the reputation that fundamentalist, evangelical churches have for moral rigidity, these Pentecostal congregations not only were relatively tolerant of moral deviations but also were more concerned with the intrapersonal than the interpersonal effects of religious commitment. To put this another way, the seeming Pentecostal ethical laxness, when compared to Seventh-day Adventists and to Holiness groups as well, is not due to an intrinsic disregard for fundamental moral standards. On the contrary, Pentecostals feel that they are more likely to observe these norms than others because they have been filled with the holiness inherent in the Spirit baptism. They are simply much more interested in the psychological qualities of sacred states of being than in the implications of religious belief for everyday conduct.

Compared to that of Seventh-day Adventism, the entire ethical subsystem of Pentecostal theology is underdeveloped. There is no set of morally sanctioned ways to employ one's personal resources, to make career choices, to use time, or to work. The Pentecostal is simply enjoined to love his fellowman; but, they insist, true love for one's friends and associates can come only from a prior love for Christ. There is usually no further specification, besides the prohibitions on the usual human vices, about those areas in which the believer who desires salvation must strive and about those he must shun.

On the whole, my informants did not endow hard work, saving, and careful investment with any extraordinary moral value. As long as a man did not squander his money on things like drink or cards and worked to support his family, Pentecostals felt there is nothing wrong in purchasing those material comforts he can afford instead of saving money for more "profitable" purposes. Willems notes that for Pentecostals in Chile and Brazil "the adoption of ascetic attitudes did not necessarily imply renouncement of all hedonistic values; the objective to be attained was not freedom from wants but the substitution of permissible gratifications for 'illicit' pleasures."[29] Although Pentecostals often admired those who were financially successful, they did not perceive the attributes of the ethically constrained businessman as similar to those which distinguish the elect. Willems points out that although Pentecostals are usually honest and hard working they lack the innovative attitudes characteristic of businessmen.

Instead of considering saving a moral necessity, the leaders of both Pentecostal congregations held that the ability to give money to others *even when you could not really afford it* was the essence of Christian charity. Sermons urged the members of the congregation to yield completely to their generous impulses because those who truly love Jesus trust him completely. Revivalists who visited the large congregation continually pressed members to *overcommit* themselves to the church building fund.

The rationale for this demand bears upon the nature of Pentecostal ideology. Pentecostals are taught to believe that God will provide for those who are willing to give themselves entirely to his care and therefore are also willing to respond immediately to the promptings of the Spirit. Innumerable testimonies were given by sect members about how they used a large sum for a worthy purpose (which usually was related to church activities) and were left without enough money for daily expenses. Miraculously, the necessary money came from an entirely unexpected source, and Pentecostals asserted that God was the force behind this gift. Of course, I never heard a testimony about unrewarded excessive generosity. Many members told stories about how they had lost their jobs and faced economic

29. Willems, *Followers of the New Faith*, p. 173.

collapse and just before they fell into despair, they got new and better jobs. They felt that their good fortune was entirely due to their complete faith in God's ability to protect and care for them, and they tended to discount the importance of any effort they made to remedy a distressing situation.

As we have seen, Pentecostal ideology does not encourage long-range economic planning and does not endow rational economic decisions with any special moral virtue. In fact, it actively discourages enduring commitments to absorbing occupational careers. From talking to Pentecostals, one gets the impression that they feel one job is much like another except that some pay more and others pay less. Unlike Seventh-day Adventists, Pentecostals would never argue that a person reveals his spiritual capacities in his job. They leave the occupational world far behind once they step across the church threshold.

This insensitivity to the ethical dimensions of work derives from the notion that the believer's first responsibility is to remain open to Jesus' influence. In concrete terms this means he should allow Jesus to determine the best uses for all his personal resources. Furthermore, Pentecostals do not postulate a relatively fixed set of priorities for the use of money, and thus their ideas about what it should be spent for are contingent upon circumstances.

At a more general level of ideological commitment, Pentecostalism encourages its adherents not to worry about their financial problems because this sort of concern invariably detracts from man's raison d'être: union with God. If a person searches for Jesus at every opportunity and places the rest in his hands, then Pentecostal ideology maintains that God will take care of his primary material needs. Pentecostal ideology does not promise, however, that God will give him great riches or even a comparatively high standard of living.

Earlier in this chapter I argued that the basic meaning of Pentecostal ideology was revealed by a positive and a negative status assertion. Positively, Pentecostal ideology declares that its members' worth should be judged on the basis of present spiritual attainments; that is, their claims to general social esteem and to a "respectable" position in the larger society are assured by their ability to communicate with God. Negatively, Pentecostal ideology claims that persons who have such a special relationship with God cannot be placed in terms of ordinary status criteria; that is, education, manners, life style, occupation, income.

These themes were often discernible in sermons and Pentecostal meetings as well as in informal conversations. For example, at meetings of the Full Gospel Business Men's Association (a nondenominational group with a decidedly Pentecostal orientation), there was almost no discussion about the connections between the members' religious teachings and those morally approved practical virtues which lead to success in the business world. Rather, they talked incessantly about the significance of spiritual baptism. They stressed its growing acceptance among some congregations which belong to the established denominations.[30] Speakers made a point of the growing number of "well-to-do" persons who attend Full Gospel conventions, and they noted that some of these normally reserved persons are sometimes overcome with the Spirit baptism in hotel elevators. Speakers would often refer to "hot" Episcopalians or Presbyterians as if to say these persons belong to prestigious and powerful denominations and yet are not afraid to recognize and demonstrate the highest spiritual knowledge available to man. They claim that "men and women of all faiths; professors, doctors, dentists, and businessmen are receiving this experience." In short, they attempt to convince themselves and others that the Spirit baptism confers unique prestige and that those who achieve something in other spheres of life are beginning to realize that this worship is consonant with their position in society—that the Spirit baptism is not a mark of social marginality.

Although this group called itself a businessmen's association, its members on the whole were not particularly affluent. Those I knew personally were skilled workers, lower white-collar work-

30. See W. A. Sadler, "Glossolalia and Possession: An Appeal to the Episcopal Study Commission," *Journal for the Scientific Study of Religion* 4 (1964), for an interesting discussion of official Episcopal reactions to glossolalia in their church.

ers, or small businessmen who did not have access to considerable capital. They buttressed their conception of their place in the societal status hierarchy by constant but guarded references to the "poor," with whom, it is hardly necessary to say, they did not identify themselves. They divided the "poor" into two groups. The first is composed of extremely poor people who are willing to make great financial sacrifices for evangelical activities. They are usually in foreign lands where people "go to bed hungry every night" and live amid great poverty, but they are capable of giving what little they have to the local missionary. The assembly was often told to emulate their generosity because they had so much more to give. In a very subtle way, this confirms the Pentecostal's perception of his status as different from that of the socially and economically disadvantaged strata. He is told that he is (comparatively) financially secure and (relatively) prosperous, and this supports his identification with the middle class. Perhaps this status protest (against identification with those strata subject to economic vicissitudes and social obscurity) explains why a group which has so little in the way of economic resources and social privileges so vehemently supports "free enterprise" and attacks "socialism, communism and the welfare state." In my opinion, this is a symbolic means of claiming membership in and allegiance to those social strata which are economically self-sufficient and which are not in a dependent relationship to private and public charity. Their interest in conservative political doctrine is generally minimal and is limited to expressions of solidarity with those who oppose "Godless communism" abroad and "creeping socialism" in this country. They are very anxious about establishing a community of symbolic interests with those who manifest the middle-class attributes of social and economic stability and reliability.

The irreligious poor were often described as people of meager means who spend much of their money on drink and other "degrading" entertainments. My informants vigorously objected to what they perceived as a pattern of frequent fighting between husbands and wives of this stratum. The minister of the small congregation was insistent on the proper relationship between husbands and wives. Wives should be retiring and obedient but not servile, and husbands should make all important decisions. According to Pentecostal opinion, this arrangement makes them unlike those working-class families where wives assert their independence to the detriment of family unity. In short, Pentecostals differentiate their own family life from what they perceive as the conflict-ridden and unstable relationships of the "lower" classes because it is yet another way of symbolically affirming their inherent respectability. Besides, there is an element of status compensation in this strong emphasis on the patriarchal family. It gives men a position of influence and importance in their homes even though they may very well occupy a subordinate position in the occupational realm. The power to make all important decisions not only gives them independence and authority they may lack on the job but also is characteristic of the general ethos of self-determination of the middle classes. To Pentecostals the capacity to assume responsibility for an entire family unit is a middle-class trait.

The same distinction between oneself and socially disesteemed groups, with whom one might be classed on the basis of purely external status criteria, is expressed in a paternalistic attitude toward the irreligious poor. Pentecostals see these people as beneath them morally and socially but not beyond the pale of redemption and social upgrading. Importantly, Pentecostals assert that the level of one's income is irrelevant to status improvement. All one needs to do is open his heart to Jesus and the transformation in his character follows almost automatically. The convert does not need to exert a great deal of effort over a long period of time to improve his habits and his everyday conduct. The baptism of the Spirit insures a life filled with holiness and hence one which is eminently worthy and admirable. The Pentecostal feels that he deserves general esteem and moral approbation on this basis alone. There is no ascetic life plan essential for salvation: the Pentecostal does not have to defer many of the ordinary satisfactions or material comforts available to him. Salvation occurs in the present; the honor of having been chosen by God as one of the elect is an immediate rather than a remote pleasure. Everything in Pentecostal ideology, then, works to assure the believer that whatever personal and spiritual gains he is to derive from religious activity, he will derive now. Consequently, he is not told that his self-esteem depends upon the end result of a long process of self-improvement; once he is filled with the Holy Ghost he is entitled to an elevated status as one of God's favorite followers of Christ.

The attitude of Pentecostals toward the irreligious poor is curiously ambiguous at first glance. Sermons are full of derogatory and often belittling remarks about these people, and yet the same speaker will urge the members to concentrate their evangelical energies upon them. In the first place, it is fairly obvious that this is one group to whom the Pentecostals can feel superior but to whom they also can feel akin. They almost can say that "there but for the grace of God go I." There is a certain implicit moral superiority in reaching *down* to save those who are unable to give their existence "meaning" and "purpose." There are few status gains to be gotten from attempting to save those who are socially superior to oneself, so Pentecostals designate those who are "down and out" as the prime group whom they can lift up through the use of Spirit baptism.

On a more speculative level, I believe that part of the significance of the Pentecostal attitude toward the disadvantaged and unfortunate is perhaps related to what they perceive as an unfair status discrepancy. Almost all the members of the groups I studied are white and literate, and yet for the most part they are socially anonymous and powerless people. They feel that they deserve more influence and recognition than our society accords them. The effect is analogous to the motive for the temperance movement. According to Gusfield, this movement lost its gradualist, reformist character once the immigrant groups it was trying to change achieved some success and influence in American society.[31] It then adopted a harsh, legalistic attitude toward drinking and tried to impose its moral standards upon the entire society in a futile effort to reestablish the dominant position that the members of this group once occupied in American society. So too, it is not difficult to imagine that many Pentecostals (who lack the economic qualifications but have the racial and religious

31. Joseph Gusfield, *Symbolic Crusade* (Urbana: University of Illinois Press, 1963).

attributes which once made identification with dominant social strata much more likely) feel that the only way to assert their rightful claim to a prestigious position in society is to transform the moral and spiritual lives of those whose entire mode of existence excludes them from respectable company. Instead of expressing their frustration against an invulnerable target, the affluent, educated middle class, Pentecostals resolve their feelings of status deprivation by expressing hostility toward those groups whose behavior and life style implicitly reject middle-class standards and by trying to convince themselves that their religious accomplishments give them the moral and social background necessary to elevate those below them. In essence, this is a vicarious way of establishing status equality with the more privileged and prestigious middle class without having to reveal the grounds on which they posit this status parity. In other words, Pentecostals do not come right out and say "although we do not have the money and social graces normally associated with a dominant status in the larger society, our spiritual excellence makes us at least equal to if not better than those whose status claims rest upon purely secular accomplishments."

Perhaps the most common and certainly the most significant theme in Pentecostal ideology is revealed by their repeated assertions that "Christ is not concerned with your color, with the way you dress, with the kind of car you drive, with where you live—just whether you are born again or not." They constantly say that all that matters about a person is whether "he is full of the Holy Ghost" and whether "he is on fire for God." This indicates their opposition to the prevailing idea that a man creates his primary status identity through his activities in the economic world.[32]

Pentecostals declare that a person establishes his primary status identity through his ability to command the special attention of God and to display and employ special supernatural

32. A person's position in the societal prestige hierarchy is most immediately related to his occupation. By a person's primary status identity I mean those personal traits and qualities which derive from his degree of competence in the occupational sphere and which our culture endows with moral significance. Hence, the greater his competence the more esteem the actor and others are likely to feel he merits.

powers which benefit mankind. For Pentecostals these talents are infinitely superior to others: "the Holy Ghost is dynamite; it is power; it blows you up." Pentecostal ideology, then, claims that a man's fundamental worth is created by his activities in the sacred rather than the secular domain. By implication, it holds that a person's standing according to conventional status criteria is irrelevant as long as he possesses the Holy Spirit and its gifts.

In summary, Pentecostal ideology lacks an ethically binding, comprehensive pattern for secular conduct.[33] It defines proper behavior but, unlike Seventh-day Adventism, it does not direct the believer to specific secular goals.[34] It does not threaten grave supernatural penalties for those who deviate from the narrow path which leads directly to a dual success—in the secular and sacred realms. Of course this does not mean that Pentecostal ideology does not invest the boundaries of permissible behavior with considerable import.[35] Although it accepts these moral

33. Wilson says that "relatively little importance is attached to ethical teaching as such in the Elim movement. . . . What the individual believes, not what he does, will be the criterion on which graduation to future existence will be decided. In particular the possession of the charismatic phenomena tends to be considered as more important than the works of supererogation. For such possession is a direct evidence of grace. That Elim members should lead especially saintly lives, devote themselves to philanthropic works, or be particularly kind and helpful, is not the subject of specific exhortation, whether in practice many members of the movement do conduct themselves in this fashion or not." *Sects and Society*, p. 77.
34. Wilson states that "earning-patterns and producing-patterns are not even considered as activity upon which religion should pronounce so long as honesty is observed; the weight of religiously prescribed restrictions falls on expenditure of leisure time, it is the sphere in which the evangelical feels himself particularly competent to judge. Leisure and leisure habits are the particular point at which activity is regarded as 'worldly': the activities of labour and money earning are simple economic necessities, and on these no stricture is made. . . . Labour is a mere contractual necessity, virtually regarded as outside the free-will area of the individual's own real interests." Ibid., pp. 79–80.
35. Wilson notes that "Elim sermons are gospel sermons, expounding the Scriptures, rather than discourses on morality, social behavior or social problems. . . . The Elim Evangel over its many years of publication has little to say about morality, except by way of condemning the laxness in the application of socially accepted standards. Good works are useless. . . . But Elim does quite pronouncedly change the activities of those who are won to the movement, by providing new occupations within the movement itself. It does not transform men's characters in conversion, and so send

standards, it nonetheless urges the believer to assess his essential worth in terms of his supernatural commitments and achievements. Therefore, as Wilson points out, Pentecostal ideology is remarkably devoid of positive ethical content because it sees the latter as the direct consequence of spiritual states of being:

The only tenet of Elim which has a distinctly ethical content is one which did not appear in the original articles of faith: It asserts that every believer "should produce the ninefold fruits of the Spirit: love, joy, peace, long-suffering, gentleness, goodness, faith, meekness, temperance." For Elim belief itself implies sanctification and this is independent of actual behavior; but these particular virtues should develop afterwards. Typical of fundamentalism, the use of these fruits of the Spirit is seen more in a religious than in a social context: "The absence of the fruit has been prolifically a cause of much damage in Church of God, especially when the inspirational gifts of the Spirit are in operation." In this regard temperance is considered of particular importance. The fruit is not regarded as an evidence of being born again, nor of the baptism of the Holy Ghost, both of which experiences are attested by inward assurance of God's touch, rather than by outward manner of living. The fruit should appear in the believer who has had Holy Ghost "in-filling," but it constitutes no evidence of such an experience, and, in any case, as a prominent Pentecostalist has put it, "fruit takes time to grow." [36]

---

them back into the world with new principles and values; rather it finds them new ways of employing their time, and this not for the good of the world, or of their work, but more specifically for the Elim movement and for evangelical Christianity." Ibid., pp. 77–78.

36. Ibid., pp. 17–18.

6 Socioeconomic Status and Sect Affiliation

The Organization of the Seventh-day Adventist and Pentecostal Congregations

This chapter describes the status trajectory of my Pentecostal and Seventh-day Adventist informants. The concept of a status trajectory refers to a person's or a group's movement through the socioeconomic order. This notion underscores the fact that status gain, loss, and maintenance is a historical process. Social honor is never bestowed with finality; no one can make future claims on the deference of others with absolute certainty. It is the variable as well as the gratifying character of social status which makes it a subject of universal fascination and intrigue. Regardless of the rapidity with which wealth and power are accumulated, they are not automatically and inevitably translated into prestige. Social status is ordinarily acquired and consolidated or diminished and lost over a considerable length of time, and it is during this period that life styles are elaborated as the symbolic tokens of material achievement. Although it is only one of a number of appropriate indexes, albeit a reliable one in this society, I shall use an individual's occupational career as the critical indicator of the direction of his status trajectory. Although I do not have systematic data on this aspect of the process, the idea of a status trajectory connotes certain intangible social techniques, such as the sort of impression management commonly associated with etiquette, that escape conventional measures of occupational mobility.

I will focus on subjective aspects of the status trajectory of these Pentecostals and Seventh-day Adventists: their view of where they have been, where they are now, and where they hope to go in the occupational system. Since my information is drawn from a small number of scheduled interviews which were definitely skewed toward the active, theologically articulate members of these groups, I cannot claim that my results are representative of these churches. Even if they are, I have no data which would enable me to determine how representative these churches are of the larger Pentecostal and Seventh-day Adventist movements in this country. Nevertheless, until it is proved otherwise by further research, it seems safe to say that these Pentecostals and Seventh-day Adventists fitted the descriptions other scholars have given of the social and economic characteristics of the members of these religious movements.

At the risk of some repetition, I would like to point out that this chapter is not meant to prove my thesis that Seventh-day Adventist and Pentecostal sect affiliation is correlated with positive and negative status expectations, respectively. Even if this is true, these are necessary but not sufficient conditions for the adoption of either a Pentecostal or an Adventist religious outlook. Nonetheless, I think that the experiences of my informants in the occupational system and their aspirations for future improvement are highly consistent with the meaning and social implications of their religious orientations.

Before examining the economic backgrounds, present occupational situations, and social aspirations of my informants, I will describe the organization of these churches, in terms general enough to disguise their identity. Since most sect members do not enthusiastically subscribe to the ethos of the public, impartial inquiry of contemporary science, in return for their cooperation I feel obligated to try to conceal the identity of these congregations.

The Seventh-day Adventist church is in a very deteriorated part of the central section of a midwestern city. The church building, however, is very substantial, well appointed, and kept in almost perfect repair. This group has been attempting to sell the church for some time but cannot find a local congregation which can obtain a bank mortgage. Besides, some members have a strong sentimental attachment to this building because they formerly lived in the area and grew up in the church. Now most of them live in other parts of the city rather far away but prefer to travel considerable distances to this church instead of worshiping in Seventh-day Adventist churches closer to their homes. They do so because they feel that this church is especially warm and friendly; many members have relatives and old friends in the congregation and the current pastor grew up there.

During the first phase of fieldwork, I spent a good deal of time visiting inner- and outer-city Seventh-day Adventist groups. I decided to study this "ethnic" inner-city group because its pastor and members were openly and deeply committed to the millenarian vision which gives this religious movement its theological distinctiveness. The style of outer-city congregations was, by contrast, so tempered that I could not easily gauge the strength of their conviction about the imminence of the Second Advent of Christ. Since the focus of the study is the social concomitants and consequences of religious doctrines, I naturally gravitated to a group whose members were obviously dedicated to its fundamental teachings. At the time I studied it, the church had about ninety members, of which a smaller group of about fifteen families provided the leadership in church activities. My informants were drawn from this group.

The ethnic designation of this and similar churches reflects the historical process of the social segregation of immigrants in American cities and the subsequent growth of voluntary organizations based upon common cultural backgrounds. The Seventh-day Adventist movement capitalized on the tendency of ethnic groups to form their own churches by sending a specially prepared evangelist to minister to the particular needs of this community.

The church itself is over fifty years old and was started by a woman evangelist who spoke the congregation's native tongue but was from an Anglo-Saxon background. She is presently viewed with great affection by the first- and second-generation members who knew her personally (she is dead now). She taught many of the older members of the congregation to read and write, and possibly even the first members of the group in this community were distinguished by their intense desire to improve themselves. Importantly, my informants did not regard her as an agent of Americanization but as a person who saw the need for an ethnic church in an area which was traditionally hostile to all forms of Protestant missionary work.

I discovered no "assimilationist" rhetoric in this group. Its members considered themselves Americans in every sense of the word and viewed their status as a natural right. All but a few of the older members spoke English without any discernible accent, and most lived in areas of the city which did not have a special ethnic character. Like many of the other American sons and grandsons of immigrants, they were interested in the country their fathers or grandfathers left and hoped to visit it as tourists. For this group, ethnicity legitimates its familial orientation. Whether the members belong to this ethnic group or not, most of them are related by ties of blood, marriage, or long-term friendship, and they want to maintain this arrangement. They value the intimacy that is associated with a common national origin but that actually rests upon kinship and friendship.

This church was predominantly drawn from people of a southern European ancestry but had a considerable number of members who were Mexican, Irish, Anglo-Saxon, and so forth, most of whom were recruited to the church as affinals of members. In my opinion, ethnicity per se had relatively little bearing upon their present religious affiliation. These people did not join the Seventh-day Adventist movement because they sought to deny their relatively lowly ethinic origins. In the first place, they are proud of their southern European background and anyone who has visited their homeland is considered a minor celebrity. Second, they do not cut themselves off from their non-Seventh-day Adventist relatives. Admittedly, close and intimate relationships are often attenuated by religious differences, but not one of my informants thought this was just cause to end contact. In fact, my informants often faced a serious dilemma. To maintain family harmony they avoided religious subjects. Yet these had to be discussed if they were to save their relatives. To resolve this problem, they would discuss salvation in general terms and leave topics such as the role the Catholic church played in the Devil's scheme for subverting Christ for those who had evidenced a desire to convert. In this way they did not completely alienate their relatives and, at the same time, fulfilled at least their minimal duties to the church. Finally, this group was known and actively identified itself as the Southern European Church in the Midwest Seventh-day Adventist movement. Although almost all the members lived closer to nonethnic churches and could easily have joined one, they preferred to maintain an ethnic subcommunity in this religious movement.

In the Seventh-day Adventist movement, it is common to form a church on an ethnic base. However, anyone is free to join any Seventh-day Adventist church as long as he meets its ethical and doctrinal requirements. There is one exception to this rule—the Seventh-day Adventist church has racially segregated congregations. However, in the church I studied one black member strenuously argued that he was West Indian and therefore not Negro. Since no one wanted to dispute the matter with him, he was accepted as a full member of the congregation, and his family was active in various church-related groups.

This church, like many ethnic churches in the Seventh-day Adventist movement, has foreign-language services for its older members. Otherwise, the worship of the church is conducted almost entirely in English, with the exception of a prayer given in the native tongue by a member of the older generation. In general, I could find no distinctive ethnic cast to the activities of this congregation beyond a desire to convert members of their ethnic group and an interest in the religious affairs of their European homeland. As in much of American life, ethnic symbolism was gastronomic; they identified ethnic origins with preference in food.

All Seventh-day Adventist churches have a denominational

institutional structure. This form of religious organization fits their predilection for orderly, predictable, and rational allocation of religious energies and economic resources. It also creates a stable, enduring source of religious authority which adjudicates disagreements within the movement. This structure is particularly resistant to ideological change. Since all doctrinal innovations must gain the acceptance of a religious bureaucracy whose interests lie in theological continuity, it is doubtful that even in times of great stress would this professional hierarchy allow any cognitive resynthesis of traditional ideology to generate a large schismatic body within the church. Although Seventh-day Adventism was originally a revitalization movement—an attempt to protect a set of beliefs from "mazeway disintegration"—it is unlikely that another visionary like Mrs. White could spontaneously reformulate Seventh-day Adventist doctrine and form a new sect.[1] All decisions about the proper theological response to changing conditions have been thoroughly institutionalized.

Besides the local church board headed by the pastor which governs its affairs, there are four separate levels of authority within the movement: the local conference covers all churches in a state; the union conference embraces churches in several states (or similar geographical areas in other parts of the world); the division conference includes the local and union conferences in a large section of the world; and finally the general conference contains all the Seventh-day Adventist churches in the world. Serious disputes or grievances are settled at each level and if one of the parties is not satisfied with the solution, he can appeal to the next higher level of authority. The world conference is the final court of appeal.

Seventh-day Adventists describe their form of church government as representative and distinguish it from episcopal organizations headed by bishops, from congregational churches, where the local group has ultimate authority, and from papal government, which is self-explanatory. Every Seventh-day Adventist member in good standing is able to vote for church officers,

1. For a cogent explanation of the role of cognitive processes in the genesis of religious movements see Anthony Wallace, "Revitalization Movements," *American Anthropologist* 58 (1958).

except for the pastor, who is appointed and is usually shifted to a new post every few years. The pastor, who is the ranking church officer, selects delegates to the local conference, the local conferences select delegates to the union conference, and so on. Each conference has full-time administrative officers who direct the day-to-day church operations and exercise considerable influence on all major church decisions.

The basis for membership in the Seventh-day Adventist church is not only a potential member's desire to join but also his ability to live up to its standards:

> Any church that votes a letter [of recommendation] to a member, and then makes a notation on the letter calling attention to some point on which the member fails, thereby confesses its own weakness and slackness in properly looking after the spiritual welfare of its members, and in exercising proper discipline where a member is not living up to his membership vows. . . . Great care should be exercised in receiving members on profession of faith, especially if they have formerly been members of some other church in the denomination. Instances are not lacking of persons disfellowshipped from some church later presenting themselves to other churches for membership on profession of faith. Without confessing their wrongs or making amends in any way, they thus find their way back into the church, and the whole intent and purpose of church discipline is outraged and set at naught.[2]

Is such an enduring structure a contradiction? How can they prepare for the imminent millennium and still construct such a permanent church organization? However, efficient organization is consonant with their principles; they extol foresight and planning in all human activities. This even applies to the member's preparation for death, although there is a note of profit for the church in the following advice:

> To dispose of one's property and to make preparations for one's future life, for the family and dependents, and for the church and the cause of God, is one of the most important and responsible acts of life.[3]

Many of the Holiness churches I visited in the early stages of the fieldwork called themselves Pentecostal (particularly some

2. *Seventh-day Adventist Church Manual*, n.p. (1932), 83–85.
3. Ibid., p. 107.

of those affiliated with the various Churches of God). It soon became apparent that the experience of the "in-filling" of the Holy Ghost was an ancillary aspect of their worship. These groups did not focus exclusively on this experience but rather sought to transform their adherents' moral outlook and social demeanor. Thus, I sought and found groups which were organized to promote the "in-filling" in *every* believer and whose service was designed to realize this end.

Incidentally, it is not easy to locate Pentecostal churches, because many do not have any connections with larger religious organizations. Negro and Puerto Rican Pentecostal churches are numerous and quite visible, but I decided not to study obviously culturally stigmatized groups, although I believe that membership in these churches is at least partially explicable in terms of the theory advanced in this study. In this case, the theory faces an additional complication. The members of these groups may very well occupy a position in the stratification system of their local ethnic communities that is not congruent with their position in societal prestige and occupational hierarchies. One would have to know how this status inconsistency affected their perceptions of their position relative to the established middle classes, and, moreover, how they felt about their prospects for advancement in the larger society. This factor, in turn, would have to be weighed against their social standing within the ethnic community before the status deprivation theory could be applied.

By spending a good deal of time visiting Full Gospel churches, I eventually discovered the kind of group I was looking for. After a few abortive attempts to establish permanent contact with various Pentecostal groups, I located a group which was, on the whole, receptive to my presence at their services. I devoted most of my energies to this small storefront church. After I was accepted by the group or, more accurately, by its leader, I could move easily at its meetings. My relationship with the leader legitimated my intrusion, and without his active cooperation the undertaking would have failed. I sought a larger group principally to check my observations of the smaller group. The larger group brought visiting evangelists to "heal" those in need of special spiritual aid and to bring into the fold those not already convinced of the unique merits of their faith.

The larger group did not keep a membership role or attendance figures. Only a small core group of about 30 persons (a rough estimate on my part) were regular members, whereas the attendance varies from 40 to 150 persons at revival meetings. Although the core of the smaller group was relatively stable, a person who returned after a long absence from the group was considered a member if he showed a desire to remain with it. Thus, the boundary between a member and a nonmember in these groups is ambiguous, and hence membership figures for the Pentecostal movement must be interpreted very loosely.

In an interesting study of the Pentecostal movement, Gerlach and Hine note that there are several modes of association between Pentecostals that bypass conventional organizational boundaries:

> In short, each individual member has a personal network or family of brother Pentecostals linked together in varying degrees of closeness. There is much crossing over of individuals who attend worship services in churches other than their own and who attend midweek Bible study and prayer groups which characteristically include individuals from several types of Pentecostal, independent, or "hidden" groups. The membership of local groups is hence far from static but rather fluctuates as members come and go from one group to another, thereby forming links between all groups.[4]

Gerlach and Hine also point to the open constituency of traveling evangelists and of "nondenominational" associations such as the Full Gospel Businessmen's Fellowship. By participating in a variety of religious activities in different organizational settings, each Pentecostal tends to develop a fluid network of contacts with other Pentecostals. In contradistinction to Seventh-day Adventism, Pentecostalism is a more or less loosely structured congeries of groups whose members feel comfortable in switching their allegiances between churches within the movement.

I will call the small Pentecostal church the Full Gospel Assembly and the larger Pentecostal church the Full Gospel

4. Luther P. Gerlach and Virginia H. Hine, "Five Factors Crucial to the Growth and Spread of a Modern Religious Movement," *Journal for the Scientific Study of Religion* 7 (1968):27.

Tabernacle, although these are not their correct names. The small Pentecostal church was located in a rented frame building in a partly industrial, partly residential lower middle- and working-class neighborhood. The church itself occupied a storefront which looked out on a major thoroughfare. According to the minister, this site was chosen partly because he felt that this area might be a fertile mission ground. Later he admitted that he had made a mistake because the area is predominantly Catholic, and the group made several moves both within and out of the city during the period when I studied it. The church had a small apartment in the back where the minister and his family lived. Even though the church was far from elegant—a naked fluorescent lamp lighted an undecorated room which contained only some used bridge chairs and an old lectern—the congregation nevertheless had considerable difficulty raising the rent money. Incidentally, I might add that part of the difficulty this group had recruiting local converts was because an Italian Pentecostal church down the street had services in that language and thus had a competitive advantage over this congregation.

In contrast, the larger Pentecostal church was situated in a well-appointed, tastefully decorated building. This large, substantial building was formerly a sports arena and was recently acquired by this group and gradually converted into a church. The church is on a large commercial street which divides a working- and lower middle-class area from a zone of expensive high-rise apartments. This area is rather heterogeneous; it has cheap rooming houses, inexpensive transient hotels, old homes and flats, some in good repair and some not; and there are obviously affluent apartment buildings as well. Although some of the members of the larger church live in its general vicinity, no one gave proximity as the primary reason for attending this or any other church I studied.

Wilson says that it is difficult to categorize Pentecostal churches in terms of extreme values of the usual sociological variables—they tend to attract more women than men, the less rather than the better educated segments of the population, and so on. The congregations I studied were largely white Anglo-Saxon, but, like the Seventh-day Adventists, Pentecostal churches draw their adherents in this country from a wide variety of ethnic groups. However, I disagree with Wilson's judgment that the socioeconomic strata from which Pentecostalism draws its adherents are so diverse that there are no positive, significant correlations between class and Pentecostalism.[5] At least in the congregations I studied, the upper class, the upper middle, and what, for want of a better term, I will call the established middle classes (persons whose education, occupation, and income assure them of a reasonably secure and comfortable, though not especially affluent standard of living) were not in evidence in these churches or in any of the Pentecostal churches I visited which firmly believed in spiritual baptism and the "gifts." Nor did I find what can properly be called the lower lower class or lumpen-proletariat—persons whose lack of occupational skills, social contacts, inherited wealth, and education place them on the very bottom rung of the social hierarchy. If we include life styles and status aspirations as legitimate diagnostic signs of membership in a distinct social stratum, the members of these congregations appeared to me to be largely stable working- and lower middle-class persons interested in a respectable, middle-class way of life.[6] These observations should, of course, be either confirmed or refuted by a systematic survey of Pentecostal groups, but they are consistent with the reports of other observers.

In chapter 4 I described the theological rationale for the

5. Wilson says that "the socio-economic class from which Elim recruits is so widespread, and so many similar movements are in the field, that no correlation of distribution of Elim churches and social classes can be shown." *Sects and Society* (London: Heinemann, 1961), p. 99.

6. This is not to say that all the members of social strata objectively marginal to the middle classes identify with them. Richard Hamilton recently found that 52 percent of clerical and sales workers consider themselves part of the working class. Of those who identify with the middle class, Hamilton says that they "report somewhat greater income improvement in recent years than the working-class identifiers. Furthermore, the middle-class identifiers are slightly more likely than the other white collar subgroup to expect future improvement. . . . We find that despite high current earnings and greater optimism, the 'traditional' white collar group show less satisfaction than the working class identifying clerical-sales group or either subgroup of the skilled." "The Marginal Middle Class: A Reconsideration," *American Sociological Review* 31 (1966: 195).

organization of the smaller Pentecostal church in some detail, and now I would like to show that the same principles are at work in the larger and ostensibly more complex church. This group originally broke off from a large fundamentalist, ethnically based church in this area. The leader of the Full Gospel Tabernacle claims that the group left the larger church without bitterness but could not remain because it had lost its spirit. For a while they met in each other's homes and even considered a storefront location, but the leader felt that "God wanted a work that would reach the entire neighborhood; if it does not our entire effort is for nothing."

They decided to buy the present building in various stages, as they had comparatively little capital in the beginning. Using only a small section of the building, they started a series of well-publicized revival campaigns. The leader emphasized that they leave all outstanding problems about mortgage money to God and that so far they have had "a miracle of finances." Although the church members see their very successful fund-raising activities as direct confirmation of divine interest in their venture, their policy of bringing famous revivalists known for their money-raising talents cannot have hurt their bank account.

According to the leader, the church has one purpose: to open people to the Spirit regardless of their formal church affiliation. Instead of raiding other congregations and building a large membership roll, they hope to convert the unchurched people living in the area while leaving their doors open to everyone to come and worship on his own terms. At the present time, the leader said he was not asking people to give up their membership in other churches but added that this was a difficult problem and he was praying for divine guidance on it.

The administrative structure of this church is purposely kept largely invisible. Organizational decisions and financial arrangements are made by the leader and the nucleus which started the church. These deliberations are not open to general congregational discussion and approval. The tone of the apparent oligarchy is informal rather than authoritarian. They believe that this part of religious activity is intrinsically trivial and should be kept that way; that is, it should not become the focus of the religious energies of the congregation. The leader plays his role in very limited contexts. The only time he exercises any authority is in planning physical improvements for the church and in raising money for church operations. Otherwise he remains in the background and allows revivalists to order the service and related activities in any way that suits them.

According to the leader, those who are with them "100 percent of the way" will become members of the church and have some say in church administration, but he also feels that too many churches "have been broken up at business meetings." He wants people "who will worship and go out and do God's work rather than worry about the details of church administration." In short, he does not want active members to become so absorbed by the details of general church policy that these issues will create factions.

This logic lies behind the church's intention to do without a permanent pastor. In the members' opinion, a permanent minister identifies the church with a specific set of people, and they prefer to get speakers who will constantly bring new people into their services. Although this congregation has a more elaborate and less egalitarian organization than the Full Gospel Assembly, it retains the same interest in maximizing spiritual freedom and emotional spontaneity. It makes no demands on those who attend its services other than that they make themselves receptive to the Spirit; it hopes that they will contribute something to the work of the church. In fact, this group stresses the idea that the church exists to "demonstrate the *power* of the Holy Ghost" and this requires a constant supply of persons who either need spiritual healing or have never had or have lost contact with Christ. The entire organizational ethos of all Pentecostal groups, then, is to avoid any administrative arrangement which would reduce their contact with persons searching for some sort of intimate relationship with Jesus.

Pentecostal and Seventh-day Adventist Status Trajectories

In this section, I will examine the general patterns which emerged out of my interview data on Pentecostals' and Seventh-day Adventists' experience in the socioeconomic order and their expectations about advancing in it. More specifically, I will concentrate on mobility patterns and on a series of interrelated queries about what they see as possible for themselves and their children in the occupational sphere. I consider my findings as notes on secular life histories rather than as statistically reliable generalizations. That is, they show trends in the sect member's background, experience, and expectations which coalesce to shape his attitude toward his present and future social status.

Adventists

I found that I could best interview Seventh-day Adventist husbands and wives together, because generally both were interested in the interview. I was able to interview eight families. For some questions I have separate answers, since the husband and wife should be counted as separate informants; for others, where husband and wife showed no significant difference of opinion, I have for all practical purposes eight informants.

To assess the present position and the social history of my informants in the socioeconomic order, I looked at their own, their fathers', and their fathers' fathers' occupations. I noticed no appreciable upward movement between my informants' fathers' fathers' and their fathers' occupational status. In all cases where they could remember, both the husbands' and the wives' paternal grandfathers were manual laborers, peasant farmers, or petty artisans in Europe. Their fathers who emigrated to this country were all either manual laborers or tradesmen. However, the absence of upward occupational mobility may mask a vital bit of horizontal mobility. The move to this country may not be an unmistakable sign of interest in greater economic opportunity, but, in line with the contemporary American ideology, their children tend to interpret their parents' desire to come to this country as an attempt to give them a better life. This provides the motivational rationale for the desire to succeed where one's parents may have failed.

Except for two informants with manual jobs (another has a small painting business), these people all have clerical, sales, and managerial jobs, usually on a relatively low level of executive responsibility with various firms. None of these men are upper-echelon executives or earn large salaries; yet they often have considerable independence and responsibility on the job. Although they are white-collar workers, they do not feel that their future is limited. Nor do they feel that their talents have gone unappreciated; on the other hand, they point out that financial rewards are not always commensurate with increases in one's duties and freedom on the job. Interestingly, these men seem to gravitate toward small family firms rather than large corporations, partly because they are attracted to jobs where they can display their ability for hard work and partly because it is easier to arrange to take Saturdays off. Nonetheless, this has its disadvantages as well. Although they can make more money in the future, and some have been offered a few shares in the businesses as a means of keeping them attached to them, they feel that it is unlikely that they will become partners—these positions are reserved for members of the families who own them. In any case, for those men in the white-collar occupations mobility has been real and significant and, equally important, they do not feel that they have come to a complete stop or dead end in their careers.

In contrast to my white-collar informants, who were in their thirties and forties, the two manual workers and the self-employed painting contractor were considerably older. These men had at most some high-school education, whereas the rest of my informants had at least some college education and some had degrees in special fields, for example, business administration. The two manual workers made a good living and, in this respect, using the ratings that their jobs receive on Duncan-Hatt scales is a deceptive way of ascertaining their status identity and the significance of their life styles.[7] One man was in a very skilled trade and had the greatest seniority in his plant, and the other was a long-distance trucker who also lived very comfortably.

These two men and the third, the painting contractor, who all

7. See National Opinion Research Center, "Jobs and Occupations: A Popular Evaluation," in *Class, Status and Power*, ed. Seymour Lipset and Rinehart Bendix (New York: Free Press, 1953) for an explanation of the logic of these scales.

remained at the same occupational level as their parents, were quite sensitive to their apparent lack of upward mobility. All of them explained that the reason they did not have better jobs was not a lack of interest or ability on their part. Since these men were older than my other informants, they grew up when it was common to go to work very young and when any family disaster would send the children out into the job market. Thus, I was told that they had only an elementary-school or incomplete secondary-school education because of exigencies such as the death of a parent. As one informant put it, the decision to leave school was not in his "power." All these men went on to say that they wanted their children to get all the education they could absorb because they themselves had not had the opportunity to do so. One remarked that "education is the only thing." None mentioned the possible relevance of the time when they joined the movement. Two of them became Seventh-day Adventists after they had left school and entered the job market, which might account for their failure to complete their education.

All my informants said they had a much higher standard of living than their fathers. This may be due largely to a general rise in real income for the working classes in recent years in America. Nonetheless, all these people felt they occupied a quite different niche in the occupational system than their fathers had. They associated their fathers' jobs with financial insecurity, rudimentary skill, and a minimal sense of accomplishment. Although they have not made a great deal of money, their jobs provide a sense of personal accomplishment. Most of them have risen within the ranks of the company for which they work. Only the truck driver did not report added supervisory or independent responsibilities since he began the job. Their present job titles—for example, sales manager, parts manager, sales representative—reflect movement upward within the white-collar category. These and other members of the church never failed to note that hard work and dependability on the job paid off financially. However, these men all saw the real opportunity to increase one's freedom and income in starting their own business, and most of them had plans to do so.

In response to the question, If you could have the same kind of job, do you think it is better to work for someone else or to work for oneself, that is, to be self-employed? without exception my informants felt that it is better to be self-employed. Independence is such an important occupational value that some informants who went into business for themselves and failed had plans to try again in the future. One of the manual workers had been in several businesses and had not prospered in any of them, and yet he still felt strongly that occupational independence is much better than working for someone else. The ideal solution for Seventh-day Adventists is to get a professional education, because then one does not have to worry about closing his business on Saturday. Although the other manual worker had a very secure and well-protected job, he too had experienced some independence as parts manager for an auto agency. He left this job, significantly, because he felt that his lack of education hampered his ability to do the paper work involved, and he too saw a professional job as the perfect realization of the value of independence.

My informant who was a small painting contractor pointed out that with pensions and welfare benefits provided for union tradesmen, the small businessman does not make much more than they do. He said that he never regrets having his own business because there is always the possibility that it will develop into something large and enduring (at one time he had eight men working for him, but now he has only one) and because there is greater "latitude" in the way you work. He specifically mentioned the tendency in his business to cheat clients who are not aware of differences in paint and workmanship. He was especially proud of the fact that as an independent operator he has never been forced to engage in shady practices to meet competition. Other informants working in firms said that company practices often compromised their own business ethics, and these informants felt that if they had their own companies they could avoid these practices.

Although these informants placed a high value on occupational independence, they were quite sensitive to the risks involved in starting one's own business. One man told me that although he saw little chance for promotion into the top ranks of management in his firm (although he saw considerable room for salary increases), he would not go into his own business unless the prospects of a large margin of profit outweighed the risks involved. This is a theme which ran through my discussions of this subject with my informants. Although they would like to start their own businesses, they all realize that anyone who wants to start a commercial enterprise must calculate the advantages and liabilities his venture will face on the open market. One of my informants, who was a sales representative for a clothing manufacturer and who worked entirely on commission, considered himself almost an independent businessman. He remarked that he experiences considerable anxiety during relatively slow periods, but the feeling of being responsible for one's success or failure and for developing one's business more than compensates for the worry. In sum, these people carefully scan the economic and occupational horizon for opportunities for advancement but, at the same time, are not likely to sacrifice their present economic security for a job or business which is highly speculative or entails considerable financial liabilities.

I elicited the same attitudes in response to these questions:

If you were offered a job with a big company or if you could go into a business of your own and make the same money at both, which would you choose? Why?

If you had your choice of the following conditions under which you could work, which one would be most important to you? Are there any that do not matter?

1. No danger of being fired
2. Big salary or income
3. Short working hours
4. Chances for advancement
5. Enjoying the kind of work involved in the job
6. Independence on the job—little supervision from above

I found that enjoying the work involved in a job was usually rated even higher than independence and income, but this is consistent with the Seventh-day Adventist orientation toward professional occupations. In general, my informants saw occupational advancement in terms of greater income and personal control over their economic destiny. In other words, they not only felt that it was desirable to move to a level where there was little technical supervision over the decisions they made on the job but also wanted a position where they could stand or fall on their own merits. Except for the older men, as I mentioned previously, all saw a good chance of making more money in their present jobs, but most doubted that they would move much higher in the managerial ranks of the firm. Even so, none revealed pessimism about the future—given their circumstances most felt that they had done reasonably well financially and that they would continue to prosper even if they stayed with their present jobs.

One indication of a person's conception of the possibilities of upward mobility is his vision of what is possible for his children and his knowledge of what it takes to succeed in our economic system. Unanimously, Seventh-day Adventists not only wanted their children to become doctors, engineers, or such, but also had what I might call reserve expectations for them. My informants often told me that if these occupations were beyond their children's natural talents, they still would like them to become teachers or technicians. The answers to the question, What do you think are their chances of getting these jobs? (those the informant would like them to get) disclosed the extent to which Seventh-day Adventists feel that upward mobility is contingent upon scholastic progress. The entire congregation not only valued education but also was sensitive to the problematic character of achievement in the competitive academic system of high schools and colleges. Although they were very optimistic about a person's chances to get the kind of job he wants if he has a college degree, they were concerned about children upon whom education did not seem to "take." One informant regretfully told me that his adolescent son, whom he had hoped would be a doctor, just did not do well in school, and thus at this point he would be happy if his son became a successful tradesman. This informant was the only Seventh-day Adventist I knew who lived in a completely working-class neighborhood. He was in the process of buying a house in a more middle-class neighborhood because of what he perceived as the deleterious effect of his son's peer group on his aspirations and interest in school. He did not want his younger children exposed to the same influences because he put such high value on their ability to do well in school. In sum, Seventh-day Adventist parents have high expectations for their children's ultimate place in the occupational realm, but they do not retain these aspirations when they are obviously unrealistic. At this point, they are willing to reduce them, but not to abandon them altogether—Seventh-day Adventist parents hope that those who cannot gain entrance to college will find some reasonably skilled and well-paying trade.

In response to the question, Is there anything a parent can do to see that his children get these jobs? (if the informant did not have a class or type of job in mind for his children, the question was rephrased in terms of getting ahead in the world), these informants stressed the importance of encouraging one's children to do well in school. Their attitudes toward less-than-satisfying academic performance did not seem punitive. They told me that they continually reminded their children that the consequences of not succeeding in school were unpleasant later in life. These informants were rather sensitive to the kinds of intellectual skills that are necessary for prospering in college. They often remarked about their children's reading habits and felt that good readers were likely to do well in school. In short, they all agreed that, as much as they wanted their children to achieve scholastically, the most a parent can do is encourage them and hope that their native desire will carry them into college. They pointed out that it is not possible to force an education on those who are unreceptive to it, but one father told me that when he saw his children's grades slipping he reminded them how hard it is to go out to work for someone else every day. Their responses to the following questions revealed their desire to protect their present economic and social gains against unforeseen contingencies and to provide for greater accomplishments in their children's careers:

Do you think people should save even if it means doing without something they really would like to have, or should they save only if they can do it without any real sacrifices?

Do you think it is a good idea to buy on time? Why?

What sort of thing do you think people ought to save their money for?

My informants' attitudes toward the proper uses of one's income were very consistent. They all agreed that it is necessary to save part of one's income regularly and that this money should be used only for very special purposes. Nor did they approve of buying on time except for purchases like cars and homes where it is unlikely that they could ever afford to pay cash. In other words, they clearly try to collect their resources for those things which are not simply items for immediate consumption: education, homes, emergencies, retirement, and, they sometimes added, vacations. Clearly, education and then homes were thought to be the most important things for which a person could spend his money, and all my informants stated that they were willing to make financial sacrifices for their children's education. They all lived in their own comfortable though not ostentatiously furnished homes. In sum, these people have made some substantial economic progress and are interested both in consolidating their gains through a cautious, moderate life style and in a judicious investment of surplus funds in those activities and objects which retain their economic value. For them, homes and education represent the prime areas of investment because they are safe, nonspeculative ways of improving one's financial and social standing in the community.

Pentecostals

On the whole, my Pentecostal informants were younger than the Seventh-day Adventists; they were in their late teens, twenties, or thirties. When possible, I tried to get informants who were young enough to be still sensitive to the real possibilities (or lack of possibilities) of movement within the socioeconomic order. Thus, I regard the bias in favor of youth as an asset, because older persons may have come to terms with their occupational destiny long ago.

Before discussing the material obtained in interviews with my Pentecostal informants, I should note that their responses to my questions were often vague, ambiguous, or other-wordly. They often responded to a question as if I had instructed them to free associate. In other words, regardless of the specific content of the questions, they were likely to use them as a vehicle for affirming their religious commitment and to restate the fundamental tenets of their belief. By and large, they also found the interview stressful. One informant half jokingly described it as the "third degree" and another remarked that my methods were not much different from the Gestapo's. To informants who are very sensitive to imputations of a lower standing than they believe they rightfully deserve, this kind of interview seems to violate some of the implicit understandings which sustain rapport with the informant and which make participant-observation such a subtle, flexible mode of research. Incidentally, I experienced a similar difficulty in a study of the same kind of religious group in a small West Indian town. I noticed that a very good informant would hesitate to express opinions in a formal interview even though he had already revealed the same attitudes in informal conversations. Perhaps the best solution to this sort of problem is to do the fieldwork in two stages; to have an "outsider" administer the questionnaire after the participant-observation phase has been completed.

I interviewed all the core members of the small Pentecostal group except one member who artfully eluded my maneuvers to talk to her in a formal context. Since this was such a small group (eight members), I interviewed two members of the larger Pentecostal group. Of my nine informants only one was married to another member of the group.

Very few of my informants remembered what their paternal grandfathers did for a living; those who did had grandfathers who were either manual laborers or small farmers. Except for the minister's father, who was a small-time gambler and part-time insurance salesman, the rest of my informants' fathers were either manual or skilled workers, and one functioned in a minor supervisory capacity. Many of the informants (five) were women, and all worked or were shortly going to work as secretaries. None reported any other occupational aspirations (except to become a missionary or evangelist), although some indicated that in the future they hoped to move into the ranks of executive secretaries; but at the time all worked as clerk-typists. Compared with Seventh-day Adventists, the Pentecostal men had complicated job histories. Seventh-day Adventists, except for ventures into private businesses, had only one or two types of jobs in their careers and had spent almost their entire occupational careers with a single firm.

The Pentecostal men had a wide range of relatively short-lived jobs. One man was in the merchant marine and the air force, and now works for a collection agency; another has had a number of sales jobs; the minister has had a long list of jobs including his service experience; the other man, who works as a carpet cleaner, has also worked in a machine shop and parking lot. All these men (except the minister) claimed that their present jobs afforded them no real satisfaction and they viewed them as merely a way of making money. The only time they showed any interest in the topic was when they related incidents on the job which brought them into contact with persons who shared their particular religious faith. None of these men had ever occupied a position of real occupational responsibility, nor did their jobs require special talents, duties, or training.

Unlike Seventh-day Adventists, who talked about their jobs in terms of the skills or opportunities they involved, Pentecostals invariably focused on the possibility of bringing others into the fold through the contacts one makes in the occupational world. For instance, the man who worked for a collection agency told how a man from whom he was trying to collect a debt told him about his alcoholic son who was the source of his financial difficulties. My informant told this man that the only solution to his son's problem was the healing powers of the Holy Spirit, and at the time he was trying to get the man to bring his son to church. My informant further pointed out that this sort of intimate dealing with a debtor violated the rules of his agency, but he felt he could not allow this chance to reach a potential convert to pass him by. Another informant who sold garage doors in poor neighborhoods told me that his most exciting experience on his job was when he discovered that a prospective customer shared his belief and they spent the rest of the afternoon praying together. He did not say whether he tried to sell him a door after they finished praying.

Following Wilson, it is possible to describe Pentecostal attitudes toward jobs and work as basically neutral. Although my informants disclosed some contempt for the kind of work they were doing, none expressed even the vaguest plans to move on to something else intrinsically more rewarding. For Pentecostals one's job is merely a way of making a living, and unless the financial benefits are great, my informants felt there was little value in thinking about the job after they finished the day's work. Not one informant whom I did not systematically interview voluntarily discussed working conditions or his job, nor was it ever a topic for discussion in the freewheeling church sermons. This did not seem to result from the low esteem accorded their jobs, since they generally had lower white-collar (sales and clerical), skilled manual (e.g., carpenter) or small-business occupations. In my estimation they did not care to discuss their jobs because they felt that their occupational role was basically static, whereas they constantly talked about their dynamic spiritual role—"growth in the Spirit."

As I mentioned previously, whenever a member of the congregation got a better paying job, he made an announcement which attributed this good fortune to God's influence. Pentecostals never seemed to relate occupational success to their ability to perceive and seize economic opportunities. In general, I noticed very little concern with concrete steps to achieve occupational success among the members of a group which tries to symbolically differentiate itself from other segments of the working class. This makes sense if one assumes that these people do not perceive a favorable, widening economic gap between themselves and the rest of the working class.

This analysis is also consonant with their response to the question, If you could have the same kind of job, do you think it is better to work for someone else or to work for oneself, that is, to be self-employed? All replied that they would prefer to work for someone else, except one informant who replied that he would prefer self-employment, albeit without any observable enthusiasm. This is not to say that Pentecostals categorically reject the idea of self-employment. First, though none of those I interviewed had small businesses, some other members of the group did. Second, they feel that they would rather work for themselves than belong to a union (in response to the question, Do you think that most people benefit from being union members or would they gain more from working on their own?). Although Seventh-day Adventist responses were similar, and although I did not systematically probe my informants' responses to the question, from the data I did get I suspect that their reasons for this choice were quite different. Pentecostals often referred to vague criminal connotations of unions which suggested that their association with a union would involve some sort of status contamination. Although Seventh-day Adventists might mention the tangible benefits of union membership, they would point out that unions place real and unalterable limits upon one's ability to rise to a higher occupational rank. In contrast, many dedicated Pentecostals believe that if a person works for someone else, he has more time and energy to invest in religious activities.

The question, Do you feel there is much chance for improvement and advancement in your present job? revealed Pentecostals' perceptions of the inherent restrictions of their present jobs and the limited vistas of their general occupational prospects. All felt that the only immediate (realistic) avenue for advancement was a salary increase. None saw a move upward into even the lower managerial ranks of the companies which employed them. Nor did any have definite plans either for getting further occupational training, for changing to another line of work, or for going into business for themselves. Similarly, their response to the question, Is the kind of work you are now doing the kind of work you will want to do for the rest of your life, or do you see yourself doing something else in the future? was quite diffuse. None mentioned any occupational goals or aspirations which would take them out of the lower middle- or working-class occupational ranks. Again, they said that although they expected to have to work for the rest of their lives (which implied that they did not envisage occupations whose incomes would provide considerable leisure), they hoped to witness for Christ at every opportunity.

In contrast to Seventh-day Adventists, who often emphasized their special job preparation, the Pentecostals' answer to the question, Has belonging to (name of group) changed your attitudes toward your job or the way you do your work? was vague. They mentioned general Christian attitudes that they brought to the job in place of the specific Seventh-day Adventist reference to qualities of perseverance and personal integrity. Their reply to the question which asked them to rate job conditions was the same as the Seventh-day Adventists'. I suspect this reflects the prevailing American ideology that the worth of a job should be judged in terms of its intrinsic value, its freedom from superfluous external controls, and, of course, the means it provides to acquire the material aspects of the good life.

Pentecostals' expectations for their children's occupations and their conception of what a parent can do to insure his child's future revealed their concern with behavior which represents a certain type of social character rather than with behavior which leads to upward mobility. In other words, they tried to instill what they thought were morally and spiritually righteous attitudes and habits—an upright demeanor—in their children rather than to nurture those dispositions essential to occupational success in our society. In response to the question, Do you think that the members of (name of church) raise their children in certain ways that may be different from most people? my informants stressed the overriding importance of teaching children how to respect adult authority, and they strongly approved of corporal punishment for young children. They said that a young child should be taught to love God and everything else will follow from this principle.

In answering the questions, Do you think that people who belong to (name of church) make certain kinds of husbands and wives? and Can you see any difference between the family life of people who belong to (name of religious orientation) and the family life of friends, relatives, and work associates who do not? my Pentecostal informants felt that there should be a clear-cut division of labor between husband and wife. The husband should be "over" the wife and the wife "over" the children. Here the emphasis is on traditional partiarchal authority in the home rather than on an instrumental, rational approach to the problems of family living. In contrast, Seventh-day Adventist parents were convinced that although physical discipline was sometimes unavoidable, it was the example set by the behavior of the parents which most deeply affected their children's attitudes and actions. Many Seventh-day Adventist parents told me that they occasionally had family meetings to talk about common problems. This difference is symptomatic of Pentecostal and Seventh-day Adventist approaches to secular difficulties. Seventh-day Adventists try to understand the particular elements involved in a situation before trying to resolve it, whereas Pentecostals firmly believe that anyone who rigorously maintains his commitment to God cannot fail to overcome obstacles because God will aid him if he proves unable to solve a difficult problem. Thus, whereas Seventh-day Adventists try to prepare their children for the struggle in the competitive occupational world, Pentecostals do not really perceive the problem and act on it. They simply hold that beneficial consequences must ultimately follow from a sincere trust in God.

Pentecostal responses to the questions, What kind of jobs would you like to see your children get? and What do you think their chances are of getting these jobs? were difficult to interpret because most of my informants did not have children. Yet even when I phrased these questions in hypothetical terms, their answers were very elusive. For instance, one young woman said that she wanted her child to be a "doctor or an actor or anything famous." Most of my informants said that they wanted their children to be the kind of person who will dedicate his life to Christ.

Their answers to the second question showed a general awareness of education as the prerequisite for occupational success. A few informants said they would give their children a good education if they showed signs of scholastic ability. A number of Seventh-day Adventist informants told me that they tried to improve their children's reading skills by taking them to public libraries and sometimes helped them with their homework. Unlike Pentecostals, Seventh-day Adventists said that the quality of the schools was a decisive factor in deciding where to live (in response to the questions, Did you move to this neighborhood for any particular reason? and What do you like and what do you dislike about this neighborhood?).

Finally, the Pentecostal response to the question, Do you think people should save even if it means doing without something they really would like to have, or should save only if they can do it without any real sacrifices? was universally unequivocal. They felt that a person ought to save regularly only if he would not have to make great sacrifices. Although Pentecostals did not approve of buying on time, their attitudes toward it were much more qualified than Seventh-day Adventists'; that is, it is all right if one does not get too indebted and if it is for an important purchase. Their answers to the question, What sort of thing do you think people ought to save their money for? do not clearly differentiate between the allocation of resources to long- and short-term goals and do not subjugate the latter to the former. Rather, Pentecostals said that people should save for anything worthwhile and frequently said that you should use your savings for purposes dictated by God.

In sum, Pentecostals do not appear to have mapped out their own and their children's chances for upward movement in the occupational world. Nor do they seem interested in investing in activities which might lead to advancement in the economic system. Their view of the proper socialization practices and of the meaning of work suggests that they see their position in the socioeconomic order as static and do not hope to change it by their own efforts. This material further indicates that they try to dissociate their image of their own social status from their prospects of upward mobility.

A glance at the questionnaire in Appendix 2 will reveal that I have not systematically exhausted all the data collected with this instrument. However, my purpose was to construct an instrument which would not only probe the actor's conception of his own status trajectory but which when employed in a survey would also yield data that would throw light on the influence of demographic variables upon differential sect affiliation. Undoubtedly, the questionnaire will have to be revised and expanded if it is used in this manner. Also, certain questions which

I thought would bring latent attitudes to the surface or distinguish Pentecostal and Seventh-day Adventist orientations toward work did not do so. Perhaps with a larger sample significant differences would appear.

There are important differences in the actual occupational experience of Adventists and Pentecostals, in their future occupational aspirations and in their expectations for their children's success in the secular order. Seventh-day Adventists have experienced a small but significant measure of both inter- and intragenerational mobility and expect that they or their children or both will continue to prosper in the occupational realm. They further think that they not only know where they are going but also know how to get there. The Seventh-day Adventists, on the whole, carefully make sure that their decisions about day-to-day secular matters fit into their larger life plans for their own and their children's success in this world. They not only want to maintain their status gains over the former generation but also want to make sure that their children will continue to do so and, they hope, will improve upon their modest occupational gains.

In contrast, Pentecostals may have experienced a small measure of intergenerational mobility, but it does not appear to have had a significant impact on their appraisal of the possibility of future advancement in the occupational system. Perhaps this is because they have not undergone any significant intragenerational mobility. Further, they seem to have tacitly abandoned any realistic efforts to rise in the occupational order, and they do not seem interested in having their children attempt what they have either failed to accomplish or avoided confronting. Rather, they seem to escape this problem through symbolic devices which proclaim middle-class respectability. This attitude fits their lack of concern with the practical routes to occupational success and their inability to perceive how one's present means can be used to underwrite future socioeconomic improvement.

7 Conclusions

Sectarian Belief and the Social Order

This book has examined the relationship between two quite distinctive sectarian religious movements and the social order from two analytically distinct vantage points. From one perspective, we can see the potent effect theologically based models of social reality have on the believer's orientation to his mundane affairs. For the believer, these assumptions about the way supernatural powers view human activity determine his conception of the kind of life he must lead. Supernatural directives set priorities for the allocation of his energies and resources and establish an unassailable rationale for his social commitments. On the other hand, it is equally true that religious ideologies are congruent with the status preoccupations and economic aspirations of their followers. Without the stimulus of material need, it seems most unlikely that they would not only accept these doctrines as true but also feel that this truth guarantees the worth of their secular hopes and desires.

The believer's conception of the right

way to achieve salvation brings discrete ethical norms into the larger fabric of cosmological and eschatological belief. The concept of salvation fuses what is possibly the believer's deepest emotional interest—concern with the ultimate fate of the self—with ideas that transcend the ebb and flow of worldly events, interests, and groups. Conceptions of salvation are never completely free of outside sources of contamination (i.e., material interests), because there is a strong tendency to see those things that are immediately beneficial to the self as crucial to its persistence after death.

Seventh-day Adventist belief pictures a harsh, demanding God who requires such a high level of moral performance from his subjects that anyone who falters or makes a misstep falls into a burning abyss. It promises success in this world and in the kingdom shortly to come to those who honor God's commands punctiliously. It equates the practical virtues which enhance one's chances for upward social mobility with the characteristics of God's elect, insuring that those who take God's stern warnings seriously will also strive to prove that they belong to this highly favored group.

On the other hand, Pentecostal theology has a very benign image of God. Anything is possible for those who open their hearts to Jesus and accept whatever provisions God makes for them. Christians who trust Jesus can attain the highest spiritual state available to man: the baptism of the Holy Ghost. This gives the believer certain knowledge of his salvation and supernatural powers which dissolve even the most recalcitrant human problems, usually those that involve considerable suffering and anguish. These spiritual gifts "heal" even those ailments which the most advanced scientific techniques cannot touch, for example, extreme feelings of despair or advanced cases of cancer. Most important, this intimate contact with God elevates the believer above the ordinary run of men and establishes his status on incontrovertible grounds. This religious system which so joyously embraces the sensate world actually flees it. It maintains that a man's accomplishments and failures in the usual affairs of life have no enduring significance; they are essentially trivial and ephemeral. Even the most saintly behavior cannot affect the truly vital area in which a person must validate his worth: the baptism of the Holy Ghost.

The social marginality of Seventh-day Adventists and Pentecostals to the established middle classes and the comparatively small positive gains of the former and the static position of the latter in the occupational system do not account completely for the marked difference in their status expectations. In my opinion, Seventh-day Adventists have slightly higher, or at least more satisfying, white-collar jobs than Pentecostals but, nonetheless, they have not undergone radical intragenerational mobility. Thus a vital factor—the economic optimism of Seventh-day Adventists and the pessimism of Pentecostals—remains open to further examination.

In retrospect, it seems that the believer's psychological reaction to doctrines which promise social support in a difficult situation are an important source of his status expectations. What psychological tendencies dispose some people to opt for belief systems which sustain either optimistic attitudes toward personal success in this world coupled with marked cosmological pessimism (Seventh-day Adventism) or pessimistic attitudes toward future success in this world coupled with marked cosmological optimism (Pentecostalism)? Unfortunately, I have only some speculations to add to this inquiry.

It is my impression that Seventh-day Adventists derive their primary gratifications from manipulating their external social and material environment, whereas Pentecostals gain their greatest pleasure from the expressive component of interpersonal relationships. Seventh-day Adventists belong to a religious organization which clearly defines concrete obstacles to happiness in this world and provides an integrated set of practical techniques for dealing with these difficulties. Seventh-day Adventists approach their internal (psychological) and external (moral and economic) environments in a highly consistent and efficient manner. On the level of religious symbolism, this is manifested in the optimistic doctrinal pronouncements on the adaptive and goal attainment levels of action:[1] material success

1. For an explication of the meaning of these terms see Talcott Parsons, *The Social System* (Glencoe, Ill.: Free Press, 1951).

is open to anyone who husbands his resources and who carefully weighs the costs of each decision he makes. Their eschatology, however, reveals great pessimism on the integrative and expressive dimensions of human association. Seventh-day Adventist theologians state that the followers of Christ are lonely beings whose moral success or failure has no effect whatsoever on even their closest relatives and friends—a man gains or loses salvation solely on the basis of the merits of his own actions. Furthermore, Seventh-day Adventist belief holds that even those presently engaged in the collective effort to save mankind from destruction may not constitute a collectivity in the future. The Kingdom of God on earth will be composed only of the righteous, and Seventh-day Adventists openly admit that this does not include everyone who belongs to their movement.

Pentecostalism reverses the psychological emphases of Seventh-day Adventism. There is ample reason for pessimism on the adaptive and goal attainment levels of social action. Here Pentecostal belief merely offers its adherents rescue from poverty or illness. It does not pretend to show a believer how to rise permanently out of his present secular predicament; it invokes God only as the last resort in great difficulty. On the other hand, Pentecostals achieve considerable success in the integrative and expressive dimensions of social life. They reach a high degree of interpersonal rapport and emotional understanding through their collective religious activity. In fact, Pentecostal theory stresses the necessity of the group's inducing collective states of spiritual well-being. One person's spiritual success increases the likelihood of (but, of course, does not guarantee) the spiritual success of others in the congregation. Pentecostal belief emphasizes the immediate consummation of a state of oneness with God, and through it of love for those who follow him. At this point Pentecostals feel a diminution of the ordinary social boundaries between the members of the group.

When searching for the psychological sources of ideological commitment, it is tempting but, in my opinion, ultimately misleading to depict the sect member's motives as forces that operate independently of the way he appraises his situation in the social order. Seen this way, his motives are constituted by imperative but only dimly perceived needs that limit his ability to consciously determine his theological allegiances. Whether the sect member's motives originate in the depths of his psyche or in the structural pressures on his life space, they presumably shape his response to cognitive stimuli regardless of his intellectual history. His motives, then, appear as innate, invariant psychological tendencies that control his perceptions of social reality, rather than as symbolic constructs which emerge out of and are frequently refashioned by his effort to discover constant meaning amid the confusion of mundane social experience.

To a certain extent, I have conceptualized the sect member's motives as concrete variables which exist in a completely definitive form before his actual contact with a particular religious ideology. Consequently, I probably have imputed greater specificity to the motives that prompt sect affiliation than was *initially* the case. The sect member often begins his quest for a permanent religious identity as a "seeker." Sometimes this is a self-conscious attempt to discover the truth; sometimes it merely involves moving from church to church to find a group that suits his religious tastes at the moment. In either case, we need only assume that ideological commitment occurs when the seeker engages in this quest to resolve problematic aspects of his social experience, and that he can do so on the basis of relatively amorphous perceptions of social reality. Although the seeker is aware of his general rank in the prestige hierarchy associated with broadly defined social strata, his exact standing in any concrete status context is frequently open to considerable doubt.

At this point in the sect member's career, he discovers an ideology that formulates his predicament in precisely those terms which enable him to extricate himself from it: it tells him what was wrong with his past life and what he must do to rectify his previous mistakes. As it enables him to evaluate his conduct from a new perspective, a sect ideology fuses a special vocabulary of motives with a new moral code. Commitment to a sect ideology not only reduces the sect member's uncertainty about his place in the social order but also delineates the praxis that decisively resolves it.

Idiosyncratic psychological dispositions undoubtedly influence the sect member's receptivity to diverse ideological appeals. Nonetheless, it is important to remember that in the process of adopting a comprehensive religious ideology, the sect member acquires a vocabulary of motives that may be only tangentially related to the needs that initiated his quest for a sacred vision of reality. Religious ideologies transform desires that are often vague into the shared goals that define both a distinctive sacred identity and a distinctive mode of secular life. Therefore, any explanation of ideological commitment that views sect affiliation as the product of the actor's needs alone will overlook the ability of sect ideologies to generate the psychological dispositions and motives that sustain their unique patterns of conduct.

Seventh-day Adventism and Pentecostalism as Transformative and Redemptive Social Movements

As I noted earlier, Seventh-day Adventists and Pentecostals do not have a large following in our society. These and other ideologically kindred religious movements attract only a small proportion of those whose positions in the social order should dispose them favorably toward these beliefs. Recent studies of conversion to "deviant" religious perspectives emphasize the role that the interpersonal relationship between the potential convert and the proselytizer plays in the recruitment process.[2] This factor explains why someone already receptive to these sorts of world views will choose a particular group from among a number of organizations which espouse similar doctrines. But here the question concerns the limited appeal of all such ideologies to persons subject to persistent social deprivation.

In some respects, the answer is quite simple. Ours is not an era when religious motives capture mens' imaginations. Even most of those who suffer from serious social deprivation are not responsive to ideologies that entail a life style at variance with the standards of the dominant culture. Few people are willing to publicly appear intellectually and socially unfashionable, even if they must forsake the enticing promises of ideologies

2. See John Lofland, *Doomsday Cult: A Study of Conversion, Proselytization, and Maintenance of Faith* (Englewood Cliffs, N.J.: Prentice-Hall, 1966).

that offer to solve all their problems. In modern societies, it is distinctly unfashionable to issue a call for complete moral reformation. And it is even more unfashionable to subjugate one's entire life style to the dictates of supernatural beings.

Furthermore, men who are habituated to segmentalized social roles tend to compartmentalize their vision of social reality. The various domains of social life—economic, political, familial—are dealt with as discrete spheres of experience. Thus, modern men learn to search for disparate solutions to what are perceived as essentially pragmatic problems, and this process keeps their gaze focused within the narrow confines of the problem's technical parameters. Hence, we can hardly expect them to be receptive to supernatural world views that demand a unified stance toward the diverse problems of living and that require personal sacrifices in the service of transcendental ideals. In place of a morally encompassing world view, secular men substitute the doctrine of freedom from gratuitous external controls over their personal lives. Roughly translated, this means that one should be free to pursue his own ends in his own way when they do not directly interfere with the goals of the collectivities to which he belongs. Inasmuch as they believe that personal choice is constrained by sacred norms, Pentecostals and Seventh-day Adventists are out of step with the modern vision of personal liberty as the pursuit of private satisfactions.

This fact, however, does not relegate them to the status of religious exotica of interest only to a specialist in aberrant intellectual developments. As we saw in the first chapter of this book, Pentecostal and Seventh-day Adventist belief has much in common with the ideologies of other social movements that occur repeatedly in societies undergoing intense change. Of the many classifications of these social movements, Aberle's recent typology is, in my opinion, one of the most stimulating and provocative.

Aberle distinguishes two dimensions of social movements: "One is the dimension of the *locus* of the change sought. The other is the dimension of the *amount* of change sought."[3] This

3. David F. Aberle, *The Peyote Religion among the Navaho* (Chicago: Aldine Publishing Co., 1966), p. 316.

logically yields four types, of which the transformative and the redemptive are relevant to the kinds of groups considered in this book. "*Transformative* movements aim at a total change in supra-individual systems. . . . *Redemptive* movements aim at a partial change in supra-individual systems."[4] Aberle points out that his types do not occur in their pure form, and that they frequently change their character during the course of their development. He then identifies the constant and variable characteristics of these movements. On the basis of their constant features, the Pentecostal and Seventh-day Adventist groups I studied undoubtedly qualify as redemptive and transformative social movements.

The Seventh-day Adventists are a classical example of the transformative type. They believe that the millennium is imminent. They see the movement of human history as an inexorable and ever quickening rush toward the final act of divine judgment. And they firmly believe in the prophetic validity of their leader's vision of the end of this world. Contrary to Aberle's type, they do not systematically disengage themselves from the larger society except on those occasions when its norms violate their moral precepts. Nonetheless, they avoid contact with the ungodly insofar as they constitute a danger of moral corruption or pollution.

Similarly, the Pentecostal groups fit Aberle's redemptive type. They are engaged in "the search for a new inner state. Changes in behavior are sought as a path to such an inner state, or, more commonly, it is believed that changes in behavior can result only from a new state of grace—that alterations of behavior require a change of heart."[5] As Aberle points out, a redemptive movement's critique of prevailing societal norms serves a primarily individualistic end: to engender the process of spiritual rebirth. Pentecostal doctrine fosters spiritual rebirth through Spirit baptism. Above everything else, the converts wants "to be born again." If Pentecostals depart from Aberle's type it is in the level of their concern with everyday conduct. Although they are not oblivious to the external signs of a change in one's inner

4. Ibid., p. 317.
5. Ibid., p. 320.

life, Pentecostals rather single-mindedly try to reexperience the "in-filling" of the Holy Ghost. Sanctification is a secondary concern, but Pentecostals are not enjoined to ignore the tasks of ordinary existence or to withdraw from social life altogether.

In drawing attention to the correspondence between Aberle's transformative and redemptive types and Seventh-day Adventists and Pentecostals my intention is not to underline the obvious—that real cases occasionally fit ideal types rather neatly. These cases bear directly on Aberle's hypothesis about the connection between the nature and source of deprivation and the content of a group's ideology. He says:

> In sum, transformative movements seem to appeal to people who have been or are being extruded from their niche—in terms of location, economic position, political position, etc., into more marginal niches, and who cannot forsee another niche which offers reasonable security—not to mention happiness. . . . Those redemptive movements with a focus on living in the world, rather than withdrawing from it, seem to appeal to groups which are being pressed to occupy a new niche, sometimes new to them, sometimes new in the society—one regarded ambivalently, or even negatively, but not hopelessly. . . . Being engaged actively in the total system through occupancy of the new niche—often engaged more economically than politically or socially—they do not tend to fantasy the dissolution of the entire system and its transformation.[6]

With respect to this hypothesis the cases at hand are clearly anomalous. It is the Pentecostals—not the Seventh-day Adventists—who have been extruded from their former niche in the larger society and who now view their economic prospects rather despondently. They are seeking to escape from the unpleasant implications of an untenable status dilemma. They desire but cannot afford a prestigious social status. Yet their general social background deceptively seems to qualify them for membership in the established middle classes. Formerly, in American society their ascriptive characteristics (their race, religion, and ancestry) would have made them preeminently eligible to take their place among the socially secure and relatively prosperous segments of the middle class. Today, their occupational prospects alone make it quite unlikely that they will ever do more than dream of

6. Ibid., p. 330.

participating in those social circles whose affluent way of life underwrites their high standing in the larger society. Pentecostals do not have the resources, education, or jobs which could significantly alter their social anonymity in the foreseeable future. With both the well-to-do and the poor contending for the center stage in our society, the socially marginal members of the lower middle class are rarely seen and almost never heard in the public arena. Their ideology reflects a fear of "falling" from a state of grace to a lower and inherently debased social status. The effort to reverse this process reveals, in my opinion, the kind of extrusion that Aberle refers to in his hypothesis on the transformative type and that is so well documented in Gusfield's *Symbolic Crusade*.

The Seventh-day Adventists conform to the hypothesis proposed for socioeconomic experience of the redemptive type. They desire to move into a new and more satisfying niche in the socioeconomic order. They work to secure all the advantages that increased education, professional status, and the like confer on the established middle classes. Their concern with the details of ordinary social and economic conduct seems adaptive to what is undoubtedly an arduous and at times disheartening effort to pull themselves up by their bootstraps. As distinguished from their severe eschatological predictions, their ideology reveals a rather optimistic assessment of the long-run possibility of moving into the established middle classes.

There are a number of possible explanations for this finding. One is that these negative cases invalidate the hypothesis. I do not think this is so. Another is that changes in a movement's aims may not be reflected in its original doctrinal charter. In this instance, however, the Pentecostal and Seventh-day Adventist groups adhere to comparatively undiluted redemptive and transformative ideologies. Aberle's distinction between an "official" and a "directing" ideology offers a clue to the answer to this conundrum.

Although Aberle's discussion of the difference between an official and a directing ideology is very brief, his meaning is clear.[7] By a group's official ideology, Aberle means those doc-

7. Ibid., p. 317.

trines or articles of faith that are accepted as formal truths but that are not necessarily held passionately or felt with deep conviction. The directing ideology does just that; it refers to ideas that organize the activities of the members of a group. By definition, a directing ideology is of utmost concern to its adherents. It points the way to the realization of values shared by the group.

In some respects, this distinction parallels the one I have urged between a religious movement's formal theology and its ideology. The distinction between an official and a directing ideology does not pause, however, to examine the way in which abstruse cognitive schemata give rise to norms that have an immediate impact upon conduct. Instead it assigns those ideas that have a concrete effect on action and those that strike the observer as "purely" formal to separate and not dynamically interrelated categories. If we look at the interaction between religious first principles and the norms operative in a given social situation, we can see how a group with a transformative ideology, such as the Seventh-day Adventists, can conform to the socioeconomic experience postulated for the redemptive type. Here Spiro's important distinction between intended and unintended and recognized and unrecognized personal motives and social functions is useful in explicating this paradoxical finding.[8] At the level of personal motives, the function of Seventh-day Adventist ideology is intended *and* largely unrecognized. Seventh-day Adventists want to increase their material well-being, whereas their perception of economic action stresses conformity to ethical norms. According to the religious actor, his conduct follows theological directives given to those who seek salvation above all else. Religious ideology not only intervenes between an actor's motives and the meaning he imputes to his conduct but also simultaneously faces in two directions. It satisfies the demands of the group's formal theology; the members of the group actively prepare themselves for the millennium. At the same time, this deeply held creed does not prevent them from scrutinizing their social environment realistically. They

8. Melford E. Spiro, "Social Systems, Personality, and Functional Analysis," in *Studying Personality Cross-Culturally*, ed. Bert Kaplan (New York: Harper and Row, 1961).

see economic opportunities and attempt to seize them. In short, the ideology sustains the group's manifest collective aims and puts the member's vision of the millennium in the service of personal motives that are common to the members of the group but that are not shared explicitly by them. The extent to which intended personal motives are unrecognized is variable. There is a peripheral recognition of the fact that their teachings lead to increased worldly success, but the members of this group do not believe that this is the raison d'être of their religious association.

The same analysis holds true for Pentecostalism. As far as their personal motives are concerned, Pentecostals want to increase their self-esteem. Their ideology allows them to make prestigious status assertions without facing their obvious economic implications. By stressing the overriding value of sacred accomplishment, Pentecostals avoid the problem of their socioeconomic position in relation to the rest of the working classes and the middle classes. In a word, their ideology conceals their social marginality. Their perception of their own action emphasizes its singularly spiritual aims and thereby defuses doubts about the sources of their self-regard in a society that puts a premium on occupational achievement.

Two discrepant cases can hardly invalidate Aberle's hypothesis. Nevertheless, this material indicates that it is hazardous to make inferences about a group's attitude toward the prevailing social order solely on the basis of its most striking doctrines. Here the criterion of salience is simply those beliefs which appear to express various degrees of alienation from societal standards. This analysis further suggests that belief systems have their own internal logic which affects the conduct of their adherents. As a general type, these beliefs have no specific meaning. It is only when particular cosmological and eschatological postulates are elaborated in an ethical code that a religious ideology has determinant consequences for behavior. In the case of transformative ideologies, for example, closer attention to the entire belief system would enable us to determine which groups were alienated from the larger society and wanted to hasten its supernatural destruction and which groups used the vision of its destruction to hasten their movement through its social hierarchy. Our typology then might encompass the historical drift of social movements that fall into this broad-scale category.

Some Theoretical Considerations

In conclusion, I would like to comment on some of the theoretical issues generated by discussions of the relationship between religious belief and social structure. I have tried to avoid the circular debate about the significance of ideal versus material factors in social life. For instance, Yinger states the problem in its characteristically polemic form:

> The only question concerns the point at which ideas and beliefs enter into the field of interaction: Are they prime movers? Can they arise independently of material conditions and help create new arrangements; or do they reinforce, rationalize and preserve the old? With reference to religion our question is: Is there a source of religious ideas and energy which cannot be traced back eventually to the material conditions or, slightly more generally, to the struggle for power? [9]

In order to escape this theoretical impasse, I have tried to look at the ways in which material factors (the believer's economic situation and status expectations) and ideal factors (cosmological and eschatological doctrines) shape the sect member's attitude toward the secular world. In this scheme, the structural (material) and cultural (ideal) elements are articulated through the agency of conceptions of the kind of behavior necessary for salvation. Here I follow Weber who, according to Parsons, sought to determine the relationships between the general value orientations contained in a religious tradition and the material interests generated by the adaptive problems faced by the social strata who espoused these doctrines:

> It was not Weber's view that religious ideas constitute the principal driving force in the determination of the relevant kinds of action. The role is rather played by what he called religious interests. A typical example is the interest in salvation, an interest which has in turn a complex derivation from, among other things, certain stresses and strains to which individuals

9. Milton Yinger, *Religion in the Struggle for Power* (Durham, N.C.: Duke University Press, 1946), p. 11.

are sometimes subjected in social situations where frustration of worldly ends seems inevitable and founded in the nature of things. But the mere interest in salvation alone is not enough. The question arises as to what kinds of specific action it will motivate. This, Weber's comparative analysis shows, will be very different according to the structure of the existential ideas according to which the individual achieves cognitive orientation to the principal nonempirical problems he faces in his situation.[10]

In another essay, Parsons notes that scholars have largely confined their discussions to the unprofitable ideal/material dichotomy because of an "undifferentiated conceptual scheme." Specifically, he claims that there is "a strong tendency not to pay adequate attention to the methodological distinction between existential and evaluative judgments, a tendency to relativize all 'objectivity' to a base in values or 'interests'," and he urges us to "follow Max Weber in his insistence on distinguishing between the motives for interest in problems, which is inherently value-relative, and the grounds of validity of judgments, which in the nature of the case cannot be relative in the same sense."[11] Following Parsons's suggestion, I have employed an analytic distinction between the ideological level of religious action, which emerges out of the actor's motives and can be derived from material or ideational sources or from both, and the theological level of religious discourse which determines the intellectual and moral validity of an act for the members of a religious community.

From this perspective, a religious ideology resides in those sacred symbols which define (but whose meaning is not exhausted by) social situations so that actors who share a common social fate can pursue their common interests without violating shared conceptions of the nature of the moral and natural universes. This definition of the ideological component or aspect of religious belief is similar to Mannheim's conception of a "general" ideology. He argued that although shared meanings arise

10. Talcott Parsons, "The Role of Ideas in Social Action," in *Essays in Sociological Theory* (Glencoe, Ill.: Free Press, 1954), p. 28.
11. Talcott Parsons, "An Approach to the Sociology of Knowledge," in *Transactions of the 4th World Congress of Sociology*, vol. 4 (Louvain, Belgium: International Sociological Assn., 1961), p. 25.

out of real social conflicts, especially out of the struggle for social dominance and recognition and out of the economic interests which align men into parties and classes, these meanings never have a solely instrumental or adaptive significance. That is, social beliefs and concepts are not restricted to the attainment of specific goals or to the solution of limited problems. They provide a metaphysical grounding, an epistemology, upon which all social action is predicated:

> In every concept, however, there is not only a fixation of individuals with reference to a definite group of a certain kind and its action, but every source from which we derive meaning and interpretation acts also as a stabilizing factor on the possibilities of experiencing and knowing objects with reference to the central goal of action which directs us. . . . The derivation of our meanings emphasizes and stabilizes that aspect of things which is relevant to activity and covers up, in the collective action, the perpetually fluid process underlying all things.[12]

General ideologies involve shared notions about the worth of certain kinds of social relationships: "The most important role of thought in life consists, however, in providing guidance for conduct when decisions must be made. Every real decision (such as one's evaluation of other persons or how society should be organized) implies a judgment concerning good and evil, concerning the meaning of life and mind."[13] This touches the ideas about the nature, meaning, and value of life which are given their fullest expression in the theological component of religious belief.

Viewed in the light of the interaction between structural and cultural factors, religion is an autonomous, though not entirely self-contained, sphere of human experience and action. Although religious ideas have their own intrinsic intellectual properties and social consequences, they are subject to ideological "distortion" owing to the pressure of social circumstances. Like other forms of nonscientific belief, religious ideas are often interpreted in ways that are congruent with the demands of social status, economic interests, or unconscious motives. Since

12. Karl Mannheim, *Ideology and Utopia* (London: Routledge and Kegan Paul, 1949), p. 120.
13. Ibid., p. 17.

religious ideas can be neither confirmed nor refuted by scientific standards of validity (which are free at least theoretically from extrinsic social and psychological considerations), there is a qualitative difference between scientific and normative beliefs. The truth of a scientific proposition does not depend upon the structural position and emotional disposition of the speaker or listener as does the truth of normative belief—moral, religious, or artistic.

Although certain forms of religious belief attract certain social strata and repel others, their meaning on the theological or cultural level is not simply a reflection of their adherents' structural positions. Cosmological and eschatological doctrines provide the intellectual and ethical grounds for concrete existential and moral judgments. They answer the questions, Is the world really like this? and Is this the right or wrong kind of action? At this level, religious notions offer what Weber termed general conceptions of meaning; that is, they attempt to make the paradoxical or incomprehensible aspects of life intelligible and morally acceptable.

More concretely, religious ideas often attempt to reduce the inevitable hiatus between the rewards accumulated by those who are absorbed by their worldly careers and fortunes and the obscurity or suffering of those who consistently follow the highest standards of moral virtue. Thus, religious ideas phrase the relationship between temporal interests and spiritual excellence in terms of supramundane dualities (e.g., the things of the soul and the things of the flesh) which urge the believer to ignore, transform, or transcend the ordinary ethical discrepancies and inconsistencies of this world. On a cognitive plane, religious ideas relate both ordinary and unexpected occurrences in the natural and social universes to immanent or transcendent principles of order, and hence impose some coherence on the alternation between regularity and disorder in human affairs. They thereby enable the individual and the community to deal with contingencies which bear upon the achievement of personal and societal ends. Human effort and striving, then, are seen in terms of more than momentary needs, desires, and impulses; they are connected to an unchanging arrangement of events, things, and purposes. Or, to put this another way, few people are able to live in a totally probabilistic world, and religion transforms a universe of chance into one where immutable values provide fixed points of orientation for action which otherwise might be inhibited by despair or apathy about the risk and uncertainty inherent in all human undertakings. Shils recently observed that the charismatic element in religion is related to the fundamental sources of order in social life. He says:

> A great fundamental identity exists in all societies, and one of the elements of this identity is the presence of the charismatic element. Even if religious belief had died, which it has not, the condition of man in the universe and the exigencies of social life still remain, and the problems to which religious belief has been the solution in most cultures still remain, demanding solution by those who confront them. The solution lies in the construction or discovery of order. The need for order and the fascination of disorder persist, and the charismatic propensity is a function of the need for order. . . . [He continues in a footnote] I do not simply know why this need for order exists. It is not simply a need for an instrumentally manageable environment, though that is part of it. It is more like the need for a rationally intelligible cognitive map, but it obviously is more than cognitive. There is a need for moral order—for things to be fit into a pattern which is just as well as predictable.[14]

Similarly, Parsons notes that religious traditions ultimately rest upon extremely general conceptions of the kind of order which pervades the natural, social, and supernatural universes. They are "the most general world-views or definitions of the human condition that underlie orientations to more particular problems."[15] Religious ideas at this level of generality do not provide the detailed outline or blueprint for social action which I have termed the ideological dimension of a religious system. As for the necessity of an ideological orientation which organizes the concrete components of action and defines the legitimate relationships between ends and means, Aiken comments:

> In science it normally suffices to state a fact, and one man may do this as well and as accurately as another. But in the sphere of conduct much more is involved. For here we have to do with matters of attitude and intention

14. Edward Shils, "Charisma, Order and Status," *American Sociological Review* 30 (1965):203.
15. Talcott Parsons, "Introduction to Part Four: Culture and the Social System," in *Theories of Society*, vol. 2, ed. Talcott Parsons et al. (New York: Free Press, 1961), p. 970.

and problems of authenticity, legitimacy, and authority. Here words must not only predict what will be but determine what shall be; they must not only inform but also prepare and initiate lines of action. And what *is* it that is being determined, prepared and initiated? This, so I contend, can be fully revealed only through the "poetry" which the ideologist may afford us. . . . Further, figurative and hence rhetorical language enables, or compels, men to perform in advance of experience those crucial symbolic actions and imaginative experiments upon which, as Dewey has persuasively argued, genuinely rational judgments of practice and of value entirely depend. . . . To disdain "rhetoric" therefore, is to disdain the very condition through which full practical understanding and judgment is possible.[16]

Seventh-day Adventist and Pentecostal cosmological and eschatological doctrines codify a reality whose full significance transcends the adaptive requirements of the social environments of their adherents. At the purely cultural level, the meaning of religious ideas is never completely contained in their reference to ways of dealing with environmental exigencies. At this level, the function of religious ideas is not concerned with the particularities of action. According to Parsons, "concepts of order and being are not things people can do; they are the grounds upon which people's actions and the concrete situations in which they occur can ultimately be made meaningful and justifiable."[17]

The ideological aspects of religious ideas emerge at a much less general level, and, as I tried to show for Seventh-day Adventism and Pentecostalism, their ideologies arise out of the adjustment of the adherent's material concerns to spiritual imperatives. The result is an ethical code which defines the road to salvation in symbolic terms, which aids his adaptation to his niche in the social order. Although moral standards are legitimated by the general evaluative and cognitive conceptions of order inherent in a religious world view, specific ethical rules are implemented in situations where real limitations invariably restrict the availability of social resources and economic facilities. Therefore, there are externally imposed restrictions on the extent to

16. Henry Aiken, "The Revolt against Ideology," *Commentary* 37 (1964):37–38.
17. Parsons, "Introduction to Part Four: Culture and the Social System," p. 971.

which moral imperatives can be realized in any society. This universal dilemma concerns the gap between what the actor perceives as the most commendable course of action and what is practically possible or desirable for him in a given situation. Since there is always some tension between what would have been morally most proper and what was in fact feasible, there must be some sort of symbolic resolution of this problem which continues to direct action despite the uncharted contingencies of all human endeavors and involvements. If this were not so, people would not continue to feel that the moral order is efficacious in governing human conduct.

Since moral norms are defined in general terms, they are usually open to different interpretations of how they should be implemented. This latitude in cultural systems enables general notions of order to legitimate ethical codes which reduce the intrinsic ambiguity of these decisions and thereby take account of both the "ought" and the "is" in human affairs. And they do this without neglecting their adherents' secular interests. Ideologies, then, define social reality so that its problems become either tolerable or alterable; moral imperatives make difficult situations endurable or changeable. Geertz makes this point in cultural theory:

> It is through the construction of ideologies, schematic images of the social order, that man makes himself, for better or worse, a political animal. . . . Further, as the various sorts of cultural symbol-systems are extrinsic sources of information, templates for the organization of social and psychological processes, they come most crucially into play in situations where the particular kind of information they contain is lacking, where institutionalized guides for behavior, thought or feeling are weak or absent.[18]

18. Clifford Geertz, "Ideology as a Cultural System," in *Ideology and Discontent*, ed. David Apter (New York: Free Press, 1964), p. 63.

Appendix 1 Methodological Considerations

> Ethnology is not a specialty defined by a particular object, "primitive societies." It is a way of thinking, the way which imposes itself when the object is "different" and requires us to transform ourselves. We also become ethnologists of our society if we set ourselves at a distance from it.
>
> Merleau-Ponty, *Signs*

The idea of urban anthropology raises serious methodological problems. Does an anthropologist have a methodological warrant for studying social action in anything as intricate and vast as a city? The anthropologist is not usually prepared to isolate and measure the influence of ecological, demographic and other supralocal factors on the social unit he observes, and for this reason he may remain ignorant of important sources of variability in the larger population under consideration. Although this is not the place to defend the varied and as yet infant discipline of urban anthropology, I shall argue that an anthropological fieldworker can grasp the meaning of participation in religious groups in a complex society.

Moreover, I hold that the method by which the anthropological observer renders religious belief and action intelligible is no different from the way any social scientist attributes specific meaning to behavior. Regardless of the complexity of the situation in which an act occurs, it is the actor's intentions and his perceptions of the salient features of that situation that constitute the meaning he imputes to his action. Our interpretation or explanation of that action is, of course, not similarly constrained by the significance the actor bestows on his conduct. Yet if we completely disregard the "inside" aspect of observable behavior, we tacitly dismiss the cultural component of human conduct.[1] From this point of view, the actor's motives and the experiential grounds upon which other actors' motives become comprehensible to him constitute his individual variant or idiolect, so to speak, of the common culture.

Anthropology has traditionally been concerned with how objective symbolic forms of a society are related to what Merleau-Ponty calls "lived experience." That is, how formalized cultural beliefs and performances are implicated in concrete systems of social action: how they take on special significance for

1. Weber's postulate that for "a science which is concerned with the subjective meaning of action, explanation requires a grasp of the complex of meaning in which an actual course of understanding action thus interpreted belongs" (*The Theory of Social and Economic Organization* [New York: Free Press, 1947], p. 95) raises philosophic questions about the relationship between thought and action. Although this is a complex issue, it is clear that we cannot disregard the actor's intentions if we are to grasp the meaning of his action. Stuart Hampshire observes that the external, purely "objective" characteristics of an act establish its potential intelligibility, but that it is the actor's motives which endow it with specific meaning: "It may seem that a person's action is independently identifiable as an event in the world, and that, however inconsistent and irregular a man may be in the reasons that lead him to act, the actions are still identifiable as actions of his, however irrational they may be. This contrast is at least questionable. A certain minimum of consistency and regularity is required in behavior, if that behavior is to be counted as intentional human action at all. There is here also the requirement of connectedness, of a trajectory of intention that fits a sequence of behavior into an intelligible whole, intelligible as having a direction, the direction of means toward an end. The external view of a particular action, as a change in the world caused by a particular person's movement, is not enough to identify the action as a case of a person's doing so-and-so, unless the intention is known or inferred." *Thought and Action* (New York: Viking Press, 1959), p. 146.

actors grappling with particular problems in a particular social setting. This approach assumes that the significance of religious commitment and action emerges out of the cultural context in which it is embedded.[2] The functions of moral norms, ritual acts, or theological doctrines are understood in terms of the meaning that an entire religious system has for its adherents. In the context of a discussion about the interpretation of ritual symbolism, Victor Turner remarks:

> Each kind of Ndembu ritual, like Nkula, has several meanings and goals which are not made explicit by informants, but must be inferred by the investigator from the symbolic pattern and from behavior. He is able to make these inferences only if he has previously examined the symbolic configurations, and the meanings attributed to their component symbols by skilled informants, of many other kinds of ritual in the same total system. In other words, he must examine symbols not only in the context of each specific kind of ritual, but in the *context of the total system.*[3]

Concomitantly, anthropologists have not usually felt impelled to operationalize their definitions of cultural variables, because they are primarily concerned with sources of meaning not realized by minute segments of observable behavior or contained in discrete attitudes. These bits and pieces of fragmented behavior become relevant to anthropological inquiry when they assume definite significance for the actors who participate in a recurrent social setting. Kluckhohn says that "form is a matter of ordering, of arrangement, of emphasis. Measurement in and of itself will seldom provide a valid description of distinctive form. Exactly the same measurable entities differ; the configurations may have vastly different properties." He

2. E. E. Evans-Pritchard says that "statements about a people's religious beliefs must always be treated with the greatest caution, for we are then dealing with what neither European nor native can directly observe, with conceptions, images, words, which require for understanding a thorough knowledge of a people's language and also an awareness of the entire system of ideas of which any particular belief is part, for it may be meaningless when divorced from the set of beliefs and practices to which it belongs." *Theories of Primitive Religion* (Oxford: Oxford University Press, 1965), p. 7.

3. Victor Turner, "Symbols in Ndembu Ritual," in *Closed Systems and Open Minds: The Limits of Naivety in Social Anthropology*, ed. Max Gluckman (Chicago: Aldine Publishing Co., 1964), p. 47.

claims that "the main unresolved problems of culture theory will never be resolved by statistical techniques precisely because culture is patterned and *never* randomly distributed, although in some cases hypotheses arrived at by pattern analysis can approximately be *tested* by statistical techniques."[4] The key term here is pattern. As I see it, the anthropologist's task is synthetic. His analysis of a situation into its component elements is a step toward the construction of a picture (or model, if a "scientific" term is preferable) of the total cultural reality within which his informants organize relationships with others, plan specific projects, and map entire social careers.

One of the principal limitations of relying solely on the survey approach is that it is difficult to prepare an adequate interview schedule without considerable familiarity with the subtleties of sect ideology. Anne Parsons came to the same conclusion in her study of an urban Pentecostal sect. She says:

> As a social scientist looking from the outside, I very often felt that it was by a noting of the selections and individual emphases made among scripture passages that I could come to my best and deepest conclusions about what was going on within the church; the method seemed far better than that of giving questionnaires or asking explicit questions that might call forth artificial or invented answers.[5]

Even if the survey interviewer asks all the right questions, he may unknowingly ask them the wrong way. Religious sects, like primitive tribes and peasant villages, have their own distinctive cultural idioms, and the outside observer must learn the language of religious discourse before he can communicate effectively with the members of the group.

Sect members ordinarily are not willing to discuss at length with outsiders what they feel are personal matters (although they often will proselytize when given the opportunity) until they are satisfied that the observer understands, even though he

4. Clyde Kluckhohn, "Culture and Behavior," in *Handbook of Social Psychology*, vol. 2, ed. Gardner Lindsey (Reading, Mass.: Addison-Wesley, 1954), p. 959.

5. Anne Parsons, "The Pentecostal Immigrants," *Journal for the Scientific Study of Religion* 4 (1965):193.

may not share, their view of reality. The dedicated sect member is passionately interested in the problem of salvation, and anyone who wants to discuss religious matters with him must realize that this interest is inextricably bound to an encompassing religious vision of the nature of the phenomenological world. In order to convince my informants that my interest in these views was not simply "scientific," I had to learn how to relax my usual skeptical attitudes toward supernatural explanations of natural events and to talk about sect doctrines in a serious and almost accepting way.

When I explained the purpose of the study to my informants, I stressed the idea that many people were not aware of the ways in which religious belief enters into everyday life and did not understand how moral commitments shape ordinary behavior. They felt that this interpenetration between sacred belief and ordinary conduct was one of their special virtues which set them apart from more conventional religious bodies. They intuitively appreciated a study which focused on the connections between belief and action because they held sacred world views which integrated complex cosmologies and conduct, and they were especially proud that religion constitutes a way of life for them and is not merely a formal gesture, an abstract form of devotion and worship.

Since they understood, to a certain degree, the kind of relationship between ideas, events, and actions for which I was searching, my informants often spontaneously supplied the vital cultural contexts which made specific bits of information intelligible. They often discussed their present belief in terms of their past religious affiliations and intellectual backgrounds and usually did not hesitate to move freely back and forth between their present and past attitudes toward a wide range of moral issues, personal problems, and religious questions. Most important, this understanding between myself and the sect members created a rationale for later inquiries into their informal social associations and into their economic decisions—areas not apparently related to studies of religious belief.

This brief discussion of how an anthropologist approaches sect belief raises a question about the nature of anthropological data.[6] Religious beliefs are hardly identical to occupation as a category for data collection. One does not solicit a person's religious beliefs as a matter of stated fact. In the course of a number of discussions an informant discloses his attitudes toward and ideas about the supernatural world. His conception of the influence of supernatural forces upon his daily life constitutes an even more subtle area of investigation. To a certain extent, these notions are contained in moral dicta. When a sect member is asked why he follows a particular religious prescription, he may justify his actions in terms of revealed commands to the faithful. However, there are instances where the connections between belief and conduct are unrecognized by the actor. Here the observer must search for the social contexts in which religious ideas seem relevant to the actor's behavior.

As a rule, anthropologists are not overly sensitive to sampling problems. Nor can I claim that in this respect this investigation is any different from a traditional anthropological field study. Colson has observed that anthropologists working in primitive and peasant societies rarely specify the degree to which the group or social unit they actually observed shares theoretically relevant characteristics with the members of a larger social universe.[7] For instance, one cannot often tell when reading an

6. Gregory Bateson astutely characterizes the nature of anthropological data in these terms: "Another peculiarity of the data collected by cultural anthropologists is the extreme complexity of each individual datum. The requirement that each datum include full identification of the individual and description of the context is perhaps never fully met in practice. The fact remains, however, that a very large number of circumstances are always relevant, in the sense that a small change in any one of them might reverse, or drastically change, the form of the behavior which we are recording. There is, therefore, almost no possibility of handling the data statistically. The contexts, the individuals, and the behaviors are too various for their combinations and permutations to be handled in this way. The units of data of which any sample is composed are too heterogeneous to be legitimately thrown together into a statistical hopper." Quoted in Kluckhohn, "Culture and Behavior," p. 960.

7. Elizabeth Colson, "The Intensive Study of Small Sample Communities," in *Method and Perspectives in Anthropology*, ed. Robert Spencer (Minneapolis: University of Minnesota Press, 1954).

ethnography how representative a particular village or hamlet is of an entire tribe.

On the other hand, the survey method also has distinct limitations. Daniel Katz remarks that "the survey always attempts to be representative of some known universe and thus attempts both in the number of cases and in the manner of their selection, to be adequately and faithfully representative of a larger population." [8] The logic of survey research constrains the interviewer to gather strictly comparable data in each interview, which means that he must ask the same questions in the same order in the same way each time. This is a rather confining procedure for studies of religious orientations where the meaning of doctrine is viewed as problematic by the observer. He searches for evaluative judgments implicit in assertions whose intent seems purely cognitive but which might link the believer's perception of his social standing to the ethical code that regulates his conduct. By ignoring the "generative" aspects of norms and beliefs, the design of many survey studies tends to assume that culture is a *constant* rather than a *variable* in the determination of social action: that culture sets the normative boundaries beyond which an individual cannot easily stray but does not further shape the direction of his activity. My view stresses the role culture plays in the creation of motives that shape the actor's choices and decisions in a multitude of social situations.

Anthropological field methods are admittedly inadequate if the problem concerns the distribution or the incidence of social phenomena in a complex society. Nor can anthropological field techniques alone measure the influence or effect of one set of social variables on another. Survey methods tend, on the other hand, to objectify the meaningful components of social action so that they can be measured. Consequently, sociological generalizations are often probability statements about the behavior of individuals in the aggregate. Since they seek to establish statisti-

8. Daniel Katz, "Field Studies," in *Research Methods in the Behavioral Sciences*, ed. Leon Festinger and Daniel Katz (New York: Dryden Press, 1953), p. 57.

cal correlations between objective social variables, social survey methods often neglect the intentional aspects of social action that arise out of and only become operative against a particular normative and intellectual background. In the survey format, the actor's motives remain obscured by a multitude of opinions which may or may not have substantial normative implications for his relationships with significant others.

As a point of contrast to the present strategy I will briefly discuss Gerhard Lenski's excellent survey study of the relationship between the content of religious belief and different patterns of social action and economic choice.[9] Lenski investigates Weber's theoretical formulation of the problem of the connection between religious belief and secular conduct. He distinguishes between the types of religious orientations and commitments found in contemporary American Catholicism, Judaism, and Protestantism. He does not seriously question the adequacy of Weber's analysis of the differences between Protestant and traditional Catholic attitudes toward work, investment, and secular conduct. He takes the subjective religious orientations toward secular concerns implicit in these traditions as given and looks at their consequences in a modern urban situation. Lenski assesses the consequences of various religious traditions on secular behavior in the city by holding other social and economic variables constant. This procedure is built into the survey design. Although he treats religious belief as an independent variable, his research design compels him to describe its effects upon conduct in what are essentially residual categories. For Lenski, those attitudes and behavioral items which cannot be accounted for by variables other than religious belief are consequences of that religious tradition. Katz, commenting on the differences between a field study and survey research, explains the methodological rationale for my decision to rely upon the former:

> The survey, to the extent that it deals with such interrelations and interaction, does so through a study of the final outcome. The on-going

9. Gerhard Lenski, *The Religious Factor* (Garden City, N.Y.: Doubleday, 1963).

> social and psychological processes are inferred in the survey from the statistical end-effects. In the field study, however, attempts are made to observe and measure on-going processes more directly. Specifically, this means that the field study either attempts observations of social interaction or investigates thoroughly the reciprocal perceptions and attitudes of people playing interdependent roles. Thus a field study will provide both a more detailed and a more natural picture of the social interrelations of the group than does the survey.[10]

I devised a questionnaire that extended beyond the range of the inquiries I could ordinarily make in casual conversations and included those that would seem out of place on informal occasions. This sort of information supports the face validity of my inferences about the content of Pentecostal and Seventh-day Adventist status expectations, but it of course does not confirm this relationship between the believer's status expectations and his sect affiliation. Such a study would undoubtedly require a sample which was representative of the Pentecostal and Seventh-day Adventist religious movements in this country and could account for major sources of variability in this population which might influence differential patterns of sect affiliation—for example, the age and sexual structure, ethnic composition, racial character, and urban, suburban, or rural location of the congregations under study.

Before the proposition that the Pentecostals' negative and the Seventh-day Adventists' positive status expectations are related to sect affiliation could be tested by survey data, it would be essential to determine whether the congregations which belong to the same religious movement vary systematically along a continuum of ideological commitment. If a religious movement is ideologically homogeneous (which is a moot point for all the groups that adopt the Pentecostal label), and if the central tenets of its belief are held with equal fervor in all kinds of churches, then we can test the proposition with a sample drawn from this population. However, in light of the geographical dispersion of these groups, it seems likely that some congregations may have abandoned some of the movement's basic teachings. If this is true, the population from which any sample is

10. Katz, "Field Studies," p. 57.

drawn should be confined to those groups who remain faithful to the movement's doctrines.

This, incidentally, raises the question of the role of social surveys in qualitative social research. Here I can do no better than quote an anthropologist with considerable urban research experience:

> The categories of quantification in them [surveys], however, should be determined by prior theoretical analysis. The findings which emerge from these surveys may then be used to test the generality of hypotheses developed because social surveys are based—or should be based—on samples so selected as to make their findings applicable to the whole population from which the sample is drawn. Quantitative methods may thus be used to refine and deepen generalizations which have been derived from other methods or to bring to light regularities which might otherwise have escaped notice. . . . In this interaction between intensive and quantitative research it is likely that fruitful hypotheses will arise most frequently out of the insights acquired in intensive studies. The appropriate role for quantitative research is to test and refine these hypotheses rather than to generate them.[11]

The questionnaire used in this study (see Appendix 2) undoubtedly touches upon what many people feel are private areas of their lives. Therefore I decided that an outsider such as myself should develop considerable rapport with his informants before asking these sorts of questions. Otherwise, I felt I would alienate them or, at the very least, get rather unreliable answers to questions about topics not covered by formal dogmas. In the first place, it is difficult for a social scientist to visit a sect and then shortly thereafter request wide-ranging interviews with the members of the group. They most certainly will place him in the social category of a stranger—a person who they think does not understand or appreciate the significance of their belief and the role it plays in their lives. My Seventh-day Adventist informants, for example, were rather relieved when they found that I was not a theology student who had come to observe the

11. J. Clyde Mitchell, "Theoretical Orientations in African Urban Studies," in *The Social Anthropology of Complex Societies*, ed. Michael Banton, Assn. of Social Anthropologists Monographs, vol. 4 (London: Tavistock, 1966), pp. 41–42.

"exotic" customs and "esoteric" beliefs of their group. They suspect that most outsiders who are intellectually interested in their belief but have no interest in joining their movement will eventually try to prove that it is wrong. In both types of sects, I frequently disclaimed any theological bias, and asserted that as far as I was concerned no religious group was theologically superior or inferior to another. Incidentally, they found this rather strange, since they believe that salvation is contingent on right belief. I referred to my Jewish background to explain my lack of interest in personal Christian salvation. Thus, I spent the early phases of the fieldwork trying to overcome the stigma of being a "stranger." Although the sects might have granted an early request for interviews, I probably would have received the standardized replies that sect members conveniently have on hand for curious or antagonistic outsiders who make such inquiries but do not appear to be potential candidates for conversion.

In my opinion, the best way to overcome this problem without actually presenting oneself as a potential convert is through the traditional anthropological method of participant-observation, although participation in this case has to be limited to verbal demonstrations of empathy with the purposes and goals of the movement.[12] Following this fieldwork tradition, I spent about six months going to services before asking what might be interpreted as personal questions, and then I ordinarily did so only with those members I knew reasonably well. In fact, one discovers which questions may offend sect members only after spending a considerable amount of time in their company. Besides, the anthropologist's rapport with his informants increases the likelihood that they will give him honest answers, and

12. Many students of esoteric religious movements have found it difficult to gain access to groups normally suspicious of outsiders. Some have resolved the problem by presenting themselves as "seekers" who are ostensibly responsive to the group's ideology or as persons who already have adopted a viewpoint similar to that espoused by the group. In my opinion, this procedure involves unethical deception about the social scientist's identity and purposes, and I preferred to lose a potential informant rather than fabricate a common bond which, in fact, did not exist. For a searching analysis of the ethical and scientific implications of this procedure see Kai Erickson, "Disguised Observation in Sociology," *Social Problems* 14 (1967).

unlike the survey researcher he checks his informants' formal statements against their behavior and informal attitudes.

This kind of rapport creates its own problems as well as bestowing its more obvious benefits upon the student of religious sects. Once the members of the small Pentecostal group discovered that I sympathized with their religious aims and that I also could empathize with their distinctive religious experience, they could not understand why I did not take the next "natural" step and become a full-fledged member of their group. They simply could not comprehend how anyone who perceived the "truth," however remotely, could resist the "innate" desire to participate in it with his whole being. I repeatedly tried to explain the case for affective neutrality and for a nonevaluative approach to the study of religious ideas. But they were so deeply committed to the idea that the crux of religious existence resides in one's capacity to understand and communicate with others about the supreme value of union with the Deity that they constantly pressed me to "move" into their special spiritual realm. They wanted me to develop what they saw as my native spiritual abilities which were manifest in my discussions of the meaning of union with the Holy Ghost.

This does not mean that they did not understand the idea of an impartial study of religious ideas. A few even found the undertaking rather attractive. The official rationale I provided for the more suspicious members of the sect was that my study would correct what they feel are the many outrageous falsehoods leveled against their belief. Fortunately, the minister was in favor of such a study, for without his cooperation it would not have been possible. Without his blessing, members refuse to engage in any collective undertaking, and they generally demand his advice in their private affairs. Since he thought it was a good idea to describe the beliefs and practices of their group as I saw them, some members of the group submitted to interviews even though they resented this intrusion into their lives.

The members of this sect simply could not restrain their impulse to try to maneuver me into group activities which served to generate the emotional solidarity which precedes conversion. I periodically had to withdraw from the group for weeks at a time when my presence became the focus of efforts to prove the efficacy of the Holy Spirit. My absences, then, were symbolic of the social distance which was part of my role as a social scientist. This reinforced the notion that I was an interested outsider and not a religious partisan. From their point of view, appearances were deceiving. If I truly understood what they were about, how could I not seize the opportunity to reach the highest level of spiritual development afforded to man? The fact that I was a Jew played an important role in explaining my inability to take the final step. The conversion of Jews is known to be especially difficult and, anyhow, it is not likely to be a very frequent occurrence until the end of this world. I should also mention that their motives in this respect were not completely altruistic. The minister, particularly, realized that the conversion of the observer would constitute overwhelming evidence of the power of the Holy Spirit to move men, such as myself, to actions (such as speaking in tongues) which their intellectual training and their desire to appear sophisticated would otherwise strenuously resist.

In contrast to the Pentecostals, Seventh-day Adventists see religious commitments as part of a more encompassing rational approach to the problems of life. Although they believe that one originally repents out of a sense of guilt for one's sins, they feel that continued adherence to a rigid moral code is simply a function of rational choice between two clearly defined alternatives. Either one sacrifices certain earthly pleasures now and, in turn, eventually gains eternal rewards or one indulges in sensual activities, which soon leave one satiated, and thereby forfeits his right to a place in the Kingdom of God. Seventh-day Adventists do not resort to emotional appeals to conversion because they believe that the correct choice is almost self-evident. They discuss this question in calm and measured, although not entirely dispassionate tones, almost as if one were buying some sort of spiritual insurance policy. They reason with but do not pressure potential converts. Ultimately they believe that an individual is responsible for his own decisions and actions and thus cannot be held even partially accountable for the decisions of his closest relatives and friends, providing he makes them aware of the alternatives which all men face. Consequently, they presented their case as cogently as possible but did not attempt to induce me to join their cause.

Appendix 2 Interview Schedule

This questionnaire was administered verbally and I restated or rephrased any question which did not seem to make sense to my informants. Also, I often tried to get an informant to elaborate his response to a question when his answer seemed shallow, unclear, or superficial. In future use I would eliminate those queries not related to socioeconomic matters. This questionnaire takes too long to administer (about one hour and forty-five minutes), and, as it now stands, the interviewer's ability to pursue the informant's occupational history and social aspirations at great length is restricted by time. Specifically, I would retain and perhaps expand items 40–62 and those items dealing with intra- and intergenerational mobility (12, 15, 18). I would omit most of the others because by the time I interviewed these people I knew them well enough to have most of the information in my field notes.

1. Have you always been a member of (name of church)?
2. (If not) To what other church groups have you belonged? For how long?

3. How did you come to join (name of church)?
4. Did you learn about the teachings and doctrines of (name of church) through an evangelist, friend, member of your family, a person you know from work, relative, or another source? (If informant came to join through multiple contacts, which were most important to him?)
5. Once you became familiar with the group's doctrines, what made you decide to join it? Did any friend or relative influence your decision? (If so) How?
6. Do you hold any office or perform any special duties for the church? (If so) What are they?
7. About how many times a month would you say you attend church and church-sponsored meetings?
8. Do you tithe? Is that one-tenth of your income?
9. In general, what are the most important differences between your present church and others to which you have belonged?
10. If a person asked you why you became a member of this particular congregation, what would you tell him?
11. Do you remember the church to which your mother's parents and your father's parents belonged?
12. Do you know what your father's father did for a living?
13. To what church or churches did your mother and father belong?
14. Do you know to what churches your mother's brothers and sisters and your father's brothers and sisters belong?
15. What does (or did) your father do for a living (principal jobs)?
16. (If married) Does your wife/husband belong to the same church as you do? (If no) Why?
17. (If married) To what church or churches do your wife's/husband's parents belong?
18. Do you know what your wife's/husband's father does (did) for a living?
19. Do you have any brothers or sisters? (If so) To what churches do they belong?
20. Are there any other relatives or close friends who are members of your church? (If friends) Were they friends before or after you joined?

21. How has (name of religious orientation) changed your life? (Or) How would life be without your faith?
22. What beliefs or teachings of your faith are most important to you? Are there any beliefs which help you deal with the problems of everyday life? (If so) How do they help?
23. Do you think that belonging to (name of religious group) has changed your attitudes toward your job or the way you do your work?
24. Do you think that people who belong to (name of church) make a certain kind of husbands and wives? In other words, do they treat each other differently from people who do not belong to this faith?
25. Do you think that members of (name of church) raise their children in certain ways that may be different from most people? (If so) How?
26. Can you see any differences between the family life of people who belong to (name of church) and the family life of friends, relatives, and work associates who do not?
27. In your opinion, what does sin consist of? In other words, what kinds of things do people do that are sinful?
28. Are there other things, that although they may not be sinful, most people do that members of your church do not do?
29. In your opinion, how do men achieve salvation?
30. What is your address?
31. Have you always lived in this neighborhood? If not, for how long have you lived there?
32. Where else have you lived and for about how long did you live in each of these places?
33. Did you move to this neighborhood for any particular reasons?
34. What do you like and what do you dislike about this neighborhood?
35. Are you thinking about moving in the future? (If yes) Where? Why?
36. If you could afford to live wherever you wanted, where would you live? Why?
37. Are you married? (Note if divorced or separated.)

38. (If married) Do you have any children?
39. Who lives in your household?
40. How far have you gone in school?
41. (If high school) What kind of course did you take in high school?
42. What kind of work do you do?
43. Exactly what does your job involve?
44. Have you ever done anything else for a living?
45. (If relevant) Have you ever been an apprentice in a trade?
46. Are there any special responsibilities or duties involved in your job or is any special training required? (If so) What?
47. If you could have the same kind of job, do you think it is better to work for someone else or to work for oneself, that is, to be self-employed? (If the latter) Do you have any plans to go into your own business?
48. If you were offered a job with a big company or if you could go into a business of your own, and could make the same amount of money at both, which would you choose? Why?
49. Do you feel there is much chance for improvement and advancement in your present job? (If yes) What would advancement mean?
50. Is the kind of work you are doing now the kind of work you will want to do for the rest of your life, or do you see yourself doing something else in the future? (If the latter) What would that be?
51. In general, do you think most people get good jobs because of hard work and ability, or do you think that the best jobs are gotten through family background and personal connections?
52. How important do you think good luck or chance is in getting ahead in this world?
53. (If relevant) Are you a member of a union?
54. Do you think that most people benefit from being union members, or would they gain more from working on their own?
55. (Use card) If you had your choice of the following conditions under which you could work, which would be most important to you? Are there any that do not matter?

a) No danger of being fired
b) Big salary or income

c) Short working hours
d) Chances for advancement
e) Enjoying the kind of work involved in the job
f) Independence on the job

56. What kinds of jobs would you like to see your children get?
57. What do you think their chances are of getting these jobs?
58. Is there anything a parent can do to see that his children get them (or get ahead in the world)?
59. Should people save even if it means doing without something they really would like to have, or should they save only if they can do it without any real sacrifices?
60. Do you think it is a good idea to buy on time?
61. Does your family keep a record of its expenditures?
62. For what sort of thing do you think people ought to save their money?

Index

Aberle, David F., 44n, 45, 46n, 217–22
Achievement. *See* Success, economic
Adorno, Theodor, 29
Advancement. *See* Success, economic
Adventist sects, 70–71, 116. *See also* Seventh-day Adventists
Affiliation, religious. *See* Sect affiliation
Aiken, Henry, 227–28
Alland, Alexander, 152n
Allen, William, 16n
Althaus, Paul, 89n
Ambition, 125–34
Amusements. *See* Vices
Angels, three, 105–8
Anti-Catholicism. *See* Roman Catholic church
Anxiety, religious, 40
Apocalypse. *See* Eschatology; Millennium; Second Coming
Ark, Jewish, 97
Army. *See* Military service
Asceticism, 14, 39–40, 88
Authority. *See* Civil authority; Hierarchy, religious; Organization, religious
Azusa Mission, 143

Babylon image, 105–6, 113
Backsliding, 60, 102–3, 104, 121, 122, 137, 140, 158. *See also* Security, spiritual
Balandier, Georges, 23
Baptism, spirit. *See* Spirit baptism
Bastide, R., 20
Bateson, Gregory, 236n
Beggary, religious, 88
Behavior. *See* Conduct
Belief. *See* Theology
Bellah, Robert, 80
Berger, Peter L., 33, 44
Bible, centrality of, 36, 57, 58, 64–65, 66, 94, 107, 150–51. *See also* Biblical interpretation; Gospels
Biblical interpretation, 74, 94–95, 150–51
Black Muslims, 109n
Bloch-Hoell, Nils, 143n
Blood, 96–97, 141
Blue laws, 106, 109, 110
Burke, Kenneth, 69
Burridge, K. O. L., 25–26
Business, 175–76, 198–200, 205. *See also* Employment; Occupation; Success, economic

Calvinists, 116
Cargo cults, 21, 24–26
Career. *See* Occupation
Carrier, Hervé, 28, 43
Catastrophes, 110

Catholic church. *See* Roman Catholic church
Charisma, 26, 59, 85, 93, 149, 155n, 158–60, 180n, 227
Charity, 173
Children: Pentecostals' expectations for, 207, 208, 209, 210; Seventh-day Adventists' expectations for, 200–201, 210
Choice. *See* Free will
Christ: as advocate, 99, 102; as intercessor, 97–99; as lightness principle, 115; as sacrificial lamb, 97; sects' idea of, 87; struggle with Satan, 112. *See also* Jesus
Christianity: and colonialism, 19–22; effect on conduct, 10; influence on non-Christian societies, 18–22; as social equalizer, 19–21
Church: as mediator, 58; organization of, 59; and social order, 57; relationship with state, 58–59, 61, 64, 107. *See also* Church membership; Church-sect typology; Congregations
Church membership: criteria for, 188; and social status, 32–34, 35–38, 45
Church-sect typology, 56–69; conservative-radical analogy, 58–59; criticism of, 56, 62–63; intellectual foundations of, 64–65
Cities. *See* Urban anthropology
Civil authority, 106, 109–12
Civil religion, 80
Clark, Elmer T., 129
Class: contrasted with status, 48–49; and church membership, 32–34, 35–38, 45; of sect members, 192; Seventh-day Adventist attitude toward, 135. *See also* Status
Clear, Val, 37n
Clergy. *See* Ministers
Collectivities, 13–14
Colonialism, 18–22, 23, 24
Colson, Elizabeth, 236
Communal ideals, 15
Communism, 11n, 167–68, 176
"Communitas," 84
Conduct: and economic success, 123–24; in employment, 74, 118, 134; Holiness attitude toward, 139–40, 142; ideologies and, 3, 5, 7, 8, 10, 78, 82; lapses in (*see* Backsliding); Pentecostal attitude toward, 71, 139, 140, 180; religion and, 40; and salvation, 36–37, 71, 102–5; 116–25, 170–72, 177; and status, 135; and Spirit baptism, 154–55, 177. *See also* Ethics; Works
Confession, 102, 104
Conflict, in groups, 146
Congregations: changes of, 146; conflict in, 146–47; importance of in Protestantism, 36–38; in study, 144–47, 158, 183–94
Consensus, ideological, 71–73
Conversion: effects of, 88; of first generation sect members, 73; necessity of, 67–68; role of minister in, 159–60; and Spirit baptism, 157, 165; as route to respectability, 165–66; of second generation sect members, 68, 73; social implications of, 21, 42–43; theory of, 42–43. *See also* Salvation
Conversionist sects, 70
Cosmology: and conduct, 51; Pentecostal, 147, 167–68; Seventh-day Adventist, 97–116
Cultic therapy, 14
Cults: characteristics of, 85–86; non-Western, 19–26
Culture heroes, 23

Dancing. *See* Vices
Dark and light, symbolism of, 115

Demerath, Nicholas J., III, 33n, 62–63
Denominations: omitted from church-sect typology, 65–66; nature of, 65–66; origins of, 66, 68–69, 71–72; religious tolerance in, 77–78; and status, 75
Deprivation. *See* Relative status deprivation
Despair, dangers of, 129
Devereux, George, 41
Devil, 106; and Communism, 167–68; as darkness principle, 115; expulsion from heaven, 112; final fate of, 114; possession by, 154; role in contemporary affairs, 99; as scapegoat, 114, 115; as tempter, 102–3, 116, 117, 119, 121, 146
Devons, Ely, 40n
Dichotomy, moral, 16
Dietary rules, 94
Discrimination, racial, 44n, 186, 189
"Divided self," 42
Divine intervention. *See* Supernatural power
Doctrine. *See* Theology
Dorcas society, 110
Douglass, Truman B., 90n
Drinking. *See* Vices
Duties of Christians, 59, 60

Economic affairs, Seventh-day Adventist attitude toward, 125–34. *See also* Business; Employment; Success, economic
Economic success. *See* Success, economic
Eddy, Mary Baker, 15
Education: Pentecostal attitude toward, 208; of persons in study, 197; Seventh-day Adventist attitude toward, 198, 200–201, 202, 208
Elect, 59, 100–101, 103, 177
Elinson, Howard, 87n
Employment: attitude of sect members toward, 87–88; conduct in, 74, 118, 134; Pentecostal attitude toward, 174, 203–7; Seventh-day Adventist attitude toward, 196–201. *See also* Business; Occupation; Success, economic
Encounter groups, 15–16
Entertainment. *See* Vices
Equality of believers, 19, 21, 24, 59, 69, 72, 84–85
Erikson, Kai, 241n
Eschatology, 70, 71; Christian, 89n; Pentecostal, 167; Seventh-day Adventist, 90–92, 95–100, 105, 109n, 112–16, 214, 220
Essien-Udom, E. U., 109n
Eternal security. *See* Security, spiritual
Ethics, 20, 21. *See also* Conduct
Ethnicity, of congregations in study, 184–86, 192
Evangelism. *See* Missionary activity
Evans-Pritchard, E. E., 233n
Evil, 99, 116. *See also* Devil

Fallers, Lloyd, 48n
Family, sect as, 60
Fieldwork, methods of, 30, 231–44
First generation sect members, 67–68, 73
Foursquare Gospel, 162–63
Free choice. *See* Free will
Free will, 5, 14, 107, 116, 117–21. *See also* Responsibility, individual
French Revolution, 111
Freud, Sigmund, 15
Fruits of the Spirit. *See* Gifts, spiritual
Full Gospel Assembly, 190, 194
Full Gospel Business Men's Association, 175–76
Full Gospel groups, 189, 190–91

Full Gospel Tabernacle, 190, 193–94
Fundamentalism, 44n, 86, 121, 138, 148–49, 181

Geertz, Clifford, 4, 7, 52, 83, 229
Gerlach, Luther P., 190
German youth movement, 12n
Gifts, spiritual, 26, 138, 139, 144, 146, 147, 149, 151, 155n, 169, 181
Giving. *See* Charity
Glock, Charles, 38n, 43n, 47
Glossolalia. *See* Speaking in tongues
Gluckman, Max, 40n
Gnosticism, 70, 86n
God, image of, 212. *See also* Christ; Holy Spirit; Jesus
Goldschmidt, Walter, 33
Goldthrope, John, 48
Goode, Erich, 62
Good works. *See* Works
Gospels: and church-sect typology, 56, 58–59, 63; interpretation of by sects, 65, 66, 86. *See also* Bible; Biblical interpretation
Government, church. *See* Hierarchy, religious; Organization, religious
Grace, 57–58, 89–90
Great Awakening (1734), 143
Group therapy, 15–16
Guiart, Jean, 21n
Guilt, 153
Gusfield, Joseph, 178, 220

Haiti, spiritual possession in, 155, 157
Hampshire, Stuart, 232n
Healing, divine, 26, 88, 147, 148, 157, 189, 212
Heaven: Pentecostal idea of, 168; Seventh-day Adventist idea of, 113–15
Hell: Pentecostal idea of, 168; Seventh-day Adventist idea of, 113
Hierarchy, religious, 59, 61, 68–69, 84, 187. *See also* Organization, religious
Hine, Virginia H., 190
"Hippie" movement, 16, 17
Holiness. *See* Conduct; Santification
Holiness groups, 37n, 139–40, 141–43, 149, 188–89
Holy Ghost. *See* Holy Spirit
Holy place. *See* Sanctuary
Holy Spirit, 138, 139; and supernatural power, 22; functions of, 148, 149. *See also* Spirit baptism
Homes, Seventh-day Adventist attitude toward, 202
Hostility, toward poor, 179

Ideologies: as adaptive tools, 52–53; and conduct, 3, 5, 7, 8, 10, 51, 81–82; credibility of, 2–3, 5–6; cult, 19–26; definition of, 1–2; and life style, 12; Marxian, 2n; as models of reality, 3, 5–6, 7, 8; and organizational change, 72; Pentecostal, 169–81; and philosophy, 6, 18; as political religions, 10–11; and politics, 10–12; and religious belief, 1–8, 12; and science, 3; and secular society, 1–2, 4, 9–17; Seventh-day Adventist, 116–36; and social problems, 4–6, 7–8, 10, 17, 18, 53, 229; and status, 38–39; and supernatural agency, 54–55; and theology, 221; vocabulary of, 12. *See also* Sect ideology; Theology
Imagery, visual, 114–15
Individualism, 146
"In-filling." *See* Spirit baptism
"Inner-directed" character type, 125

Interpretation, biblical. *See* Biblical interpretation
Introversionist sects, 70
Investigative process, 100–103, 112. *See also* Judgment, final
Isichei, Elizabeth, 72
Isolation, social, 77

Jamaica, 20n
James, William, 15, 42
Jehovah's Witnesses, 86n
Jesus: as center of Pentecostal worship, 145; functions of, 145, 148–49. *See also* Christ
Jewish ritual, relevance of, 95–96
Jobs. *See* Employment; Occupation
Johnson, Benton, 142
Judgment, final, 98, 99, 105. *See also* Investigative process
Justification by faith, 90n, 138; *See also* Salvation

Kahl, Joseph, 44n
Katz, Daniel, 237, 238
Kelsey, M. T., 143n, 150n, 155n
Kentucky Revival of 1799, 143
Kiev, Ari, 152n
Kingdom of God, 113–15, 136
Kluckhohn, Clyde, 233–34
Koch, Sigmund, 50–51
Kroeber, A. L., 19n

Lamb, sacrificial, 97
Lanternari, Vittorio, 23
"Last days," 105. *See also* Eschatology; Millenium
Law, 102, 120, 123, 124, 139
Lenski, Gerhard, 238
Lichtheim, George, 2n
Lickey, Arthur, 106n
Light and darkness, symbolism of, 115
"Liminals," 84
Lipset, Seymour, 34n
Lockwood, David, 48, 49
"Lumpen-bourgeoisie," 45
"Lumpen-proletariat," 75, 192

McCarthy, Joseph, 11n
Mair, Lucy, 20n
Mannheim, Karl, 2n, 3–4, 224–25
Marginality, social, 8, 45–46, 77
"Mark of the beast," 106
Marriage: Pentecostal attitude toward, 176–77, 207; Seventh-day Adventist attitude toward, 131–32
Martin, D. A., 65–66
Membership, church. *See* Church membership
Merleau-Ponty, Maurice, 27, 232
Merten, Don, 16n
Messianic hope, 17, 23–26
Methodology, research, 27–30, 195, 203, 231–44
Middle class, characteristics of, 44–45, 49–50. *See also* Respectability, desire for
Military service, 74, 109–10
Millenarianism, 71, 90–92, 108
Millennium, 22, 105, 108, 112–16, 218
Miller, Walter, 165
Miller, William, 90–91
Millerites, 90–92
Mills, C. Wright, 45
Ministers: function of, 59, 66, 73, 144, 151, 159–60, 188, 194; in study, 145, 146, 150, 151, 157–64, 171, 176, 189, 193, 194, 204, 242, 243
Missionary activity, 18–19, 21, 60–61, 69–70, 74, 88, 121, 164, 166–68, 178, 206
Mitchell, J. Clyde, 240
Mobility, upward, 42, 44, 45, 50, 71, 109n, 126, 133, 135, 195–200, 206, 209, 210, 212, 213. *See also* Status expectations; Success, economic
Monasticism, 87, 88
Money. *See* Saving; Success, economic

Morality. *See* Conduct; Ethics; Works
Motives: obscured by survey method, 238; for behavior, 28; for sect affiliation, 38–41, 215–16, 222
Movies. *See* Vices
Mystery religions, 17
Mysticism, 47, 85, 87, 88, 93–94, 153

Negro Christ, 23
Negroes, 186, 189
Neighborhoods, of congregations in study, 184, 191
New Jerusalem, 114. *See also* Kingdom of God; Millennium
Niebuhr, H. Richard, 67, 68–69
Nock, A. D., 17n

Objectivity, limits of, 9
Observer, relationship with sect members, 234–35, 240–43
Occupation: of persons in study, 195–99, 203–4; and social status, 179n, 183. *See also* Employment
Oikumenê, 19
144,000, the, 94–95
Optimism: cosmic, 15; of Pentecostals, 137, 214; of Seventh-day Adventists, 50, 128–29, 137, 213–14. *See also* Pessimism
Organization, religious, 72, 144, 186–88, 193–94
Orlinsky, David, 16n

Paganism, 19
Parsons, Anne, 234
Parsons, Talcott, 4, 13n, 48n, 169, 213–14, 223–24, 227, 228
Participant observation, 27–30, 234–35, 240–43
Pastors. *See* Ministers
Patriarchal family, 177
Peale, Norman Vincent, 15
Pentecostalism: background of, 9–10; attitude toward conduct, 71, 139, 140, 180; compared with non-Western religions, 22, 25; compared with Holiness groups, 139–40, 141–43; cosmology, 147, 167–68; and economic situation, 42, 44, 46; eschatology, 167; formal organization of, 143–44; history of, 143; ideology of, 169–81; lack of formal theology, 167–68; as Redemptive movement, 216–20, 222; and secular affairs, 87–88; statistics on, 9n; theology of, 138, 143–69; and traditional Christianity, 86–88. *See also* Sect ideology; Sect members; Sects
Perfection of believers, 57, 102–5
Persecution of Christians, 105
Pessimism: of Pentecostals, 50, 138, 213; of Seventh-day Adventists, 137, 214. *See also* Optimism
Philosophy, and ideology, 6, 18
Pleasures, proscribed. *See* Vices
Polak, F. L., 53, 54
Polanyi, Michael, 29
Politics, ideology and, 10–12; Pentecostal attitude toward, 176; Seventh-day Adventist attitude toward, 108–12
Poor, Pentecostal attitude toward, 176–79
Pope, Liston, 67n
Pope, as agent of Devil, 106
Power, supernatural. *See* Supernatural power
Prayer, function of, 94, 104, 117, 153
Predestination, 39
Prejudice: ideological, 2n; racial, 44n, 186, 189
Primary group, sect as, 60, 77

Problems, social: and ideology, 4–6, 7–8, 10, 18, 53; sacred solutions to, 47; secular solutions to, 47
Professions, Seventh-day Adventists' admiration for, 126, 198, 199
Prophecy, 26, 145, 147. *See also* Speaking in tongues
Proselyting. *See* Missionary activity
Protest, other-worldly, 67n
Protestant ethic, 39–40, 71, 116
Protestantism: doctrinal diversity, 35–38; proliferation of sects within, 64–65; and social class, 32–34, 35–38
Psychodrama, 77
Psychological tendencies of sect members, 41, 213–16

Quakerism, 72
Questionnaire, 209–10, 239–41; text of, 245–49

Radicalism, religious, 58–59, 86
Ramano V., Octavio, 93
Rapport, David, 41n
Rapport, of observers with sect members, 234–35, 240–43
Ras Tafari, 20n
Reality, models of, 3, 5–8, 51–52, 78, 83, 90, 226
Reason, 118, 133
Redemptive movements, 216–20, 222
Reformation, 110–11
Relative status deprivation, 8, 40–41, 45–46, 47, 48
Religion: and conduct, 40; furtiveness of, 18; political, 10–11; relation to secular life, 30–31, 38–39; and social status, 32–34, 35–38; subjective values of, 63; and technology, 18. *See also* Christianity; Ideology; Sects
Remmling, Gunter W., 2n
Respectability, desire for, 44–45, 50, 135, 165–66, 174, 176–79, 192
Responsibility, individual, 59, 99, 117–21, 136, 214, 243
Revitalization movements. *See* Separatist religious movements
Revolution: and ideology, 10–11; Seventh-day Adventist attitude toward, 108–12, 116, 120
Rewards and punishments, material character of, 113
Rieff, Philip, 14–15, 17
Riesman, David, 125
Rites of passage, 84
Ritual: functions of, 79–82, 84; Jewish, 95–96; lack of, in sects, 59, 147; place of in modern society, 80–81, 84; promoted by clergy, 66; relation to belief, 82, 83; and social differentiation, 33–34
Roman Catholic church: as Devil's agent, 105–8, 111, 186; doctrinal unity of, 35–38; hierarchy, 61
Roman Empire, religious milieu of, 17

Sabbath, as proper day of worship, 92, 106, 110, 113
Sabbath school, 94, 95
Sabbath School Lesson Quarterly, 95, 103
Sacraments, 58; in Catholic ritual, 35–36
Sacrifice, ritual, 96–97
Sadler, W. A., 175n
Salvation, 1, 5, 18; and communal purpose, 13–15; and conduct, 36–37, 71, 100–101, 104, 116–25, 140, 170–72, 177, 212; and free will, 107, 116; and history, 53–54; individual responsibility for, 59, 99, 117–21, 136, 214, 243; by

faith, 90n, 138, 164; importance of correct theology, 77–78, 87, 89, 94–95, 97; as openness to experience, 16; persistence of idea of, 13–14, 17; Protestant idea of, 17, 89; through Spirit baptism, 138, 139
Sampling, 236, 239–40
Sanctification, 138, 143, 181, 219
Sanctuary, 91–92, 95–100; cleansing of, 95–96, 97–100; Jewish, 95–97
Satan. *See* Devil
Saving, 130, 135; Pentecostal attitude toward, 173; 209; Seventh-day Adventist attitude toward, 201–2
Scapegoat, Devil as, 114, 115
Scholem, Gershom, 153
Schools, Seventh-day Adventist, 130–31
Scriptures. *See* Bible
Second Advent. *See* Second Coming
Second blessing. *See* Sanctification
Second Coming, 105, 108, 112–16; date of, 90–92, 95–96; description of, 112–15; imminence of, 106–7; Pentecostal view of, 167–68. *See also* Millennium
Second generation sect members, 67–68, 73
Sect affiliation: motives for, 38–41; prediction of, 41–42; and relative status deprivation, 40–41; and social status, 42, 44, 58, 62, 152; and social structure, 35; theology and, 77, 83
Sect ideology: as compensatory mechanism, 76; and conduct, 73, 78, 82, 88; and medieval philosophy, 78; as model of reality, 51–52, 78; 83, 90, 226; and salvation, 77–78; variations in, 75, 76. *See also* Ideologies; Pentecostalism; Sect members; Sects; Seventh-day Adventism
Sect members: attitude toward observer, 234–35, 240–43; duties of, 59, 60; economic situation of, 42, 44, 46; exclusion from middle class, 46; first generation, 67–68, 73; psychological tendencies of, 41, 213–16; second generation, 67–68, 73; social identity of, 67–68; social status of, 68. *See also* Pentecostalism; Seventh-day Adventism
Sects: attitude toward social order, 57, 61, 65, 69–70; biblical emphasis of, 57, 58, 64–65, 85; classification of, 69; conservative-radical analogy, 58–59, 86; diversity of, 67, 77–78; distinguished from cults, 85, 87; established, 72; missionary activity of, 60–61; otherworldliness, 88; as primary group, 60, 77; as refuge, 67; relation to Christian tradition, 86–87; role of ritual in, 81–82, 84; separatism of, 61; and social status, 75, 88; solidarity, 60–61, 73, 84, 214; as voluntary community, 60. *See also* Church-sect typology; Pentecostalism; Sect affiliation; Sect ideology; Sect members; Seventh-day Adventism
Secularization, 10, 13, 18
Security, spiritual, 102, 122, 139. *See also* Backsliding
Segregation, racial, 44n, 186, 189
Self-abnegation, 81, 88
Self-employment. *See* Business; Employment; Occupation
Self-improvement, 123, 131
Self-realization, 14–17
"Sensitivity training," 15–16

Separatist churches. *See* Separatist religious movements
Separatist religious movements, 18–26
Seventh-day Adventism: attitude toward conduct, 71, 116–25; attitude toward economic affairs, 125–34; attitude toward employment, 196–201; background of, 9–10; compared with non-Western religions, 22, 25; cosmology, 97–116; and economic situation, 44, 46; eschatology, 90–92, 95–100, 105, 109n, 112–16, 214, 220; history, 90–93 ideology, 116–36; latitude in biblical interpretation, 94–95; organization, 144, 186–88; political attitudes, 108–12; and secular affairs, 87–88; and social order, 129; statistics on, 9n; theology, 91–116; and traditional Christianity, 86–88; as Transformative movement, 216–18, 220–22. *See also* Sect ideology; Sect members; Sects
Shils, Edward, 12n, 93, 227
Sin: Pentecostal idea of, 71, 153; Seventh-day Adventist idea of, 71; universality of, 169; venial, 171. *See also* Conduct; Ethics
Sincerity, 125
Sinners, fate of, 113–14
Smelser, Neil, 7n
Smoking. *See* Vices
Social order: relation of religion to, 226–27; Pentecostal attitude toward, 212; Seventh-day Adventist attitude toward, 129
Solidarity, sect, 60–61, 73, 84, 214
Sommerfeld, Richard, 38n
Speaking in tongues, 81, 143n, 145, 149–50, 152, 154, 167. *See also* Prophecy
Spirit baptism, 138, 139, 140, 143, 145, 150, 151–52, 153, 219; benefits of, 22, 153, 155–57, 169, 175; description of, 152, 154, 155–56; effect on conduct, 154–55, 171–72, 177. *See also* Holy Spirit
Spirit of the Times, 90
Spiritualism, 93–94
Spiritual possession. *See* Spirit baptism
Spiro, Melford E., 83, 221
Stark, Rodney, 43n, 75n
Stark, Werner, 2n
State: as agent of Devil, 106; church and, 58–59, 61, 64, 107
Statistics on sect members, 9n
Status: sacred measures of, 46, 179–80; contrasted with class, 48–49; defined, 48; desire of sect members for, 88, 176–79; and economic position, 176; of Pentecostals, 174–75, 219–20. *See also* Respectability
Status deprivation. *See* Relative status deprivation
Status expectations: and sect affiliation, 41, 42, 44; and conduct, 50. *See also* Mobility, upward; Success, economic
Status trajectory, 44n, 182–83, 209
Stratification, social, 32
Stress. *See* Problems, social
Study groups. *See* Congregations, in study; Ministers, in study
Success, economic, 47, 50, 126–35, 170, 205; related to conduct, 123–24; Pentecostal attitude toward, 172–74; Seventh-day Adventist attitude toward, 111, 221. *See also* Mobility, upward; Status expectations
Sunkler, Bengt, 26n
Supernatural powers, 18, 26, 46–

47, 54–55; access to, 22–23, 79, 81, 85
Survey method, 234, 237–38, 240
Symbolism, 23, 25, 80; Pentecostal, 141; Seventh-day Adventist, 115, 134–35. *See also* Ritual

Tabernacle, Jewish, 96
Talmon, J. L., 11n
Tawney, Richard H., 78
Technology, and religion, 18
Temperance movement, 178
Temptation, 116, 117, 119, 121. *See also* Free will
Ten Commandments, 97, 104, 106
Theology: and conduct, 82–83; consensus on, 94–95; as explanatory variable, 82; formal, 51; function of, 81–82; Pentecostal, 137, 143–57, 166–69; relation to ideology, 221–22; and sect affiliation, 77, 82; Seventh-day Adventist, 91–116. *See also* Ideology
Therapy: cultic, 14; group, 15–16
Thorner, Isidor, 47n
Time, sacred conceptions of, 53–54
Tongues speaking. *See* Speaking in tongues
Transformative movements, 216–18, 220–22
Trinity, 86n, 87, 145, 149
Troeltsch, Ernst, 36n, 56, 57n, 58, 60, 61, 62–63, 64–65, 67, 69
Tucker, Robert C., 159
Turner, Victor, 80, 84, 233

Underhill, Evelyn, 35–36
Unions, 135
Urban anthropology, 231–44
Utopianism, 23, 53, 54

Variables, intervening, 50–51
Vices, 71, 73–74, 121–22, 135, 166, 171

Wallace, Anthony, 187n
Warburton, T. R., 142, 143
Watchtower movement, 20n
Weber, Max, 36n, 39–40, 48, 49, 71, 223–24, 226, 232n, 238
Weisberger, Bernard, 143n
Weslyan movement, 142, 143
White, Ellen G., 91, 92–93, 94, 95–98, 101, 110–11, 116, 121, 122
Will. *See* Free will
Willems, Emilio, 156, 165–66, 173
Wilson, Bryan, 66, 69–71, 72, 76–77, 82, 108, 145, 148, 149, 180n, 181, 191–92, 204–5
Winter, Gibson, 32, 34
Witchcraft, 18
Witnessing. *See* Missionary activity
Word, the. *See* Bible
Works, 90, 100, 170. *See also* Conduct
Worldly pleasures. *See* Vices
World view. *See* Reality, models of

Yinger, Milton, 71–72, 223
Youth's Instructor, 130–31